GRE&GMAT
阅读难句教程

杨　鹏 ➡ 编著

浙江教育出版社

图书在版编目(CIP)数据

GRE&GMAT阅读难句教程 / 杨鹏编著. —杭州：浙
江教育出版社，2015.2
ISBN 978-7-5536-2437-2

Ⅰ.①G… Ⅱ.①杨… Ⅲ.①GRE—句法—自学参考资
料 ②英语—句法—研究生—入学考试—自学参考资料
Ⅳ.①H314.3

中国版本图书馆CIP数据核字（2014）第262988号

GRE&GMAT阅读难句教程

编　　著	杨　鹏	
责任编辑	孔令宇	
责任校对	蔡　歆	
责任印务	陆　江	
封面设计	大愚设计	
出版发行	浙江教育出版社	
	（杭州市天目山路40号　　邮编：310013）	
印　　刷	北京精乐翔印刷有限公司	
开　　本	880×1230　1/16	
印　　张	17	
字　　数	380 000	
版　　次	2015年2月第1版	
印　　次	2015年2月第1次印刷	
标准书号	ISBN 978-7-5536-2437-2	
定　　价	35.00元	
联系电话	0571 - 85170300 - 80928	
电子邮箱	bj62605588@163.com	
网　　址	www.zjeph.com	

——目　录——

──前　言──

　　本书之所以将 GRE（美国研究生入学考试）和 GMAT（美国管理专业研究生入学考试）文章中的难句收录在同一本书中，是因为笔者在新东方学校兼任 GRE 与 GMAT 阅读教师的教学实践中，发现这两种考试（还可以加上 LSAT）的阅读文章从题材选择、文章写法、句子结构到出题思路和解题技巧等各个方面，都是完全相同的。究其原因，两种考试都是由 ETS（Educational Testing Service）主办的英语考试，考查的对象又都是经过四年大学本科教育之后希望到美国的研究生院或商学院深造的人，因此这两种考试的阅读实际上大同小异。中国的 GRE 考生在准备考试的过程中常常使用 GMAT 或 LSAT 的阅读文章来进行训练，而对于 GMAT 的考生来讲，GRE 的阅读文章几乎就是唯一的课外阅读资料。然而我们的考生遇到的一个问题是，当今 GRE 和GMAT 的参考书目虽多，但真正从根本上研究其阅读部分的规律性的认真之作却少得可怜。

　　众所周知，GRE 和 GMAT 考试中的阅读过程至关重要，因为除了狭义的 Verbal（语文）部分中的阅读（Reading Comprehension）之外，数学、逻辑以及 GRE 的 Verbal 中的填空各部分都对考生的阅读能力提出了较高的要求。这很好理解，因为本来 GRE 和 GMAT 考试的考查对象就是那些申请到美国大学去读硕士或博士学位的人，要在美国学习、生活，用英语做研究、写论文、查阅资料，当众做 Presentation（演讲性陈述），没有一定水准的中高级英语阅读能力，在美国的研究生院或商学院里是混不下去的。因此 ETS 在 GRE 和 GMAT 考试中着重考查这方面的能力，不但是对美国的教育机构负责，也是对考生负责。我们中国考生，甚至一些出国考试的教学培训机构以前对此问题的认识存在着某些偏差，以为全凭一些考试中的阅读技巧先把 GRE 或 GMAT 考试给对付过去，到了美国那个英语环境中再真正提高阅读的能力也来得及。平心而论，此话不无道理。以中国考生之聪慧，适应能力之强及学习之刻苦，大多数考生确实可以到了美国再补上这一课。可是正因为我们优秀的中华子孙的这一长处，绝大多数人犯了一个可悲的、没有任何意义的错误。

笔者当年上大学时，世人并无今日对英语学习的狂热态度；同学中虽也有极其个别的人学习 TOEFL，但全被视为另类。我也乐得下围棋、打桥牌，过一种惬意悠闲的生活。毕业后于外贸公司浑浑噩噩生活，每日花天酒地，再不学习。虽然做国际贸易常用英文，但仅限于品名、价格、信用证条款，谈判口语也极其简单，全凭吃些老本便足以应付。日复一日，年复一年，于此种活法愈发厌倦：虽也有纵横商界的成就感，但更多的是陷入到公司日常人际关系的内耗中。几乎有一年的时间，每天早晨一醒来就发愁，对于去公司面对那些丑恶嘴脸从内而外地感到恶心。天生我才，该不是要整日谄媚领导、压制下级、与同事勾心斗角地过一辈子吧?! 我不相信这个世界上有谁会在不是走投无路的条件下主动选择此种活法。于是我萌生了出国读书的想法。然而想法易有，决心难下。首先，我已有八年未接触正规的考试英语，拿出大学四、六级的词汇本，发现认识的单词不到三成，至于语法已经彻底忘光。第二，多年的外贸工作已经令我懒惰无比，心中不静，杂念如潮，要面对繁难的出国考试，与20岁左右的、视书海与考试为家常便饭的年轻人（家兄称之为"生荒子"，笔者以为传神）竞争，颇有廉颇老矣之感。不但如此，当时已经做到部门经理的我，放弃这份工作就意味着放弃了一切：稳定的收入、即将到手的房子、多年奋斗打下的客户基础、在公司的积功晋职的机会。一旦失败，必将懊悔不已，结果不堪设想。然而多年的商海经验令我陡增胆识。无予无取，先予后取。只要我付出足够多的努力，且无论艰难险阻，决不放弃，必能得到我想要得到的东西。至于要放弃眼前的既得利益，确实是一个痛苦的抉择，但是为了更大的目标，这也是惟一的抉择。我见过了世界上太多的有志之士，空有满腔豪情，然而不敢于放弃各种鸡肋、面对未知的奋斗，终于饮恨终老，可悲而不可泣。

于是，抱着"失去的只能是锁链，而得到的是整个世界"的信念，我义无反顾地踏上 GRE 和 GMAT 的不归路。两年之后，当我站在新东方的讲台上，看到同学们殷切而执著的目光的时候，想起当初破釜沉舟的我所发的绝大誓愿，不禁仍为当年所做出的决断而自豪。而两年来所承受的种种起先想像不到的困难和挫折，那些个长夜孤灯、食不甘味、夜不能寐的日日夜夜，那些个自信心被无情地击得粉碎的刹那，那些个痛苦得一个人独坐阳台见东方渐白的最黑暗的时刻，一瞬间涌上心头，令我眼眶为之湿润，嗓音为之失声。即使是现在，想起其中所受之苦，灵魂所受之考验，仍心有余悸；不知如果现在重新选择，是否仍然敢走这条路。不过路走过来之后，蓦然回首处，发现自己已迥非出发时的自己，此中的种种收获是没有此经历的人所不能梦见的，实一言难尽！

与精神上的涅槃相比，在英语水平上的飞跃还算是副产品。然而我之所以到新东方教课，除了有一种受人点水之恩，必当涌泉相报的心理之外，还有另外一个重要原因：自以为在 GRE 和 GMAT 的学习中颇有所悟，特别是在两种考试的最大难点——阅读上有独到的心得体会，如果不能传授予仍在奋争中的后来者，总觉心有不甘。

中国考生在 GRE 和 GMAT 考试中遇到的主要难点是 Verbal，Verbal 中的两只拦路虎：一是词汇，二是阅读，而阅读又是二者中较难突破的，几乎是所有中国考生的一块心病。究其原因，词汇虽然难背，但毕竟是体力活，功到自然成。而且词汇在 GRE 考试中的考法又相对固定，新东方对其研究已经极其透彻，所出的有关书籍亦多；而经过新东方的不懈努力，这些考法对于中国考生来讲已无半点秘密可言。所以同学们一旦了解了其规律性，经过数月的努力，绝大部分人均可以有所突破，到了备考的后期，很少有人觉得词汇考题难。GMAT 考试对词汇的要求更简单，绝大多数的关键词汇都是四、六级词汇和托福词汇，个别考题中虽然要求认识一些中高级的英语词汇，但是也都不要求考生对其做精确理解。

而 GRE 和 GMAT 的阅读却是中国考生们心中永远的痛。从广义上来讲，GRE General Test 中除了 Verbal 当中的阅读文章之外，Quantitative（数学）和 Verbal 中的填空都要求考生具备较强的阅读能力和较高的阅读速度。而中国考生的阅读能力较差，也正是我们在这几部分中失分的主要原因。尤其是 GRE 和 GMAT 考试改成计算机考试之后，逻辑单题的阅读量大大增加，更使得考生们解题的速度和正确率大打折扣。狭义的 Verbal 部分的阅读文章更是难上加难，即使是经过长期认真复习的 GRE 考生，往往到了考试的前夜，也仍然为阅读担心不止。笔者当初准备 GRE 时，只用了 17 天的功夫就把红宝书背熟。（此非吹牛，我班里的学生有人听完我讲的背词法以后，仅用 10 天就基本把单词搞定。背词法可参考《17 天搞定 GRE 单词》。）可是由于阅读能力迟迟无法提高，笔者考期一拖再拖，苦恼至极：自从能把阅读题在一定的时间内做对 2/3 开始，足足有三个月的时间水平无法提高。直到有一天，恼羞成怒，抛弃了几乎所有的从权威那里听来的阅读方法，以个人所悟重修 GRE 阅读之法。

　　笔者另起炉灶，从难句和抽象词入手，用一个月时间以文火培元固本；再花 15 天用集中突破法辅以 LSAT 资料以武火锤炼，其过程虽然苦如炼狱，但奇迹终于发生了：忽有一日，所读文章的英文词句在眼中似乎消失了，只有文章作者的思想在我心中流淌，其感觉妙不可言；读至一处，感觉作者的思想与自己不谋而合，拍案叫绝。读完文章后再做后面的习题，长文章的题目全部做对，而且连读文章带作题，花的时间也不多。自此，阅读关被彻底攻破。回头再看以前所读文章，似乎原文意思大变。又一个月后，在最后两套 GRE 题的模考中，规定的时间内阅读题目全部做对。

　　正因为笔者是从基础最差的条件下，以五体投地之姿势一步一步爬出来的，所以对于 GRE 考生们的心理及其在复习中所遇到的困难有着深刻的切身体会。又因为自己多年的阅历，所以敢于挑战市面上已经成了权威的说法。如果是错误的说法，则越权威，越为人们所公认，其杀伤力越强。比如说，笔者认为最害人的一种说法，就是："GRE、GMAT 的阅读水平是不可能在两三个月内大幅度提高的"，或者有人说得更直接，"GRE、GMAT 的阅读在考试现场用规定的时间全部做对是不可能的"。用不着我出手，且看我的学生来反驳此两种说法（学生来信）：

杨老师：

我是您新东方上海寒假班（1月15日至2月7日）的学生，不知您还记不记得我（g004班，就是老是缠着你问No.题阅读的那个，呵呵）？您在您的最后一次课上说的一席话很让我震动，从那以后我更加拼命学习，尤其是阅读，用您说的集中突破法仔细研究No.题，虽然很烦闷，但想到您，还是坚持了下来。阅读总算有了很大提高，到最后做99.4模考时阅读题目只错一道，很激动！昨天（4月26日）考完了试，虽然状态很不好，但还是老天帮忙，题目较简单，得到了2340的高分，verbal考了760分的满意分数，当时特别激动，付出总算有了回报。谢谢您对我精神上的巨大启发，谢谢您了!!不知老师现在是否还在上海，还是已回北京，将来有什么打算吗？

我打算8月考托福，申请明年秋季入学，不知有什么建议？

祝 节日快乐！

　　工作开心！

林蓓蓓

我说权威说法有害，就在于如果考生们坚信自己是永远达不到最高境界的话，他（她）就永远不可能达到最高境界，永远在胜利之前的那个最黑暗的夜晚放弃努力，终于只能一辈子仰望险峰绝顶，而体验不了那里的无限风光。还有一种说法，本来荒谬已极，居然招摇于世，叫做"GRE和GMAT的学习，只能提高考生的应试技巧，不能提高考生的英语水平。"怎么可能?! 背下了上万个高级英语实用单词，精读了200多篇逻辑严密、论理清楚、结构复杂的高级英语阅读文章，英语水平会没有提高?! 难道像笔者那样，抱着一种"登泰山而小天下，学GRE而小英文"的学习者，在高分通过GRE考试之后对英语听、说、读、写、译的飞跃性的提高都仅仅是一种幻觉？更有一个号称"傻"字当头的"高手，高手，高高手"跑出来演讲，宣称考完GRE后再考大学四级，才考了60多分，以此证明GRE的学习与提高英语水平没关系，简直就是人如其名。

然而当今出国培训的最大症结就在于此。笔者前面所讲到的很多人所犯的可悲又没有必要的错误亦在于此。很多人受种种流行说法所误导，虽然花了大量时间来学习GRE 和 GMAT，但是由于指导思想错误，阅读能力一直无法提高。这些人过分相信技巧至上，而不从最根本的阅读的基本功入手，不从人的记忆规律、认知规律、阅读习惯出发，不肯痛下功夫认真地对阅读文章进行系统的训练，从而真正地体会到 GRE、GMAT 阅读中包含的规律性的东西，就想有大的提高，好比痴心妄想，痴人说梦。古人说得精辟，无欲速，无欲小利；欲速则不达，欲小利则大事不成。按照笔者系统的训练方法，很多学生除了 10~15 天要全心投入用集中突破法训练之外，其他时间每天仅花两到三个小时来训练阅读，在短短两三个月之内阅读能力都得以飞跃。说起来也许令人难以置信，最快的方法，往往就是最"笨"的方法！此处所说的笨，并不是不讲学习技巧的一味的笨，而是从阅读的基本功出发，老老实实、按部就班地循序渐进，注意总结自己的每一个心得体会，到了一个特定的水平线以集中突破法为手段，以摧枯拉朽之势征服 GRE、GMAT 阅读这只拦路虎。笔者抱憾于不能把所研究的成果广播于天下，唯有夜以继日笔耕不辍，谨以此书作为阅读基本功训练教程奉献给中国的有志于出国求学的莘莘学子们，愿大家有志竟成！

本书之出炉，得益于俞敏洪校长的大力支持和宝贵意见；在成书的过程中，又得到很多同学提供的第一手资料，在此鸣谢！

由于时间紧张，水平有限，本书必有缺憾，还请大家批评斧正。笔者的 e-mail 是：complex-sentence@21cn.com

杨　鹏

——再版前言——

承蒙朋友们的厚爱，《GRE&GMAT 阅读难句教程》一书反复再版、重印，这一次新东方大愚文化的编辑让我写几句话，也使我有机会对本书的使用方法再做一些补充说明。

本书初次出版，是在笔者到新东方授课满一年之时，书中还有些许零碎的错误。经过几次修改，可以说已经大致无误了，但是心中的遗憾，却与日俱增。如果是今天来写此书，恐怕会面目全非了。这并不是说原书的写法不对：经过这么长时间的考验，此书仍然被广泛使用，已经证明了书的质量，也令笔者感到莫大的欣慰。当初写的时候，一字一句，纯是出自我心，虽然写得很苦，但也希望能够成为经典。至于书出版之后，引来一片"难句"出书风潮，从四、六级、考研难句到 TOEFL、IELTS 难句，倒是笔者始料未及的。不过即使是今天来看这本书，仍然不显得过时，可以说基本上实现了当初的目标。但是近些年来，随着阅历和年龄的增加，又幻想着如果重写此书，可能会写得更好；就好像我们常常幻想如果能够再活一遍，一定会活得更精彩一样。只是我们终究无法再活一遍，就像我现在无法再写书一样。所以幻想终究只能是幻想，所能弥补的，是在这里再提醒一下我们的读者，什么是正确的练习难句的方法。

笔者教过的上万名同学中，使用难句训练提高水平最大、最快者，都是背下30～50个难句子的同学，他们的方法超出了笔者的"每个句子反复阅读"的要求；进步中等的同学是按照笔者所说的方法一个句子反复阅读的同学；而绝大多数同学只是走马观花，把每个句子分析一下语法、看一看解释就了事，所以收效不多。我的一个学生把书读了一遍，了无所得，来找我问为什么进步不大？后来考 GMAT 失败，方才想起来我当初的"把句子熟读、烂读"的要求，狂读了一个月的难句子，第二次考出770 的高分，特意又来找到我讲述这段经历。古人说，惟上智与下愚者不移，意思是只有最聪明和最傻的人才能坚持到底、矢志不移。而能够傻练到底的人实在太少了！所以最好本书的读者能够把每个句子都至少读到 20 遍以上，不要管读不读得懂——反复读，就是最好的学习方法。因为语言是一种习惯表达，是没有道理的，熟悉了就会懂；如果不熟悉，就算了解了其中所有的语法，读起文章来照样是不懂。请读者们切记！

我还要向读者们道歉：我原来的计划是要再写两本书，一本《17 天搞定 GRE 单词》在 2001 年底就已经出版了，但是另外一本《GRE 阅读集中突破法》，这些年一直没有时间写。所以每当有读者写信来问什么时候可以见到这本书的时候，我都惭愧得无以复加，感觉就像欠债不还一样。不过我想将来还是有可能写的，毕竟，老师是我一生的职业，当我没有很多机会在讲台上教课的时候，写书可能是我与同学们交流的更好的方式。

最后，感谢同学们多年来对我的支持，祝愿每一位学习英语的同学都能迅速提高自己的英语水平，祝愿每一个追求自己理想的人都能够实现自己的梦想！

杨 鹏

本书写作原则及读者学习指导

◎ 大原则：以实战的要求为目的

任何一本以考试学习为目的的教学书籍，如果不能贴近实战，必为废品。笔者认为，写书者如不能心系天下考生，而以个人著书立说、名利双收为主要目的，浪费了读者们宝贵的时间、精力与金钱，则该书不写也罢。

本书有两个目的：第一，训练读者在现场迅速读懂 GRE 和 GMAT 考试中出现的难句子的能力。请注意，我说的不是阅读文章中的难句子，而是所有考试中出现的难句子。尽管本书中所录仅为 GRE 和 GMAT 考试中出现的阅读文章的难句，但是考生只要能够克服它们，那么一切在考试中所出现的对于句子的阅读就都不在话下，因为在考试中阅读文章句子的难度很大。

第二，本书也可以用作复习 GRE、GMAT 考试阅读部分的参考书，同学们可以在此查找到在文章中最难以理解的句子的详细解释（包括中文翻译和语法分析）。抱歉的是，由于时间紧张，本书中只收录了最难的一百多个句子，肯定有一些值得解释的句子漏网。同学们如果遇到在理解上感到困难的句子，可以注明在教材中的页码和行数，请发 e-mail（e-mail 地址见前言）给我，我会在再版时将其补充进去。

◎ 原则一：迅速读懂

"迅速"和"懂"之下都加了重点号，是因为在考试现场，这二者缺一不可。其实 GRE 和 GMAT 中没有真正意义上读不懂的句子，只要时间够用，反复阅读之下，最终都可以读懂。但是这对于考生来讲没有丝毫意义，因为在考试现场根本就没有那么多的时间反复来读同一个句子。本书的最终目标就是训练考生们一遍读懂句子的能力。

◎ 原则二：利用语法，不靠语法

由于中国考生从小接受的英语教育就是碰到一个英语句子就分析它的语法结构，因此在阅读中也对英语语法过分依赖，这是同学们在考试现场阅读速度上不去的一个重要原因。英语语法的最基本的功能有两个，一是规定造句者所写或说的英语句子结构的规范，二是避免读者或听者产生错误的理解。我们当然应该承认，语法学习对于初学英语的人打好英语基础、理解英文语义有着不可替代的作用。

然而对于实用英语、尤其是 GRE 和 GMAT 考试中的英语来讲，过多的强调语法的作用弊大于利。首先，语法的最主要功能是约束那些书面语的写作者（如 ETS 的出题者）的，对考生而言，一句话的语法是否严密、哪个词（或词组）来充当主谓宾定补状等成分都不是我们需要关心的问题。更有些同学无法摆脱多年英语学习和考试中形成的惯性思维，一看到句子，就本能地想去分析其语法结构，忘了自己是在考大学四、六级考试还是在考 GRE 或 GMAT 的阅读。这一点虽然说起来可笑，然而却是很多人都会犯的一个惯性思维的错误。请本书的读者永远记住，在 GRE 或 GMAT 考试中，考生永远也不需要在考场上分析一句话的语法成分，也不要想这句话有没有语法错误：考生的惟一任务，就是现场快速地将其读懂！而且在考试中的阅读材料中，其语法也永远是对的，即使你发现某些语法与你多年所学不合，你也不要怀疑其正确性：如果你在阅读中发现了问题，一般来讲，是你水平不够；特殊情况下，即使你坚信你是正确的，你也不要在这上面费神，因为出题者是游戏规则的设计者，而你不得不按照这一规则玩下去。千万不要忘了你正在做的是阅读题。而且，没有人能够不花时间就把一句话的语法分析明白，尤其是 GRE 和 GMAT 的难句子，就算是花了时间，你也不一定能搞清楚。而以 GRE 和 GMAT 考试之难，现场阅读量之大，一分一秒的时间浪费都是考生承受不起的。

另外一方面，笔者又不得不在本书中对所有的难句子做一些简单的语法分析。原因有两个：第一，初学 GRE 或 GMAT 的中国考生如果看不懂句子的结构，往往会感到烦躁不安，心情沮丧；或大脑溜号，连文章都读不下去，更谈不上对文章有所理解了。因此，适度的语法解释可以给学习者以信心，让大家感觉到："哦，这句话原来如此，我是可以看懂的。"第二，笔者在书中做语法分析的目的，是想让读者们熟悉各种 GRE 和 GMAT 阅读中常用的（但是对初学者来讲却是极为生僻或不习惯的）语法结构，熟悉到见怪不惊的程度；再配合以各种训练方法，最后达到能够熟练掌握各种句式结构，不必做语法分析就能一遍读懂的目的。也就是说，我们利用语法来学习、掌握难句的规律，一旦达到了这一目的，就要抛弃它。就好比每个中国人在认字之前都要学习拼音一样，学拼音并不是目的，用拼音是为了认识那些我们还不掌握的字；而一旦字认得差不多了，没有谁还会死抱着拼音不放，都会把拼音扔掉，独立地来认字。

◎ 原则三：学练结合，以练为主

说到底，阅读能力还是一种实战要求很高的技能。不管考生语法知识有多丰富，英语词汇量有多大，但是如果不能在看到句子时迅速看懂这句话的含义，哪怕他（她）是英语专业的博士生，在 GRE 和 GMAT 的考场之上也一样会败下阵来。仅仅从理论上进行探讨是纸上谈兵；只有配合了一定强度的合理的训练，才能拥有一定的技能。笔者长期以来一直为没有合适的、能够针对考生的英语阅读习惯而设计的阅读材料而苦恼，现在终于轮到笔者来写书，能够有机会把本书设计成为一本学练结合、以练为主的实用书籍，真乃幸事也！

　　本书的训练分为三类：1. 难句阅读训练；2. 阅读理解力训练；3. 阅读速度和阅读习惯训练。对于难句本身阅读的训练，自是本书的第一要务，其训练方法作者将在后面第三章"克服 GRE、GMAT 难句"中详述，在此不多费笔墨。关键是后两类阅读能力的训练，一直令笔者在教学中耿耿于怀，心情沉重，又无计可施。大家可能注意到了，所谓第二类"阅读理解力训练"，就是上面笔者反复用重点号标出来的那个"懂"字，而第三类"阅读速度和阅读习惯训练"，其实就是标了重点号的"迅速"二字。有些考生在以上的两点上已经病入膏肓、积重难返，不大剂量施以猛药，不足以去根。

　　我们从小学习英语，从老师到学生都形成了这样一个观念，那就是："学英语是为了考试"。此观念不能说它对，但是谁也不能不承认这个观念管用。在应试教育之下，分数就是一切；我们当然也知道运用英语的能力很重要，但是我们的时间和精力虽然有限，考试的科目却多，所以对于能力的培养还是放一放再说吧，什么"高分低能"的帽子戴它一段时间又有什么了不起，等到挤过了高考这座独木桥，到了大学再培养能力也来得及。问题是到了大学，一些学习习惯和思维定势已经形成，而考试仍多，很多不良习惯既改不了又没有必要改，于是又把真正提高英语能力的希望寄托到毕业以后。然而毕业后大家都比较忙碌，少年时的梦也渐渐的淡了。偏偏 GRE 考试又是一种能力考试（Aptitude Test）！

　　应试教育对英语阅读产生的负面影响体现在以下两个方面：

　　1. 刻板地死记硬背单词，看到单词时的第一反应就是背出单词本上与它对应的中文释义，对英语句子乃至文章的理解也仅停留在翻译的层次上。这也难怪考生，本来我们的英语学习从来就不是为了实际的使用，惟一目的就是为了应付考试。而我们的考试是规定了一大堆标准答案的；你不把单词的中文释义背得一字不差，即使能说对意思，还是要算你错。记得有一个在英国长大的华人小女孩，八、九岁的时候被带回到中国生活，有一次小学里考英语，她放学后哭着回家，妈妈问起来，她说是因为有一道题考汉译英，"这是真的吗？"，标准答案是"Is it true?"，被她答成了"Really?"，结果被老师批了一顿。小女孩不能理解：在英国大家都说"Really?"，没有人会说"Is it true?"，怎么到了中国就反过来了？这种考试和这种教育的结果就是大家全部脱离了学习英语的真正目的，在一个自己塑造出来的虚幻的封闭系统里搞出来一套中国英语，过分地强调一些意义并不大的东西：比如说，我们为什么要学英语？是为了搞懂外国人说什么或者写什么，还是为了成为语法专家或蹩脚的翻译家？我们语法的考试能力很强，但是一旦我们开口说话，或写点儿什么东西，语法错误不断，令美国人百思而不得其解。实际上，对于英语语法的学习，包括对英文单词的中文释义的记忆和对英语句子的中文翻译，都只是我们学习英语的辅助工具：我们最终的目的，是为了提高对英语的实际使用能力。具体到 GRE 和 GMAT 考试的应用上，就是看到英语句子时，正确的做法不应该是现场先分析出其语法结构、再背出每个单词的中文释义，再把这些中文单词串成句子，最后才根据翻译出来的中文来想这句话的意思是什么，而是读到每一个词、每一句话的时候，大脑中的第一反应是其意思而不是中文释义。这种反应才是现场最合理、最准确也是最节省时间的反应，是考生在现场对于自己英语技能的最高层次的应用：这才是我在前面反复强调的迅速读懂的不二法门！（请参阅附录三"阅读抽象词提速法"）

2. 应试教育对英语阅读产生的第二个负面影响，是学习者忽视了许多考试以外的能力的培养，因此从学习英语的第一天起，就养成了许多不良习惯。拿阅读能力来讲，以英语为母语的受过一定教育的人读文章的读法与我们根本就不一样：精读、泛读、跳读、略读、读意群、横读、竖读，根据阅读材料的不同，可以用最快的方式汲取到所需要的信息。正是因为他们需要使用英语的阅读能力为每天的学习、工作和生活服务，所以才能训练出种种快速有效的阅读技巧来。美国是最早研究速读法的国家，很多美国人的阅读速度可以达到每分钟几千个英文单词，甚至还有人能做到每分钟读 20,000 个词。比如说《华盛顿邮报》每期 300 多版，而大多数有一定知识水平的美国人利用喝早茶的时间就能过一遍，要让我们的同学来读，恐怕没有几个月读不完。而我们从小学习英语，从来就不是以这种实战的快速阅读为目的的，从来我们拿到的英语阅读材料就都是既少又重要的精读文章，我们被要求认出其中的每一个单词，做对其后的每一道题，遇到读不懂的单词就拿出字典来查，久而久之，我们形成了一大堆臭毛病。阅读过程中的生词或专有名词我们不习惯于、也不敢于用合理化原则来推理出其意思；阅读中某词不太理解，就反复重读，不管三遍五遍，读懂为止；到后来干脆一个词、一个词地细抠，生怕出一点纰漏：分数低可是上不了重点学校的！如此一来，学生们的阅读速度奇慢无比。结果，我们的英语考试的出题者考虑到学生的阅读速度较慢又不得不延长考试时间，这样考生就更没有必要提高阅读速度，形成一种恶性循环。不但如此，我们从小就被家长和老师拎着朗读英语，到最后出声朗读几乎成了我们惟一的阅读方式，也就是说我们阅读的单位不但达不到竖读和意群，甚至连单词都不是，我们读的是音节！造成的结果，就是不但无法达到 GRE 要求的阅读速度，连 TOEFL 阅读的要求也无法满足。

在以上所述的两大类毛病中，前者相对较易改过来。只要读者对前面所述内容多加思考，再结合 GRE 考试的实际要求自己加以印证，只要想通了，改变自己的固有观念，都可以很快纠正过来。不过为了进一步夯实此点，笔者在此向读者们提出第一个要求：

要点一：请读者们在对本书的难句进行阅读的过程中，只以在大脑中反应出所读英文的意思（不是中文释义！）为惟一目的。什么时候读者发现自己完全消除了在阅读时在大脑中的中文翻译和语法分析过程，此要求即已达到。

然而对于笔者上文所说的第二大类的诸多毛病来讲，想要纠正却要下一定的功夫了。需要说明的一点是，在 GRE 和 GMAT 的考试中，基本不需要英美人士所常用的泛读、跳读、略读等方法，因为 GRE 阅读文章属于精读类型。但是中国同学长期以来所养成的回视、读音节等不良习惯却是要坚决克服的，因为这些习惯是绝对无法满足 GRE 和 GMAT 考试的时间要求的。笔者尽管反复在课上强调这一点，但是同学们往往积习难改；而且改掉一种不良习惯的惟一方法就是用一种好习惯来代替它。为此笔者特别在本书中设计了以下四种训练方式：

    a. 意群训练

    b. 不回视训练

    c. 合理化原则推理训练

    d. 速度与理解力的平衡点训练

四种训练的详细解释如下：

意群训练：前面讲过，多年朗读英文造成的悲剧性后果就是很多同学不把看到的东西念出声来，他（她）就读下去，看不懂文章。这样的阅读其实是在读音节，而其阅读速度会大大减慢。正确的读法是读意群（word group）。所谓意群就是指几个相邻的表示同类意思的词，而读意群就是说把这几个词用一眼看下来，可使阅读速度成数倍地提高。如：

例句：
> The methods that a community devises to perpetuate itself come into being to preserve aspects of the culture legacy that that community perceives as essential.
>
> （注：此句属于难句例句之一，此处读者先不必读懂，后面有详解）

像这么一个句子，我们完全可以不必一个单词、一个单词来读，因为英语中有很多虚词，只有语法意义而无实际意义；还有很多词组，只有几个词放到一起才有完整的意义，这些成分我们都可以在现场合并到一起来读。如例句中的前三个单词 The methods that，实际上读者完全可以一眼看下来，因为这三个词说的其实就是一个 methods。整个例句如果用意群的方法来读，可以分成 8 眼看下来：

The methods that a community devises to perpetuate itself come into being to preserve aspects of the culture legacy that that community perceives as essential.

原来眼睛要停留 25 次的句子，如果现在只停留 8 次，阅读速度即是原来的三倍。问题是，有的同学看到此马上就会问一个问题，你说得头头是道，但是真的可行吗？我怎么看着不习惯呢？先说可行不可行的问题。我告诉你，美国人可以一眼看一行，你信不信？你要是不信，我告诉你我读中文可以一眼看一行，这回你信不信？你可能回答我说，读中文的话我还能一目十行呢。问题出来了。大家都知道中文是世界上语法最复杂的语言，而且单个字的信息量也最大，一行中文翻译成英语可能要两行，为什么你读中文可以一目十行，可是改成读英文的时候就连三个词都不能一眼看下来呢？所以我在课上反复对同学们说，读意群是一个习惯问题，而不是能力问题。读意群的另外一个重大的好处，就是它可以克服很多同学的出声读、读音节的问题。不信你试试看，眼睛在三个单词上停一下就走，你怎么把三个词给我同时念出来？

再说习惯的问题。首先，我在此向本书的读者提一个要求：从今天开始，就请不要出声朗读任何阅读材料。这是克服读音节的前提条件。还没完，很多同学知道出声读不好，但是阅读时仍然在心里出声读。请这部分同学有意识地压抑住内心的声音和喉头及嘴唇的颤动。然而光靠这一点是不够的，解决有声阅读的最关键的一点是：

要点二：眼睛在阅读材料上移动的速度要比自己在心中或喉部出声阅读的速度快上一点点。

笔者承认，这种阅读习惯的改变是非常痛苦和困难的。笔者原来也有在心里出声读的毛病，在念大学期间几番要改，但是都无功而返，因为当时还没有遇到像 GRE 或 GMAT 对阅读速度要求这么高的考试。后来为了考 G，笔者痛下决心，不到一个月就彻底改成了读意群，到现在已经可以不分意群地用眼睛横扫了。其实只要是练到读意群的程度就已经足以应付 GRE 和 GMAT 考试的要求了。不过读者在按照上面所讲的方法改变阅读习惯的初期，会感觉按照上面的要求，什么都看不懂。这是正常现象：由于练习者要花很大心思在克服错误习惯、使用新的阅读方法上，无法把注意力都集中于所看到的句子的内容上，因此在理解上必然会产生一定问题。但是请大家不必在意，看不懂也不要回去复读（回视），坚决地按照读意群的方式读下去，一段时间后新习惯已经养成，注意力又可以回到文章上，就能够既快又好地理解文章。至此，读意群的能力就已练成。

苦于目前市面上还没有专门为 GRE 和 GMAT 考生设计的、针对意群训练的阅读材料，笔者在此书中将所有收录的难句以意群格式重排，附于每个难句的详解之后，希望能够方便那些想提高 GRE 或 GMAT 阅读速度的同学。注意：笔者建议初学本书的读者可暂不练习读意群，最好是学到 15～20 个句子之后，基本摸到了 GRE 的语言规律之后再进行集中训练，效果较好。否则，本来句子就读不懂，再用一种不熟悉的方式来读，容易丧失学习信心。

需要提请大家注意的是，一旦基本养成读意群的习惯之后，就不必太拘泥于读意群；尤其是有些同学练习到后来，在阅读的时候不去读文章的意思，而是去想现在有没有读意群，这简直是舍本逐末、买椟还珠。其实，阅读意群的最高境界就是不分意群，大脑中思考的是文章的意思，而眼睛则在文章上横扫。所以请同学们注意，只要你在阅读的时候不是在一个一个单词地读，一眼可以看两个以上的单词，则只要能够读懂句意，则就算符合要求。

不回视训练：中国考生阅读速度上不去的另外一个重要的原因就是喜欢回视。表面上回视的原因只有一个，就是第一遍没看懂，可是实际上回视的真正原因却有两种：最主要的原因是第一遍看得不认真，其次才是真的有些单词或结构不懂。前者是一种极其不好的阅读习惯，究其来源，就是前面笔者所述的应试教育的必然结果：我们既不需要在日常生活中做大量英语阅读，考试时时间又很宽裕，回视几乎就是天经地义的。再加上考分历来的对中国人的重要性，使得我们向来不太相信自己的眼睛，还是多看几遍来得稳妥。这样一来，回视又产生了另一个坏毛病：第一遍阅读时注意力不集中。人人都有惰性，既然可以读三遍才懂，何必费那么大的力气苛求自己上来就非要读懂呢？结果溜号、走神，以至于非要回视不可。最终，回视和注意力不集中形成了一个恶性循环的怪圈。而打破这个怪圈的方法就是：

要点三：在阅读本书，以及其他任何英语材料时，都请注意杜绝整句的回视现象，坚持一遍读下来。

这种训练的道理在于，抛不开拐棍的人，永远学不会独立行走。一旦失去了支撑，摔得鼻青脸肿，真正疼了，才会注意认真走路。训练不回视也是这么个过程，刚开始，一遍读下来读不懂，又不能回头看，心中痛苦；有过几次这样的经验，再读东西的时候，就自然而然的会肃然为戒，下意识地告诉自己，我这一辈子只有这一次机会看到这个单词和句子，注意力就会高度集中，看到真正不懂的东西就地用合理化原则推断出其大致含意，这样一来，理解力大为提高，回视也就没有必要了。

笔者可以负责地告诉读者，只要大家可以做到以意群为阅读单位，并且能够在阅读的过程中基本不回视，就已经可以达到 GRE 和 GMAT 考试现场的阅读速度要求。只要同学们坚定信念，都可以在较短时间内形成这些良好的阅读习惯。

合理化原则推理训练：在阅读过程当中往往会遇到真正不认识的单词或词组，有的同学立即怒火中烧，愤而跳过；有的人顿感天旋地转，如堕五里雾中；还有人感觉如冷水浇头，豪气顿消，在一种郁闷的情绪下读完全文；更多的人心乱如麻之下，反复阅读，回视了三、五遍之后，还是不明所以，把时间白白地浪费掉了。这些反应同样是我国多年以来英语教育的片面性所造成的：我们泛读训练几乎为零，而阅读教材上的精读文章之前，都要先把所有生词全部背过才行。结果是大家天生的合理化原则的推理能力在英语阅读中全部退化，学生们成为字典的奴隶。实际上，在 GRE 和 GMAT 考试中出现的大部分生词或专有名词，都可以利用合理化原则推理出其大致含意，而不会影响对文章的理解。所谓合理化原则推理，就是指根据看不懂成分在句中的位置以及它与上下文中读者可以看懂的其他成分的关系，推理出其大致意思和特点及其在文中起到的作用；对于专有名词，还可以用词头、词根推断出其大概含意，如果还是不行就对它做首字母提炼，先知道这里有这么个东西，后面很有可能作者会再做说明，或者考到时知道回来找就可以了。这个合理化原则说白了，就是在文中，一个词该是什么意思，它就是什么意思。

例句：
> Many theories have been formulated to explain the role of grazers such as zooplankton in controlling the amount of plank-tonic algae（phytoplankton）in lakes.

有很多人一读之下立即背过气去：不定式中 explain 的长宾语中居然有三个词不认识（zooplankton、planktonic、phytoplankton），这文章怎么读啊！其实如果认识词头词根的话，zoo-是动物的词头，phyto-是植物的词头，二者的关系是前者控制后者，都生活在湖里，肯定是前者吃后者的关系。-plankton 是浮游生物的词根，前后一拼就出来了：肯定是浮游动物吃浮游植物。即使这些词头、词根你都不认识，前面的 grazer 和后面的 algae 总该认识了吧?! 前面是食草的动物，后面是水藻，那么那个叫 Z…的东西一定是个水虫，后面的叫 P…的玩意儿必是一种水草，这篇文章讲的一定就是水虫控制水草的机制的。

其实上面的推理是任何人都能轻易做出来的，但问题是初学 GRE 的同学根本就没有想到要自己去作推理，以至于在阅读现场或反复回视，或不知所措，就是不肯自己开动一下脑筋。我们说，灵活的运用合理化原则来阅读，这是一种主动阅读的方式，能够表现出考生在阅读时的积极的心态。

要点四：读者在练习本书难句时，凡遇到不懂的成分，请就地用合理化原则进行推理。

速度与理解力的平衡点训练：阅读理解毕竟是一种实际能力，需要同学们不断在训练中调节自己的状态。在实践中，有的同学片面追求速度，有的同学片面追求看懂，其实单独强调任何一方面而忽视了另一方面都是不现实的，不能满足 GRE 和 GMAT 考试的实战要求。总体而言，现场阅读的速度和对所读内容的理解力成反比关系，即速度越快，则理解越下降；理解越透，则速度越慢。这个公式很好理解，关键是我们怎么利用这个原理。它给我们提出了两点要求。第一，同学们要在阅读的实践中不断摸索出适合自己的在阅读速度与理解力之间的平衡点，使得自己在满足考试时间要求的前提下，对阅读材料达到一个最佳的理解程度。第二，读者应该在阅读中根据所读内容的难度和重要性的不同，调整自己的现场阅读速度。因此笔者希望读者学到本书的后半部分，基本掌握了难句的规律和已经能够习惯于用意群进行阅读的时候，在读本书的过程中能够注意寻找一下自己在阅读中的速度与理解力的平衡点，并注意在阅读文章时，读到文章主题和重要的启、承、转、合点或较难的句子时适当放慢速度。

本书的学习进度：作者写本书的目标是争取让读者在 20 天到一个月的时间内彻底攻克 GRE 和 GMAT 难句，并形成正确的阅读习惯，为最终征服 GRE 或 GMAT 阅读打下坚实的物质基础。笔者希望读者一次将本书前面讲解难句规律的部分读完；第二天将第一天所讲的要点简要地复习一下，接下来按部就班地按照第二章的难句训练法所述，每天花半小时左右进行系统训练；练习到 20 句之后开始加入意群训练和不回视训练，到本书的后半部分时再加入速度与理解力的平衡点训练。注意在全书的学习过程中，都要自觉地灵活运用合理化原则做推理训练。还有一点请读者注意，那就是：

要点五：本书的学习贵在每天坚持，雷打不动，不半途而废，只有这样才必有效果。

从某种角度上讲，整个 GRE 和 GMAT 考试就是考阅读。好的阅读能力是考出较为令人满意的分数的前提条件。希望同学们能够以坚定的意志和坚强的决心坚持训练，彻底粉碎难句这块顽石，以期为最终完成阅读能力的飞跃扫清障碍。

第一章　GRE、GMAT 难句概论

1.1　什么是 GRE、GMAT 难句

GRE 和 GMAT 考试的一大特点，也是一大难点，就是充斥着一些或很长、或很怪异的句子，我们称之为 GRE、GMAT 难句。从这些句子在考试中所起到的作用和它们对考生的影响来讲，以阅读和逻辑单题中出现的难句对考生杀伤力为最大。其中又以阅读中的难句最难，请看 GRE 阅读中所出现过的最长的句子：

例句：
> Theses questions are political in the sense that the debate over them will inevitably be less an exploration of abstract matters in a spirit of disinterested inquiry than an academic power struggle in which the careers and professional fortunes of many women scholars—only now entering the academic profession in substantial numbers—will be at stake, and with them the chances for a distinctive contribution to humanistic understanding, a contribution that might be an important influence against sexism in our society.

尽管这句话远算不上是 GRE 和 GMAT 考试中最难理解的句子，然而可以想像当我们的考生在考场上发现原来这篇长文章的第三段原来就是一个长达 10 行的大句子的时候，其欲哭无泪的心情。句子，作为任何阅读材料中最基本的阅读单位，其重要性不言而喻。可是 GRE 和 GMAT 阅读中的句式之繁难，超出其他所有的英语考试的范畴，其长度更令人瞠目，往往读到句末，已经忘了前面在说些什么，令很多初学者困惑不已，不得不放弃真正读懂文章的想法。因此，在学习 GRE 和 GMAT 的早期阶段用较短的时间打掉难句子这只拦路虎就成了摆在众多有志出国的 GRE 和 GMAT 考生面前的一

个很现实的任务了。

1.2　GRE、GMAT 难句的由来

谈到这些句子的来历，不得不说一下 GRE 文章和 GMAT 文章的来历。

GRE 和 GMAT 考试中所出现的所有阅读文章都是来自于英语国家，主要是美国的各种最新的科学杂志中所收录的学术论文，由 ETS 的阅读测试专家将这些原始资料根据考试要求进行了重新改写。其改写有两种方式，一是为了出题而在原文中加上了对应答案的选项的语言重现。二是大量的删节与压缩。因为美国科学杂志上刊登的学术论文长度动辄上千行、最少也要有几百行，要压缩成几十行的 GRE 和 GMAT 文章，就必须用最小的篇幅来运载最多的信息。原文的一段或几段变成了现在的一个句子，结果就是改写后的句子奇长无比，信息量大，而且没有什么废话与重复，因此对其中任何一个单词的理解出了问题，都有可能造成对整句话理解的错误。但是如果把账全算到 ETS 身上也不公平，因为这些美国科学家所撰写的论文本身就非善类。试举一例：

例句：This simplest kind of black hole—one formed by the contraction of nonrotating, collisionless matter with spherical symmetry—is called a Schwarzschild black hole, after the astronomer and mathematician Karl Schwarzschild, who devised the first known solution to Einstein's equations of general relativity.

此句子与 GRE、GMAT 文章的句子何其相像！看来我们的同学研究一下难句不仅仅对考试有好处，我们到了美国原来也要天天读这些东西，有些同学说不定哪一天自己也要写一些这类东西！

1.3　GRE、GMAT 难句与文章的对应关系

笔者经过长期观察发现，GRE 和 GMAT 的各种文章中，句子的难度与文章的内容往往有一种对应关系，即：文章越难，句子就越简单——如生命科学和自然科学题材的文章，由于其内容较难，细节较多，因此绝大多数的情况下这类文章的句子相对文科文章而言较短，较容易，以降低文章难度；而文章本身越简单，其句子也就越难——如文学评论和社会科学的文章，因其内容较少，作者态度较为明确，因而难句通常既多又难；我们很多考生因为无法读懂这些句子，反而认为这两种文章比生物、物

理文章更难。因此，对文学评论型文章比较害怕的同学们下一番功夫攻克 GRE 难句，就显得更为重要了。

1.4 理解难句对于做题的影响

在前面举过例子的那篇长文章中，有一句话，叫做：

例句：
Studies by Hargrave and Geen estimated natural community grazing rates by measuring feeding rates of individual zooplankton species in the laboratory and then computing community grazing rates for field conditions using the known population density of grazers.

文章后面出了一道题，问 Hargrave and Geen 在其实验中干了什么事，很明显正确答案一定是原文刚才那句话的同义改写。后面的五个选项分别如下：

(A) They compared the grazing rates of individual zooplankton species in the laboratory with the natural grazing rates of these species.

(B) They hypothesized about the population density of grazers in natural habitats by using data concerning the population density of grazers in the laboratory.

(C) They estimated the community grazing rates of zooplankton in the laboratory by using data concerning the natural community grazing rates of zooplankton.

(D) They estimated the natural community grazing rates of zooplankton by using data concerning the known population density by phytoplankton.

(E) They estimated the natural community grazing rates of zooplankton by using laboratory data concerning the grazing rates of individual zooplankton species.

看明白应该选哪个选项了吗？请读者们读到此处先不要往后看，假设你自己就在考试现场做题，你选哪个选项呢？

还有，你想一想 ETS 出这样一道题，是为了考你什么东西呢？

世界上没有任何人，也没有任何技巧能够使考生在现场读不懂原文的那句话就能够把这道题做对。这道题是摆在那些技巧至上（注意：笔者并非说技巧一点儿用处都没有）的鼓吹者面前的一座不可逾越、又无法绕开的大山，是那些不肯下功夫真正攻克英语阅读难句的人的致命伤。

从这道题里面，我们清晰的听到了 ETS 的声音：

"提高你们的阅读能力吧！"

其实文中所说的就是这么一个简单的事情：

实验室单位速率×野外密度＝野外群体速率

可以想一想，如果出题者想把这句话说得简单或者想让你把这道题做对，他（她）能不能做到？实在太简单了。ETS 的用心不必笔者再费笔墨了吧？

本题答案选（E），请读者们自行琢磨。

第二章　GRE、GMAT 难句的语法突破

首先笔者声明一点：本书所有的（当然也包括此处的）任何的语法分析都只是一种帮助读者理解并掌握难句的规律的手段，而不是暗示或鼓励任何人依靠语法分析来进行现场阅读。在本书中，语法是手段而不是目的；笔者是利用语法这只船把读者们渡到熟练掌握难句规律的彼岸，让大家明白这些难句结构的原理和其所要表达的语义，而一旦读者们熟悉了这些常用的难句表达方式，就一定要勇于抛弃语法，轻装前进。因为现场做语法分析，既影响速度又无必要；同学们在现场阅读时的真正要务是迅速读懂。再啰嗦两句。笔者希望读者了解并熟悉了某一种语法结构在难句中表达的意思之后，就要忘掉与该语法有关的一切，只要再看到难句中的同样结构时能正确地反应出其意思即可。如果读者读完本书后养成了读文章时下意识地分析其句子的语法的恶习，笔者将无颜面对天下 GRE、GMAT 考生！

由于笔者向来坚决反对在阅读理解的过程中做语法分析，而且向来也认为在现场阅读中，对语法分析的过度迷恋不但起不到太大的作用，反而对考生的阅读速度有负面影响，因此在本书中作者只做最简单的语法解释，只以把问题说清楚为目的，而避免使用任何有可能使读者陷入语法争论的说明。我用语法的目的只是让大家知道："原来在难句中这么说是这个意思"，下次看到这样的结构就会立即正确地理解其语义。

本书对每个难句的解释使用以下格式：

1. 首先列出难句原文。
2. 用各种符号做标志将难句中需要解释的较难的部分分解成有意义的单元，使读者一目了然。而不需要解释的地方笔者不会特别标出，以免显得杂乱无章。各种标志的用法如下：

主语：加阴影；谓语：加下划线；宾语：波浪线；插入语：加双点下划线；修饰成分：括号按修饰的层面由大到小用 ‖ ‖、[ ] 或（）表示；表示并列、转折

等的连词：**黑体字**；省略：*斜体字*。长状语：∕ ⋯⋯∕；从句引导词：│that│

例：The methods （│that│ a community devises to perpetuate itself） <u>come into being</u>∕to <u>preserve</u> aspects of the cultural legacy （│that│ that community perceives as essential） ∕.

其实读者此处不必硬记这些符号，读过几个句子自然就记住了。

3. 汉语译文。

4. 难点分析（会用到语法说明）。

5. 意群训练。

2.1 GRE、GMAT 难句的分类详解

GRE 和 GMAT 难句虽然为数众多，但是类型较少，很容易掌握。从实战的角度，一共分为四种类型：

第一类：复杂修饰成分

说明：句子本不难，但是修饰成分多且长。修饰成分大致有以下几种：

1. 从句（包括主语从句、宾语从句、定语从句、状语从句、同位语从句等等）；

2. 介词短语修饰；

3. 分词修饰；

4. 不定式修饰。

经常是在同一个句子里有一种以上的修饰成分，且每一种修饰成分也可能不止一个。

例句：The methods that a community devises to perpetuate itself come into being to preserve aspects of the cultural legacy that that community perceives as essential.

标志：The methods （│that│ a community devises to perpetuate itself） <u>come into being</u> ∕ to <u>preserve</u> aspects of the cultural legacy （│that│ that community perceives as essential）∕.

译文：（一个社会设计出来保存自己的）方法得以形成／来保持（那个社会认为是最重要的）文化遗产的一些方面／。

规律：此类难句之所以难，就只是因为长。而之所以长，是因为前面说过的 ETS 要对原文进行压缩的原因，句子必须携带大量的信息，造成对句中的某些成分的大量修饰。我们可以想像，原文在被压缩前可以是这样的一段话：

> All communities seek to perpetuate themselves. They apparently do so by preserving their cultural legacy. But when they don't have the ability to preserve all the aspects of their culture, they choose those aspects that they perceive as essential. Thus, although many diverse methods come into being to serve this purpose, they all share one common feature.

我们知道，中文也是可以通过增加修饰成分无限扩展下去的。比如说，我们完全可以把一句最简单的话，"他看书"，变成一句奇长无比的结构复杂的难懂的句子，如：

困倦的他在看一本旧书；

一夜没睡的困倦的他目光呆滞地在看一本发黄了的旧书；

斜靠在沙发上，没有血色的嘴唇上叼着一只不知在什么时候就早已经熄灭了的雪茄烟，一夜没睡的困倦的他目光呆滞地借助一盏时明时暗的摇曳的残破油灯绝望地在无精打采地看着一本发黄了的、却保存得颇为完整的现在市面上很难买到的名叫《准备考试的你能看得懂这句不但无聊之极而且无耻之尤的话吗？》的旧书。

相信如果同学们感兴趣，想把这句话继续延长，恐怕可以写上数千字。当然以同学们的汉语水平，读这样的句子应是轻车熟路；可是你能想像一个母语不是汉语的、正在学习中文的美国人读到这句话的时候的惊恐不安吗？笔者的一个教对外汉语的朋友告诉笔者，其美国学生如果在考试中读到这样一句中文，其痛苦程度要远远高于同学们读到 GRE、GMAT 难句时的感觉。

读法：对于这种类型的难句，初学者可以先抓出句子的主谓宾等主要成分来，回头把修饰成分补上。比如刚才所举的例句，主语是 The methods；谓语：come into being；后面是一个以不定式 to 引导表示目的的状语；回头看 that a community devises to perpetuate itself 作为一个定语从句是修饰主语 methods 的，我们就知道是（一个社会设计出来保存自己的）方法，后面不定式中的主干是 preserve aspects of the cultural legacy，来保持文化遗产的一些方面；在 legacy 之后有一个定语从句 that that community perceives as essential. 此处的两个 that，第一个是定语从句的引导词，第二个 that 是指"那个"，此从句修饰 cultural legacy，［来保持（那个社会认为是最重要的）文化遗产的一些方面］。

然而这种读法绝不是我们难句训练的最终目的。我们评价一种阅读方法的好坏的惟一标准，就是它是否利于实战。此读法虽然能使我们读懂，但是速度较慢。我们所要训练出来的最后的正确的读法，就是按照英语原文的语序直接读。请读者不要怀疑自己是否具备这种能力，请问刚才读那句长得离谱的中文句子的时候，又有谁是先挑出主谓宾来读呢？都是直接读下来的，不也都理解得很好吗？中文能做到，英语亦然。至于怎么做到，是我们训练的手段问题。后面的"克服 GRE、GMAT 难句"一章中有详述。

第二类：大段的插入语或同位语

说明：这种难句是初学者感到最不习惯的一种难句。因为在汉语中几乎碰不到这种表达方式，而且就算是以前在英语学习中偶尔见过一些插入成分，但是像在 GRE 和 GMAT 考试中这么不分场合、不计后果的高频率地使用插入语，还是前所未见。所以中国学生初学 GRE 或者 GMAT 的时候，往往一看到长句子中出现了插入语，就发生思路混乱，感觉句意支离破碎，要看上几遍也不一定能把整个句子的意思有序地组织起来。

此类难句之所以难，在于其插入成分在句中打断读者的思路，割裂插入成分前后之间的句意，造成理解上的困难，我们称之为"打岔"。就好像一个人在说一句话时，总有人不断地打断他，结果讲话者因为现场思路受到严重干扰，最后自己想要说些什么都想不起来了。GRE 和 GMAT 中的插入语堪称语言表达的极端现象，不但长度极长——最长可以达到四、五行，而且可以在一句话中的任何地方出现，更增加了阅读者理解的困难。

例句：Moreover, I can feel strong emotions in response to objects of art that are interpretations, rather than representations, of reality.

标志：Moreover, I can feel strong emotions ［in response to objects of art（that are interpretations，rather than representations，of reality）].

译文：而且，我能够感觉到强烈的感情，[这些感情是对（现实的解释）的艺术目标做出的反应而不是对现实的描述的艺术目标做出的反应。]

解释：在 in response to 引导的、修饰 emotions 的介词结构中，介词宾语 objects of art 被由 that 引导的定语从句所修饰，而定语从句中的表语 interpretations of reality 被插入语 rather than representations 所分割，造成读者在看到 object of art that are interpretations 时大脑中反应出来的是"艺术的目标是解释"，看到 rather than representations 时大脑中又想到"艺术的目标是解释而不是描述"，此时突然看见 of reality，顿时大脑混乱，大叫"怪哉！"哪里来的 of reality，什么的 reality！

其实在 GRE、GMAT 考试中插入语的频繁使用是这两种考试的阅读材料本身的需要。笔者前面讲过，因为考试中阅读文章的篇幅有限，所以这些资料都是高度压缩得来，而使用插入语的一大好处就是可以节省篇幅。比如我说：

今天我去新华书店（不是教育书店）买了一本书。

如果我不用插入语，我就必须在句子后面补上一句话，变成这样：

今天我去新华书店买了一本书。我去的是新华书店，而不是教育书店。

后者的篇幅明显远远长于前者。固然可以把原话改成：我今天去买书的地方是新华书店而不是教育书店，但是此句与原句的语义有差别：原句强调的是买书的行为，而这句话却是强调去何处买的书。所以并不是所有的文章中的插入语都是出题者故意为考生所设置的障碍。但是在客观上这种语言结构确实给考生们带来了很大的麻烦。上面英文例句中的插入语属于 GRE 和 GMAT 考试中出现的最短的插入语（当然不算是最简单的插入语），但仍然能够起到割裂句意、干扰读者的作用，更不要说那些三、四行的大段插入语了。那么，现场遇到这种语言结构的时候应该如何处理呢？

读法：插入语的标志是成对出现的逗号。建议初学者凡是在阅读中遇到成对出现的逗号时，或是发现句意尚未完整时出现了逗号，先跳过插入语，将其前后的内容连起来读；待句意读完整后再回头读插入语。当然本书的目的不止于此。与第一类难句一样，经过系统训练之后的考生在一般情况下（插入语长度不超过三行）是可以将此类难句按照原文的语序直接读下去的（后面会详细谈到此点）。但请注意，如果插入语达到三行或三行以上，即使训练到了最后，大家读难句的能力已经很高，还是一定要先跳过，回头再把它看全。

第三类：倒装

说明：本书所提到的"倒装"结构与普通语法书中所说的倒装结构完全不是一回事。GRE 和 GMAT 中的语言结构的复杂程度远远超过了国内现有语法书所讨论的范畴，而笔者又不愿再造一些新的专有名词，宁愿旧瓶装新酒，借助现有的语法称呼解释一下 GRE 和 GMAT 中的这种常见的语言现象。

我们以前所说的英语语法中的倒装主要是指动词或助动词被提到主语前面，如"Here comes a bus"或"Were she here, she would support the motion"等等。这些东西我们从小就烂熟于心，不过在 GRE 和 GMAT 的考试中很少出现；即使出现，我们的考生也熟视无睹，不会对理解文章造成任何不利影响。而在这两种考试中对我们的考生造成真正威胁的常见的语序变化却是大段成分的后置：

例句：That sex ratio will be favored which maximizes the number of descendants an individual will have and hence the number of gene copies transmitted.

标志：That sex ratio will be favored [which maximizes the number of descendants (*that* dividual will have) **and** hence *maximizes* the number of gene copies (transmitted)].

译文：那种［能够*最大化*（一个个体的后代的）数目并且因此可以*最大化*（被传播的）基因的份数的］性别比率将会是有利的。

解释：像本句这样的语法结构在我们的大学教育中或是 TOEFL 考试中都是从来没有过的。本句的正常语序应当是：That sex ratio which maximizes the number of descendants an individual will have and hence the number of gene copies transmitted will be favored. 但是因为主语 That sex ratio 之后的以 which 引导的修饰它的定语从句太长，如果按照以上语序，则有头重脚轻之感。所以原文将此长长的从句倒装到谓语 will be favored 之后。

笔者之所以不愿意把上面那句话的语法结构叫做定语后置，是因为在 GRE 和 GMAT 考试中还有大量的难句与上面的句子虽然有着共同的特点，但是后置的成分不同，而笔者希望把这些句子归为一类，便于同学们迅速掌握，所以宁愿把所有这些句子都叫做倒装。其共同点在于：由于应该放在句子前面的成分太长，为了避免头重脚轻而把这些成分倒装到句末。再看下例：

> 例句：Black Fiction surveys a wide variety of novels, bringing to our attention in the process some fascinating and little-known works like James Weldon Johnson's Autobiography of an Ex-Colored Man.

上例中在逗号后的分词中，bring 的宾语应该是 some fascinating and little-known works like James Weldon Johnson's *Autobiography of an Ex-Colored Man*，然后才应该是 to our attention in the process，但是这样句子就显得重心不平衡，于是被放到了句末。本书中将所有因为此原因而造成的语序颠倒都叫做倒装。

读法：如果说现代汉语还从西方引进了一些类似于插入语的语法的话，那么 GRE 或者 GMAT 考试中的这种倒装可以说几乎是一点影都没有，因此同学们对此感到不习惯是十分正常的。在本书中所归类的这四种难句中，倒装可谓最难。对于这种句子，初学者不妨先按正常语序读，等到后面的难句训练中，熟悉了其表达方式之后，再按照原文的语序来读。

第四类：省略

说明：相对以上三种难句中的语言结构来讲，省略比较简单，由于中国学生的英语语法基础大多都极为坚实，所以如果在短句中出现了省略，大家一般都可以轻易看出。但是本书中所收录的这种省略都是在长句子中出现的，特别是当其与以上三种之一种甚至几种同时出现的时候，往往会给同学们带来意想不到的困难。如上面在倒装类型中所举的例子中的省略：

That sex ratio will be favored [which maximizes the number of descendants (*that* an individual will have) **and** hence *maximizes* the number of gene copies (transmitted)].

在 which 的从句中，有两处省略：第一处是在 maximize 的第一个宾语 the number of descendants *that* an individual will have 中，an individual will have 是修饰 descendants 的定语从句，但是因为 descendants 在从句中做 have 的宾语，所以引导词 that 可以省略。第二处省略是在第二个 the number of 之前，省略了与前面一样的成分 maximizes。"and hence" 在此表示后面的成分作为前面"最大化一个个体的后代的数目"的结果。

　　根据笔者长时间的学习及后来的教学经历，以上四种形式已经在语法意义上完全覆盖了 GRE 和 GMAT 考试中的难句类型。然而问题并不这么简单。

　　首先，在阅读理解的意义上而言，仍然有些文章中出现的句子、甚至是文章之后的题干和选项令人感到难以理解或是令人容易误解。笔者结合了自己的教学经验，在本书中收录了一些比较特殊的从理解上容易出问题的似易实难的句子、题干和选项，就是出于这一点考虑。

　　其次，仅仅了解了这些难句在语法上的特点，并不能保证读者在实战中看到难句时能够看懂其意思。而且，利用语法分析来读懂一句话也无法适应考试现场的时间要求，因此也不能成为笔者写本书的真正目的。要想以符合考试要求的方式真正地克服这些难句，必须在熟悉这些难句的语法结构的前提下，进行连续的、有一定强度的系统训练，以达到最终能够在现场不借助语法而一遍读懂所有考试中出现的难句的目的。

2.2　GRE、GMAT 难句的典型结构

1. 长成分

　　GRE 和 GMAT 考试中的句子之所以难，最主要的原因就是其惊人的长度；而整句的长度又取决于构成句子的各种成分的长度。形形色色的各种长成分是本书所录难句的一大特色。经常出现在考试中的比较典型的长成分有四种：长从句、长状语、层层修饰和并列成分。

1）长从句做主语、宾语或其他成分

A. 主语从句

例句：　That each large firm will act/with consideration of its own needs/ **and** thus avoid selling its products /for more than its competitors charge/ is commonly recognized by advocates of free-market economic theories/.

　　句首出现了一个由 that 引导的长长的主语从句，一直延伸到谓语is commonly recognized 为止。像这样的主语从句，现场阅读时可以把整个从句理解成一个名词，做句子的主语。初学者如果感到不适应，这里推荐一个简单的操作方法，就是读完该从句的

意思后，在它后面加上一个词"这一点"。比如本例中的主语从句可以这样来理解：每一个大公司都将出于对各自的利益的考虑而行动，而且因此将避免把其产品卖得比其竞争者更昂贵这一点通常被自由市场经济理论的支持者所认识到。

B．宾语从句

例句：

The historian Frederick J. Turner wrote /in the 1890's / that the agrarian discontent（that had been developing steadily in the United States since about 1870）had been precipitated /by the closing of the internal frontier—[that is, the depletion of available new land（needed for further expansion of the American farming system）] /.

本句包含了一个超长的宾语从句，从第一行的 that 开始一直延续到句子结束。不过与主语从句不同的是，我们中国读者从来不害怕宾语从句。究其原因，是因为在我们汉语中其实有着相同的表达方式。上面的句子用中文来说，就是：

历史学家 FJT/在 19 世纪 90 年代/写道，（自从 1870 年开始就在美国持续发展的）农民的不满是被内部边疆的消失所加剧的，[而内部边疆的消失即指（所需进一步扩展美国农业系统的）可资利用的新土地的枯竭]。

我们可以看到，就主句和宾语从句的衔接而言，英语中的宾语从句的语序和中文的语序是完全对应的。此类长从句直接读下来即可。

2）长状语

长状语在 GRE 和 GMAT 难句中十分常见。由于状语可以用来说明的东西特别多，如时间、地点、方式、程度、数量、原因、结果、背景、条件和位置等；而且也不像句子那样有严格的结构要求，可以出现在句子的任何位置，因此是出题者很喜欢使用的一种成分。往往又由于压缩文章篇幅的要求，出题者喜欢把状语、定语、插入语或其他成分捏在一起，形成一个长状语，如下例：

例句：The appreciation (of traditional oral American Indian literature) has been limited, /hampered by poor translations **and** by the difficulty, even in the [rare (culturally sensitive and aesthetically satisfying)] translation, (of completely conveying the original's verse structure, tone, and syntax) /.

3）层层修饰

这是难句构成的最主要途径。笔者在前面讲到复杂修饰类难句时说过，可以通过不断地增加修饰的成分把一个句子的长度无限制地延伸下去，其实讲的就是这里的层层修饰：

例句：(A very specialized feeding) adaptation (in zooplankton) is that of the tadpolelike appendicularian { who lives in a walnut-sized (or smaller) balloon of mucus [equipped with filters (that capture and concentrate phytoplankton)] }.

实际上本句的主架构很简单，就是adaptation is that of the tadpolelike appendicularian，其他所有成分都是附加的修饰成分。尤其是对宾语的层层修饰，从 who 开始一层套一层，一共套了三重修饰。

4）并列成分

并列成分的使用是 ETS 的出题者增加句子的长度的又一种常用方法。另外，使用并列成分还有一个好处：能够省略掉一些不必要的重复成分。见下例：

例句：They were fighting, albeit discrectly, to open the intellectual world /to the new science /**and** to liberate intellectual life from ecclesiastical philosophy **and** *they* envisioned their work as contributing to the growth, **not** of philosophy, **but** of research in mathematics and physics.

本句中出现的两个 and 连接的三个成分不属于同一层面：第一个 and 连接两个并列的不定式；第二个 and 的级别较高，连接前后两个并列的句子。and 之后相当于省略了主语 they。

2. 常见倒装搭配

1）及物动词加介词

在某些词组的固定搭配下，经常会出现倒装结构。这些词组通常由一个及物动词加上一个介词组成，如 bring to，当其表达为 bring A to B 的时候，则有可能被倒装成 bring to B A，如：

例句：**Yet** Walzer's argument, however deficient, does point to one of the most serious weaknesses of capitalism—namely, that it **brings** /to predominant positions in a society/people [who , no matter how legitimately they have earned their material rewards, often lack those other qualities (that evoke affection or admiration)].

主句宾语的同位语从句中固定搭配 bring A to B 被倒装。如果把这句话恢复成正常语序，则是 it **brings** people [who , no matter how legitimately they have earned their material rewards, often lack those other qualities (that evoke affection or admiration) /] **to** predominant positions in a society/。

类似于这种容易在考试中被倒装的固定搭配，还有 throw over、insert into、import into、infer from、establish for、advocate as 等。

2）及物动词加副词

Friedrich Engels, however, predicted that women would be liberated /from the "social, legal, and economic subordination" of the family//by technological developments (that **made** /**possible**/ the recruitment of "the whole female sex into public industry) /."

本句后面的宾语从句中的第二个状语 by technological developments 后面跟着的定语

从句中出现了倒装：| that | **made possible** the recruitment of "the whole female sex into public industry." 的正常语序应该是：| that | **made** the recruitment of "the whole female sex into public industry." /**possible**/，固定搭配 make ... possible 中的副词 possibe 被倒装到了前面。

3. 省略的几种情况

1）重复的成分

由于笔者前面提到过的 ETS 对科学论文做改编和压缩的需要，以及尽量使文章中的语言简明扼要的要求，所以如果在句子中出现与前面或后面重复的成分，文章中基本上会把能省略掉的东西全部省略掉。请看下例：

> 例句： The correlation of carbon dioxide with temperature, of course, does not establish whether changes in atmospheric composition caused the warming and cooling trends or were caused by them.

标志：The correlation (of carbon dioxide with temperature), of course, does not establish **whether** changes (in atmospheric composition) caused the warming and cooling trends **or** *changes* (in atmospheric composition) were caused by them.

在最后的 or were caused by their 当中，or 之后省略了与 whether 一句中相同的主语 *changes (in atmospheric composition)* ；最后的 them 指代的是 or 之前的 warming and cooling trends.

2）让步转折的省略

根据英语的语法，表示让步和转折语气的词汇在同一个句子中只能出现一次，而且在绝大多数的情况下，都是让步在前转折在后：

> 例句： **Although** many of these historians have accepted the earlier assumption that loyalists represented an upper class, new evidence indicates that Loyalist, like rebels, were drawn from all socioeconomic class.

可以很清楚的看出，前面的分句与后面的分句意思上的巨大反差。句首的 **al-though** 引导的表示让步的分句在说保王党是上流社会，而后面在说保王党是三教九流无所不包。明显后面的分句是一个转折语气；而且明显作者在强调后面的转折的内容。但是因为刚才说过的原因，**although** 与 **but** 在本句中都只能出现一次，所以后半个分句中的 ***but*** 被省略。

同样，如果后面出现了 but（yet，however 等表示转折的词汇），同样意味着在句首有一个表示让步的词汇（如 although，while 等）被作者省略。

在 GRE 和 GMAT 考试的阅读现场，以上思维至关重要。我们以前接触的英语阅读中虽然也有这种语法，但是因为句子通常较短，句义也都很清楚，所以用不着把让步和转折都补全，就可以准确的理解作者想要表达的语气。但是 GRE 和 GMAT 阅读中的句子奇长无比、结构复杂，所以读者如果不在阅读现场把让步和转折的语气在大脑中有意识地补齐，读到后半个句子的时候很有可能忘了前面的语气。所以笔者在此要求读者从现在开始养成一个良好的习惯，只要是在前面的分句中看到表示让步的词汇，就立即在后面的分句前补上一个 **but**；看到后面有表示转折的词汇，立即给前面的内容加上一个 **although**。

笔者为了培养读者的阅读习惯，在本书中的难句讲解中都用黑体和斜体字标出了被省略的 ***although*** 和 ***but***。让步和转折，几乎是 GRE 和 GMAT 考试中最为重要的语言点，请读者关注。

3）定语从句引导词的省略

本来这是我们中国学生熟知的一个语法现象，即：如果被定语从句修饰的成分在从句中做宾语，则从句的引导词可以省略，如：the book that I read 中的 that 可以被省略，直接说成是 the book I read。在一般的英语阅读中，这种省略是可省可不省的，而且在容易发生句义混淆的情况下通常不省。但是由于 ETS 出题者对压缩文章篇幅的近乎狂热的追求，几乎在所有的 GRE 和 GMAT 文章中都是能省就省，根本不管考生是否能看懂；而且当被修饰成分在从句中做介词宾语、甚至是不定式宾语的时候，也要省略引导词：

例句：
> Because the potential hazards pollen grains are subject to as they are transported over long distances are enormous, . . .

先不必理会逗号以后的成分，句首的这个分句中修饰主语 the potential hazards 的定语从句的引导词 that（或 which）就被省略掉了，因为被修饰的主语是从句中的介词 to 的宾语。这个分句的结构标志如下：**Because** the potential hazards (*that* pollen grains are subject to /as they are transported over long distances/) <u>are</u> <u>enormous</u>,...

例句： In order to understand the nature of the ecologist's investigation, we may think of the density-dependent effects on growth parameters as the "signal" ecologists are trying to isolate and interpret,...

the "signal" 后面实际上是一个修饰它的定语从句，但是由于 "signal" 在从句中做不定式 to isolate and interpret 的宾语，所以从句引导词 that 被省略。句子的结构标志是：/In order to understand the nature of the ecologist's investigation, /we <u>may</u> **think of** the density-dependent effects (on growth parameters) **as** the "signal" (*that* ecologists are trying to isolate and interpret,...

4）定语从句中的引导词与系动词的同时省略，变成后置定语

例句： qualities (such as "the capacity for hard work") essential in producing wealth

这种结构的典型形式是：名词 +形容词 +介词结构。

其原型是：名词 +定语从句的引导词 + be +形容词 +介词结构，然后同时省略从句的引导词和 be。如上面的例子，补全所有的成分应该是：

<u>qualities</u> (such as "the capacity for hard work") (*that are* <u>essential in producing wealth</u>)

这种省略的结果，就是形容词 +介词结构被放在名词之后充当该名词的后置定语。需要说明的是，之所以会出现这样的结构，关键的原因是后面的介词结构。如果不是因为这个介词结构的原因，修饰名词的形容词可以被直接置于名词之前来起到修饰作用，上例就可以简单的说成 essential qualities (such as "the capacity for hard work")。由于介词结构的极其广泛的语法用途，所以在 GRE 和 GMAT 的阅读中对这里所讲的名词 +形容词 +介词结构进行了充分的、大量的使用，成为出题者增加句子长度、层层修饰的重要手段。

4. 短语被分割

　　由于 GRE 和 GMAT 难句的超常的长度和其复杂的结构，造成了一些短语或固定搭配被分割得很远，以致即使是我们熟知的结构，阅读现场也辨别不清。这些短语有 such as, so that, too... to, more than, from A to B, between A and B 等。

　　例句：**Such** variations in size, shape, chemistry, nconduction speed, excitation threshold, and the like **as** had been demonstrated in nerve cells remained negligible in significance for any possible correlation with the manifold dimensions of mental experience.

　　例句：Under the force of this view, it was perhaps inevitable that the art of rhetoric should pass **from** the status of being regarded as of questionable worth（because although it might be both a source of pleasure and a means to urge people to right action, it might also be a means to distort truth and a source of misguided action）**to** the status of being wholly condemned.

5. 多重否定（双重否定、三重否定）

　　各种否定的频繁使用是 GRE 和 GMAT 阅读的另一个特色。这种使用除了行文的需要之外，更多的体现了出题者对于考生语言能力和思维能力的考验。我们知道，其实任何多于一重的否定都可以用肯定的方式说明白，像下面这样的句子就更没有必要：

　　例句：Despite these vague categories, one should not claim unequivocally that hostility between recognizable classes cannot be legitimately observed.

　　从这个例子中可以看出，句子的难度也不全是与其长度成正比。比如这句话，既不算长又没有什么不认识的单词，但是偏偏很难看懂。其原因，是写文章的人使用了三重否定：should not, unequivocally, 和 cannot。在这里，可以明显看出 ETS 在考查我们的阅读能力，因为如果想把句子说成肯定的语气而不改变句子的意思是很容易的，其实就是：

Despite these vague categories, one may still claim definitely that hostility between discernable classes can be validly observed.

其实这种结构并不难，因为我们在理解中文的多重否定的时候都不会有问题。克服这种难句的方法也很简单，就是通过多读、多练来熟悉其语言表达以及逻辑方式。对于一切语言的掌握，无不遵循熟能生巧的原则。只要本书的读者能够按照本书所讲的方法和原则坚持训练、持之以恒，一定可以迅速攻破难句这个堡垒。

第三章　克服 GRE、GMAT 难句

尽管在 GRE 和 GMAT 中出现的上述难句看上去确实令人恐惧，然而，这些所谓难句决非不可攻克；事实上，只要训练方法得当，并且能够坚持每天抽出半小时左右进行练习，这些难句完全可以在一个月甚至几周内被攻克，而做到此点，对我们的考生有以下四点重大的意义：

第一，所有长句子只读一遍就懂，避免了反复阅读造成的时间浪费，可以大大的提高大家的阅读速度；

第二，可以顺利地做出机考中的高分值题，因为与难句对应的阅读题，包括数学和逻辑中读起来较难的题目，一定对应着比较高的分值；

第三，可以增加同学们阅读文章时的理解力，提高对文章整体的把握能力；

第四，可以增加我们的自信心，产生一种阅读中的顺畅的愉悦感，也使我们在学习过程中不再沉浸在一种烦躁的情绪之中，真正地与文章的内容和作者的思路打交道。

3.1　难句考点与突破（ETS 考查的各种能力详析）

与托福考试形成鲜明对比的是，GRE 和 GMAT 考试考查考生的最核心的素质不是其英语水平。这两种考试作为能力考试，名义上是考查考生在专业上的学术能力的高低。但是这种说法本身存在很大问题。这两种考试的考生都来自包括文科和理科的很多种专业，而且其考试成绩又被美国大学的很多不同专业用作重要的录取依据，所以考题本身就没有任何的专业内容，其数学考试甚至基本上就是一些初中数学的内容，这样的考试又怎么能考查考生在专业上的学术能力呢？惟一的合理的解释，就是 ETS 通过这样一种考试，不是考查考生在某一个具体专业上的现有的学术功底，而是要考查受试者在所有专业上的发展潜力。既然是所有专业都要有的能力，就意味着这不会是

一种细化的专项能力，而是一种最最基本的又最最重要的能力。那么人类身上什么能力是最最基本的又最最重要的呢？从这个答案中不难得出：大脑的思维能力。在对考生的这种能力的考查上，ETS 在 GMAT 考试中测试的角度与在 GRE 考试中并无不同：以前很多美国大学都接受申请者用 GRE 成绩代替 GMAT 成绩来申请 MBA，即使到了现在，仍有少数大学的 MBA 允许考生用 GRE 成绩来申请。

关于 ETS 在两种考试的阅读中对考生所具备的各种具体的大脑能力的考查及其考法，不是本书所讨论的目的，笔者将在另一本专述 GRE 和 GMAT 阅读的规律性的书中做全面阐述。这里仅讨论在难句中 ETS 考查考生的一些能力。

我们都知道，阅读理解尽管也涉及到一些类似眼睛的视幅和眼睛的移动速度等与感官技能有关的能力，但是从本质上来讲，不管是对什么语种、什么材料的读物所作的阅读，主要还是一种大脑活动。当读者抱着想去搞清楚一份阅读材料说了什么内容为目的来进行阅读时，其眼睛所起到的作用仅仅是把需要阅读的字符输送到大脑，而真正要对这些文字进行解码而理解其含义，则完全要依靠大脑才能做到。如果这时大脑不能对这些符号进行有效加工，或者在其解码过程中出现错误，使大脑发生了混乱，则阅读者所表现出来的状态就是"视而不见"。

而利用 GRE 和 GMAT 阅读中出现的难句来考查考生大脑的基本能力就成为了出题者的一个相当好的选择。由于这些句子结构复杂、长度惊人、断断续续、语序颠倒，再加上用词抽象，考生想要读懂这些句子，大脑在以下几方面必须具备较强的能力：

1. 大脑的容量
2. 大脑的抗干扰能力
3. 大脑的排序能力
4. 大脑的联系能力

大脑的容量：在第一类难句（复杂修饰成分）和第二类难句（插入语）中对此类能力的要求最高：前者需要应试者不仅仅记住主体词，还必须记住其复杂的、冗长的修饰成分；后者对考生的要求更高：如果考生希望以最快的速度把句子读下来的话（即不跳过插入部分，而是按照原文语序直接读下来），他（她）就必须在大脑中另开辟一个记忆区（其作用与计算机的内存相仿），将插入部分暂时存储于此，而注意力集中于把插入部分之后的内容与插入之前的内容联系在一起的工作上。没有经过一定训练的初学者是很难做到这一点的。

大脑的抗干扰能力：主要体现在出题者在对第二类句子（插入语）的使用上。就像笔者前面所说的那样，插入语可以出现在句子中的任何位置，将本该是连续出现的句子成分割裂开来，因此它可以对读者起到一种强烈的负面的干扰作用。因为笔者在上段所提到过的那个原因（即速度原因），为了提高速度而按原文顺序阅读的考生见到插入语时，必须把对插入语之前的内容的记忆保持到读完插入语之后，这样才能够把插入部分前后的意思联系在一起。同时，考生大脑中对插入语的内容又要做出理解，因为插入语的内容出题时经常会考到。所以考生在顺序阅读插入语的时候，其大脑的运作类似于一心二用，而上述两种任务彼此之间又很容易互相干扰。这对考生的抗干扰能力的要求是很高的。

大脑的排序能力：主要在倒装类句子中考查考生的这种能力。这一点很好理解，笔者不做赘述。

大脑的联系能力：其实读每一种难句都需要大脑的这种能力。因为大多数的难句都较长，读者需要将整个句子联系到一起，才能对句子的整体有一个全面的和正确的理解。ETS 对考生的这种能力的考查，尤以在插入语和省略句中表现的最为突出。在插入语中，读者被要求把被长长的插入部分隔了很远的两部分的意思联系在一起，而在省略句中读者需要根据意思来判断缺了某种成分的部分与其前后部分的关系，对大脑的联系能力提出了更为苛刻的要求。

以上对 ETS 在阅读难句中考查考生能力的分析，只是笔者试图破解 ETS 出题原理的一部分从理论角度的心得体会。这些分析同时也是笔者的难句训练法的理论依据。不过笔者需要说明的是，本书所讲的难句训练的方法尽管是笔者当年闭门造车所得，但是此法绝对是笔者亲身使用、并收效显著的一个训练方法：不但使笔者迅速攻克了阅读中出现的难句，而且也使笔者迅速提高了阅读速度和理解力。不仅如此，此法在所有笔者授课的班级上均收到了非常突出的效果，笔者方敢示之于野。

3.2 难句训练原理

笔者在本书中的训练法的理论基础有两条：

第一，我们的大脑是无所不能的；

第二，经过训练的大脑的能力是可以迅速提高的。

首先，我们大脑的能力远远超出我们自己的想像。当然作为当今自然界的最大谜团，大脑的运作方式是笔者所不敢妄言的，不过笔者对大脑对语言的强大的加工能力确实深有体会。具体到对句子结构的理解上，这种能力的最突出的表现就是，当我们对某种很生僻或很怪异的语言结构足够地熟悉了以后，我们的大脑可以在瞬间以一种潜意识的方式，在大脑中自动的把其变成一种阅读者可以很容易理解的语序，从而使读者能够读懂这句话的涵义。

本书的难句训练法就是基于大脑的这种超凡的能力。而我们训练的关键就在于要使大脑对前述的四种难句足够的熟悉。

比如说，初学者通常对 GRE 和 GMAT 考试中所出现的长句子大为头痛，常常是看到后面的内容，却搞不清楚与前面的成分的关系。其实这类句子之所以长，主要是因为修饰成分太多（即第一类难句），而初学者对这种一个接一个、有时甚至是一层套一层的修饰语感到不习惯，所以才感到无法读懂。然而此处就出现了一个重大的问题，难道我们真的读不懂有复杂修饰的句子吗？看前面举过的例子：

例句：斜靠在沙发上，没有血色的嘴唇上叼着一只不知在什么时候就早已经熄灭了的雪茄烟，一夜没睡的困倦的他目光呆滞地借助一盏时明时暗地摇曳的残破油灯绝望地在无精打采地看着发黄了的、却保存得颇为完整的现在市面上很难买到的一本名叫《准备考试的你能看得懂这句不但无聊之极而且无耻之尤的话吗?》的旧书。

笔者之所以旧例重提，是请同学们考虑一个问题，那就是为什么我们可以不费吹灰之力的读懂一个远比 GRE 和 GMAT 考试中的句子复杂得多的中文句子，却无法读懂结构相似、且长度相仿的英语句子呢？

上面的例子告诉我们，本书的任何一个读者都是有读懂阅读难句的潜力的。中文作为世界各种语言中进化时间最长的语种之一，其词义之抽象、结构之复杂及其语法变化之难以掌握都要远远超过英语，大家既然能够轻易读懂上面的句子，就意味着大家也都有潜力读懂英语考试中的难句，只不过是我们采用什么方法来训练的问题了。

笔者以为，英语长句子之所以难以读懂，惟一的原因就是我们的大脑不熟悉英语的这种句子的表达习惯（语序）！

首先，由于中国的大学本科学历以上的同学无不对中文文章进行过大量的阅读，对于中文中所出现的语言结构了如指掌，而且多么长的句子都见过，以至于对中文长句子熟视无睹，在读上面那句话时恐怕根本就没有想过这句话是长是短。可是由于我们以前在英文阅读时从来没有见过类似于 GRE 和 GMAT 考试中所出现的那么长的句子，所以当我们的大脑在处理这些超出其习惯的长度的句子的时候就出现了各种错误，或者每读几个词就发出"怎么这个句子还没完"的信息，或者出于阅读短句的习惯而做出一些错误判断。其机理有些类似于电脑在遇到所需处理的数据超出其规定范围的时候，或者输出错误结果，或者死机。例如：

例句：... She wished to discard the traditional methods and established vocabularies of such dance forms as ballet and to explore the internal sources of human expressiveness.

在阅读本句的时候，有很多同学由于不习惯长句子中的复合成分，读到不定式中 discard 的宾语 the traditional methods and established... 的时候，大脑根据多年来学习英语短句所形成的定式，判断到 methods 的时候 discard 的宾语已经完整，and 之后的动词只能是与前面 wished 或 discard 并列的成分（其实此两种理解在语法上都不成立，请读者自己分析），而做梦也想不到 established vocabularies 居然是与前面的 the traditional methods 并列的、做 discard 的宾语！

在笔者的教学过程当中经常会接触到同学们的这种大脑的思维定式。最可笑、同时也是最发人深省的一个例子是，有个学生一次来找我，说按照我的难句训练法认真地训练之后，阅读中超过四、五行以上的句子看得就非常懂，可是三行以内的短句子却看不懂了，总觉得那个句子没有写完，应该再写上两行才看得舒服。尽管这是一个极端的例子，但是它告诉我们，大脑对所处理的信息使用的判断原则是：**熟悉的就是对的；习惯的才好理解。**

读者难以读懂复杂修饰类难句的另一个原因是，与中文的长修饰成分不同的是，在英语中稍微长一点的修饰成分都要放到被修饰成分的后面。因为中文的修饰成分永远放在主体词之前，所以当我们读英文的时候，不管放在主体词之前的修饰语有多长都不会感到困难（如 all new black American leather shoes，我们读得很习惯），而对于后置的修饰成分，我们的大脑总是不习惯于把它联系到前面的词汇上去。这属于母语对英语学习的负干扰。

上面所说的大脑对所读信息的处理模式同样适用于其他三种难句。如果大脑不习惯插入语、倒装或者省略等句式，读到它们的时候我们的脑子就罢了工，拒绝做出反应（其实它也不知道如何做出反应）。反过来，如果我们的大脑越熟悉一种语言结构，对它的反应就越快；这种反应的速度完全与大脑对这种语言形式的熟悉程度成正比。与大多数人的想法不同的是，在现场的快速阅读中，这种反应的速度和准确性与读者的语法能力却没有太大的关系，因为大脑在刹那间的判断方式是依据以前的经验，而非抽象的语法。

以难句中最令人头疼的倒装为例，举一个中文的例子，比如"如之奈何？"一句，学过古文的同学都知道此句实际上是"奈何如之"的倒装，意思是"如何来对付它"？然而读完"如之奈何？"这句话，再按照语法把它恢复为正常语序"奈何如之"，最后在根据正常的语序才能理解其含义，这只是初学古文者的做法，真正经常看古文书的人是不会这么读的。因为他天天都读这种语言，早已熟悉了这种结构，不管读"如之奈何"还是"奈何如之"，不管这四个字以何种语序出现，他都知道就是在问怎么办的问题；要是你在他读完之后问他为什么是这个意思，语法结构是怎么会事，他可能还真答不上来，因为刚才他读的时候也根本没有想过这句话的语法。

其实语言本身就是为了运载含义的，只要你明白句子的意思，其语法结构不提也罢。我们训练 GRE 和 GMAT 难句，就是要在短时间内达到上面所谈的这种高级读法的境界，即：不管是什么句子，都是按照原文的语序直接读下来（除了 3 行以上的插入语），就知道句子的意思。当然，这种读法必须以反复的、针对难句的训练为前提。

本书的难句训练法的第二个理论基础是，经过训练的大脑的能力是可以迅速提高的。请大家回顾一下我们从小学习英语的全过程：最初我们背单词，一次只能记住几个、十几个；到了中学，一次就能记住二三十个了；上大学以后，一次能背下的词汇翻了一翻，达到了五六十个；到我们学习 GRE 和 GMAT 的时候，我们发现一次背它二三百词似乎也不是很困难。也就是说，在背单词的过程中，大脑对于单词的记忆能力也在不断的提高。不但如此，在强烈的欲望和坚定的信念的支持下，训练者大脑的这种能力可以在短时间内还可以迅速的提升。笔者班上有很多同学都与笔者一样，是工作了很长时间以后才重新学习英语的，初背单词感觉什么都记不住，而坚持训练几天之后，背单词的能力就会大大增加。

背单词的能力如此，读难句的能力亦是如此。初读长句，感觉说的内容太多，大脑容量不够，这时读就会清晰的感觉到句子的长度超过了自己的大脑所能承受的限度。然而按照笔者的训练方法不间断的练上两周以后，很少还有人会去考虑这个句子是长还是短；也就是说，大脑的容量扩大了，对所读句子的长度范围不再设定限制标准。再比如说，初读插入语，大脑不知如何处理，立即发生理解障碍；而经过短期的专门训练，大脑就能够发展出两种能力：1. 阅读过程中如果发现当句意不完整的时候出现了逗号（有时是括号或破折号），大脑在潜意识中会自动的判断这部分内容是插入部分，而且马上会把插入语义前的内容固定，并在阅读插入部分的同时等待插入之后的内容的到来；等到插入部分完成后，自动地把插入语前后的内容连在一起。2. 在等待插入部分之后的内容的时候，大脑会自动的把插入部分的意思与前面读过的某个成分（大多数情况下就是插入与前面的那个词）的意思合并，以简化阅读理解的过程。需要说明的是，以上过程在真正的现场阅读中并非有意识的过程：一切都是在潜意识中瞬间完成的自动化过程。倒装句也是这样，经过训练的大脑并不是看到一个单词以后马上给这个单词在句中的作用划上一个句号，而是在大脑中时刻留有一种"后面出现的内容可以修饰前面所说过的内容"的可能性，看到被倒装了的成分，立刻就会把它的内容追溯到前面看过的成分上。同学们经过一段时间的训练就会明显的感觉到自己在阅读时的大脑运作方式产生了变化：不再是一看到什么东西就马上就对其语义及其在句子中的功能做出结论性的判断，而是**把做出判断的时间点大大的向后延迟了**，等到这部分叙述完整后再进行判断。

3.3　GRE、GMAT 难句训练法

训练方法：请读者在一个月左右的时间里，每天花半小时左右时间，对本书所列难句进行训练。或者，读者凡是读到 GRE 或 GMAT 文章中在现场读一两遍读不懂的句子，也请摘录下来补充到本书中，按以下方法，进行训练：

首先，对本书中自己无法一遍读懂的句子反复阅读。此时注意不要一读不懂就去看后面的译文和解释，而是一定争取自己读懂它（否则会养成一种惰性），如果五遍以后还读不懂，再看后面的详细解释。

这个句子读懂后，请不要马上读下一句，一定要继续坚持把此句话读通、读顺。就像笔者前面分析过的那样，之所以当初读者读不懂这句话，一定是因为其语言结构不符合阅读者大脑的思维习惯，是大脑不熟悉的东西；而解决这个问题的方法，就是用大量的重复，让学习者的大脑熟悉这种语言结构。当读者继续反复读这同一个句子的时候，随着大脑对其结构的熟悉程度不断增加，读者会感觉这个句子没有什么不通的地方；再读下去，读者会感觉这种句子的写法很好、很正确，就该这么写；如果是自己来写这个句子，恐怕也要这么来写。读到这种程度，就可以开始下一个句子的训练了。再过几天，等读者又练过了十几个句子之后，要再回头看一看前面练过的句子，读者会发现原来读的很顺的句子又显得别扭了，这时要再一次反复阅读，直到读得很通顺为止，这样重复几次，等到读者很久不读这个句子，可是一看到就能够迅速地一遍把它读懂，对这个句子的训练就可以永远的停止了。其中的道理，古人概括的非常精辟，正所谓：熟读唐诗三百首，不会作诗也会吟。

在笔者的指导下，很多考生都在一个月内用这种训练方法大幅度地提高了阅读的速度和对文章的理解力。这里面的道理在于，就像笔者在前面论证过的那样，人的大

脑对于语言的处理方式是高度自动化的。一旦大脑熟悉了某种语言结构，它就会对以这样的结构出现的语句进行自动地处理，哪怕句子是语序颠倒的，阅读者也能在瞬间知道其正确意思，绝无混乱之感。然而有以下几点需要说明，请同学们在训练中注意：

1. 本书中收录的 GRE 难句的难度高于 GMAT 的难度，GRE 考生可以把 GMAT 难句作为检验自己难句训练成果的练习题，而 GMAT 考生则可以参考一些 GRE 难句，作为一种提高难度的课外训练。

2. 希望本书的读者把难句练习与阅读训练的进度结合起来，最好能在练习某个难句之前，先读过原文，这样就可以有的放矢，把重点放在现场理解最难读懂的句子上；而且这样一来，读者对句子含意的理解以及这句话在原文中所起到的作用都有一个全面的视角。

3. 随着读者水平的不断提高，大家到了能够读懂大部分难句的时候，可以注意按照前面"本书写作原则及读者学习指导"一节中所提出的几个原则进行训练，以使自己的阅读方法及阅读习惯满足考试的要求。

4. 如果水平较高的同学们发现本书中所收录的有些句子在文中可以顺利读懂，可以不予理睬，而只标出读不懂的句子，加以训练；反过来，如果文章中某句读不懂，而本书没有列入，也可以补充进来。本来千人千面，各人之间不应强求一致，但是最重要的，是对于自己的薄弱之处，集中优势兵力，加以突破。

5. 希望提请大家注意的是，对这些难句的训练一定要以读意思为主、看语法为辅；只要能不去分析其语法，就不要去分析语法；训练初期考虑一些语法，训练后期一定要完全抛弃语法！

6. 笔者最希望本书读者注意的是，对本书的训练切不可浅尝即止，半途而废。经过我的调查，凡是能够真正坚持用这种方法训练的同学，无一例外地在数周之内，阅读能力和阅读速度都得到了大幅度地提高，兴奋地来找我，告诉我再没有完全读不懂的文章了。而大多数同学只练了几天就放弃了，实在可惜。对本书的正确的学习方法，应该是坚持每天不间断地训练，才能强化大脑对各种语言现象的熟练程度，而三天打鱼、两天晒网的练法，必然事倍功半，效率低下。切记，贵在坚持！希望同学们持之以恒，尽快摆脱 GRE、GMAT 难句的困扰，早日达到与阅读文章的文字下面所隐藏的思想神交的阅读的真正目的！

第四章　GRE、GMAT 阅读难句详解

【**说明**】　本书每个难句的格式如下：

序号　（标明序号）

原文　（难句原文）

难句类型　（主要按前述四种难句分类）　　难度　（分为 1~5 等）

标志　（将原句按句子的语法结构对需要解释之处做出拆分标志）标志如下：

主语、形式主语以及后面的真正主语的引导词：加阴影；

谓语、系动词：加下划线；

宾语、介词宾语或表语：加波浪线；

插入语：加双点下划线；

长状语：/… …/；

修饰成分：括号—按修饰的层面由大到小用 ‖‖、［］或（　）表示；

表示并列或转折等的连词：黑体字；

某些固定搭配的、被分割开的词组：黑体字；

部分需要重点解释的词汇：黑体字；

省略：*斜体字*；

从句引导词：[that]

译文　（中文翻译）

解释　（分析句子的难点及重点。本书中所用的英文释义取自 Marriam-Webster 和 Webster's New World Dictionary）

意群训练　（按意群格式将原句重排）

4.1 GRE 阅读难句详解

序号：001

> That sex ratio will be favored which maximizes the number
> of descendants an individual will have and hence the num-
> ber of gene copies transmitted.

难句类型：倒装 + 省略　　难度：5

标志： That sex ratio will be favored ［which maximizes the number of descendants *(that* an individual will have）**and** hence *maximizes* the number of gene copies（transmitted）］.

译文： 那种［能够最大化（一个个体所拥有的）后代的数目并且因此可以最大化（被传播的）基因的份数的］性别比率将会是有利的。

解释： a. 本句的正常语序应当是：That sex ratio which maximizes the number of descendants an individual will have and hence the number of gene copies transmitted will be favored. 但是因为主语 That sex ratio 之后的以 which 引导的修饰它的定语从句太长，如果按照以上语序，则有头重脚轻之感。所以原文将此长长的从句倒装到谓语 will be favored 之后。

b. 在 which 引导的从句中，有两处省略：第一处是在 maximize 的第一个宾语 the number of descendants *that* an individual will have 中，an individual will have 是修饰 descendants 的定语从句，但是因为 descendants 在从句中作 have 的宾语，所以引导词 that 可以省略。第二处省略是在第二个 the number of 之前，省略了与前面一样的成分 maximizes。"and hence" 在此表示后面的成分作为前面"最大化一个个体的后代的数目的"结果。

意群训练： That sex ratio will be favored which maximizes the number of descendants an individual will have and hence the number of gene copies transmitted.

序号：**002**

> Hardy's weakness derived from his apparent inability to control the comings and goings of these divergent impulses and from his unwillingness to cultivate and sustain the energetic and risky ones.

难句类型：复杂修饰 + 省略 + 抽象词　难度：3

标志： Hardy's weakness derived /from his apparent inability（to control the comings and goings of these divergent impulses）/ **and** *derived* /from his unwillingness（to cultivate and sustain the energetic and risky ones）/.

译文： 哈代的弱点来源/于其明显的不能够（控制这些不同冲动的来去）/，同时也来源/于他的不愿意（去培养和维持那些有活力和大胆的冲动）/。

解释： 介词 from 的宾语有两个并列的部分，由 and 所连接。在 and 之后的第二个 from 前，省略了与前面一样的谓语动词 derive。本句之所以难，有两个原因，一是 derived from 后面的成分太长，初学者难以一下子看下来；二是作为一篇文科文章，用词抽象，难以迅速理解。

意群训练： Hardy's weakness derived from his apparent inability to control the comings and goings of these divergent impulses and from his unwillingness to cultivate and sustain the energetic and risky ones.

序号：**003**

> Virginia Woolf's provocative statement about her intentions in writing *Mrs. Dalloway* has regularly been ignored by the critics, since it highlights an aspect of her literary interests very different from the traditional picture of the "poetic" novelist concerned with examining states of reverie and vision and with following the intricate pathways of individual consciousness.

难句类型：复杂修饰 ＋ 省略＋ 抽象词　　**难度：**5

标志：（Virginia Woolf's provocative）statement（about her intentions in writing *Mrs. Dalloway* ）has regularly been ignored /by the critics/，/since it highlights an aspect { of her literary interests [*that is* very different from the traditional picture of the "poetic" novelist（concerned with examining states of reverie and vision **and** *concerned* with following the intricate pathways of individual consciousness）] } /.

译文：（VW 的挑战性的）（关于其在写作 MD 一书时的意图的）陈述通常/被评论家们/所忽视，/因为此陈述突出了这样一个方面，{此方面是其文学兴趣中的/[非常不同于传统的、所谓"诗性的"小说家的情况（这些人关心的是审视白日梦和幻想的状态，并关心去追寻个人意识的曲折历程）]}/。

解释：本句逗号以前只有复杂修饰的长主语有些难，但总的来讲比较好懂，since 引导的原因状语从句较难。

a. Since 之后的 it 指前面的 statement。Highlight 的宾语 an aspect 之后有两个修饰成分，一个是（of her literary interests），另一个是以 that 引导的定语从句 *that is* very different from the traditional picture of the "poetic" novelist，都是修饰 an aspect 的。Novelist 后面又有由 and 连接的两个介词结构 concerned with doing 修饰 novelist。

b. 句中有两处省略。一是在 her literary interests *that is* very different from 当中，修饰 interests 的定语从句中引导词 + be（that is）被一起省略。第二处在 **and** 之后，由于 *concerned* with 与前面的 concerned with 重复，所以 concerned 被省略。

c. 本句另外一个难懂的地方，就是使用了大量的抽象词。这是文学评论题材的文章的一个特点。

意群训练：Virginia Woolf's provocative statement about her intentions in writing *Mrs. Dalloway* has regularly been ignored by the critics, since it highlights an aspect of her literary interests very different from the traditional picture of the "poetic" novelist concerned with examining states of reverie and vision and with following the intricate pathways of individual consciousness.

序号：004

> As she put it in *The Common Reader*, "It is safe to say that not a single law has been framed or one stone set upon another because of anything Chaucer said or wrote; and yet, as we read him, we are absorbing morality at every pore."

难句类型：抽象词、抽象词组 + 比喻　　**难度：**5⁻

标志：／As she put it in *The Common Reader* ／, "*Although* it is safe to say that not a single law has been framed **or** one stone set ／upon another／ ／because of anything Chaucer said or wrote／; and **yet**, as we read him, we are absorbing morality at every pore."

译文：／就像她在《致普通读者》一书中所表达的那样／，"尽管可以毫无疑问地说，没有任何法律被制定出来、也没有高楼大厦被建立起来／是因为乔叟说了什么或写了什么／；然而，当我们读他的书的时候，我们身上每一个毛孔都吸满了道德。"

解释：很多人读这句话的时候，虽然字字句句全都认识，而且句子结构似乎也能读懂，可是就是不知道作者在说些什么。这是因为本句不但用词抽象，而且还使用了比喻的修辞手法。

先解释两个词：句首的 as she put it in *The Common Reader* 中的 put...in... 不同于普通所理解的把……放到……中；在此 put 的意思是在 *The Common Reader* 一书中，用语言来表示或表达某种思想或意图，其英文释义为：to convey into another form <I want to put my feelings into words>。作者用引号引用的 "*Although* it is safe to say that..." 是 VW 在书中所写的原话，其中 It 是形式主语，真正的内容在不定式中。safe 在此也不是普通所说的安全的意思，而是其引伸义：毫无争议的、没有问题的，其英文释义为：unlikely to produce controversy or contradiction。

在本句中，作者连续使用了三个比喻："没有任何法律被制定出来、也没有高楼大厦被建立起来"这两个比喻，指没有因为乔叟的言论而产生任何实际的行为规则或政治机构；而"我们身上每一个毛孔都吸满了道德"，则比喻我们受其影响之深，以及其影响力之大。本句的意思是说，乔叟影响读者的方式不是明确地规定，硬性地灌输，而是潜移默化地陶冶。

意群训练：As she put it in *The Common Reader*, "It is safe to say that not a single law has been framed or one stone set upon another because of anything Chaucer said or wrote; and yet, as we read him, we are absorbing morality at every pore."

序号：005

> With the conclusion of a burst of activity, the lactic acid level is high in the body fluids, leaving the large animal vulnerable to attack until the acid is reconverted, via oxidative metabolism, by the liver into glucose, which is then sent (in part) back to the muscles for glycogen resynthesis.

难句类型：复杂修饰 + 插入语 + 专有名词　　**难度**：4⁺

标志：/With the conclusion of a burst of activity/, the lactic acid level is high /in the body fluids/, /leaving the large animal /vulnerable to attack/ /until the acid **is reconverted**, /via oxidative metabolism/, /by the liver/ into glucose, [which is then sent (in part) back to the muscles for glycogen resynthesis] //.

译文：/随着爆发出来的运动的结束/，/在体液中乳酸含量会变得很高，/使得大型动物/处于容易受到攻击的状态/，/直到乳酸被/通过有氧新陈代谢的方式/由肝脏/转化成葡萄糖，[葡萄糖接下来又会被（部分地）传送回肌肉中重新合成糖原] //。

解释：本句中的修饰成分极多，以分词修饰和介词结构修饰为主，作各种类型的状语。前面的状语和主句还好理解，从 leaving 开始句子变难：leaving 引导的直到句末的结构来做整个句子的状语；分词中又包含了三个状语，其中的两个（/via oxidative metabolism/，/by the liver/）又起到了插入语的作用，把 **be converted into** 拆成两段。
　　本句的另外一个特征是其中充斥着专有名词。其中的 body fluids、oxidative 和 re-synthesis 通过字面的意思或者根据词头、词根，我们是应该猜出其意思的；lactic acid、

metabolism 和 muscle 这三个词在生物类文章中极其常用，大家应该背下来；而 glycogen 这种东西则没办法，只能作一个首字母提炼。但是请记住，GRE 和 GMAT 文章中只要出现了这种专有名词，出题者是一定会在文章中把它在文章中所用到的词义解释清楚的，所以读者遇到文章中做了解释的专有名词，应该力求把解释看懂。

本句验证了笔者的一个观点，那就是：阅读现场与其分析句子的语法，倒不如光看句子的意思来得更方便。不信看一看本句的标志，令人眼花缭乱。

意群训练：With the conclusion of a burst of activity, the lactic acid level is high in the body fluids, leaving the large animal vulnerable to attack until the acid is reconverted, via oxidative metabolism, by the liver into glucose, which is then sent (in part) back to the muscles for glycogen resynthesis.

序号：006

> Although Gutman admits that forced separation by sale was frequent, he shows that the slaves' preference, revealed most clearly on plantations where sale was infrequent, was very much for stable monogamy.

难句类型：插入语　　**难度：**3$^+$

标志：Although Gutman admits that forced separation by sale was frequent, *but* he shows that the slaves' preference, revealed most clearly on plantations where sale was infrequent, was very much for stable monogamy.

译文：尽管 G 承认由于出售奴隶而造成的强迫分离是经常会发生的，*但是他指出*奴隶们自己的偏好（此偏好在很少出售奴隶的种植园中表现得最为明显），还是很喜欢一夫一妻制。

解释：由于本句中插入语的使用（即 revealed most clearly on plantations where sale was infrequent），后半个分句中的主语 the slaves' preference 与系动词 was 离得太远，造成阅读的困难。

意群训练： Although Gutman admits that forced separation by sale was frequent, he shows that the slaves' preference, revealed most clearly on plantations where sale was infrequent, was very much for stable monogamy.

序号：007

> Gutman argues convincingly that the stability of the Black family encouraged the transmission of—and so was crucial in sustaining—the Black heritage of folklore, music, and religious expression from one generation to another, a heritage that slaves were continually fashioning out of their African and American experiences.

难句类型： 复杂修饰 + 插入语　　**难度：** 4

标志： Gutman argues convincingly that the stability of the Black family encouraged the transmission of—**and so** was crucial in sustaining—the Black heritage (of folklore, music, and religious expression) /**from** one generation **to** another/, [a heritage (that slaves were continually fashioning out of their African and American experiences)].

译文： G 令人信服地论证道，黑人家庭的稳定性鼓励了——因此也在后者的保持上起到了重要的作用——（包括民间传说、音乐及宗教表达的）黑人遗产/从一代到另一代的/传播，[这是一个（奴隶们不断地从其在非洲和美国的经历中塑造出来的）遗产]。

解释： 在 that 引导的宾语从句中，encouraged 的宾语the transmission of the Black heritage 被同时表示并列和转折的 **and so** 分开，给读者造成了阅读上和理解上的困难。最后一个逗号后面的部分是修饰前面的 Black heritage 的同位语。

意群训练： Gutman argues convincingly that the stability of the Black family encouraged the transmission of—and so was crucial in sustaining—the Black heritage of folklore, music, and religious expression from one generation to another, a heritage that slaves were continually fashioning out of their African and American experiences.

序号：**008**

> This preference for exogamy, Gutman suggests, may have derived from West African rules governing marriage, which, though they differed from one tribal group to another, all involved some kind of prohibition against unions with close kin.

难句类型：复杂修饰 + 插入语　　**难度**：3⁺

标志：This preference for exogamy, Gutman suggests, may have derived /from West African rules（governing marriage），[which , though they differed from one tribal group to another, all involved some kind of prohibition（against unions with close kin）] /.

译文：这种对于异族通婚的偏好，G 认为，有可能是来源/于（管辖婚姻的）西非的规定，[该规定 尽管从一个部落到另外一个部落各不相同，但都涉及到一些（反对近亲结婚的）禁忌] /。

解释：本句有两个插入语，第一个插入语 Gutman suggests 割裂了主句的主语和谓语。West African rules 后跟着两个修饰成分，第一个是分词修饰（governing marriage），第二个是以 which 引导的非限定性定语从句，从句中出现了第二个插入语 though they differed from one tribal group to another，又割裂了从句引导词与从句谓语之间的联系。

意群训练：This preference for exogamy, Gutman suggests, may have derived from West African rules governing marriage, which, though they differed from one tribal group to another, all involved some kind of prohibition against unions with close kin.

序号：**009**

> His thesis works relatively well when applied to discrimination against Blacks in the United States, but his definition of racial prejudice as "racially-based negative prejudgments

against a group generally accepted as a race in any given region of ethnic competition," can be interpreted as also including hostility toward such ethnic groups as the Chinese in California and the Jews in medieval Europe.

难句类型：复杂修饰＋插入语＋抽象词　　**难度**：4⁺

请思考：*如果 but 引导的分句难以看懂，是否可用合理化原则推理出其意思？*

标志：His thesis <u>works</u> /relatively well/ /when applied to discrimination against Blacks in the United States/, **but** his definition of racial prejudice [as "racially-based negative pre-judgments against a group (generally accepted as a race) in any given region of ethnic competition,"] <u>can be interpreted</u> /as also including hostility toward **such** ethnic groups **as** the Chinese in California and the Jews in medieval Europe. /

译文：他的论点/被应用于针对美国黑人的种族歧视时候/，/相对来说较为/管用，但是他的对于种族偏见的定义［即"在任何特定区域里用基于种族的负面的先入之见来反对某人群（此人群通常被认作一个种族）"］能够被解释/成也包括对以下民族的敌意，比如加州的华人和中世纪欧洲的犹太人/。

解释：本句长度惊人，插入部分比较长，再加上又不乏抽象词，所以较为难懂。在表示转折的后半个分句中，长长的插入语［as "racially-based negative prejudgments against a group (generally accepted as a race) in any given region of ethnic competition,"］作为主语his definition of racial prejudice的同位语，使分句中的主谓相隔千山万水。除此之外，本句用词抽象，语义难以理解，对读者的词汇功底要求亦高。考试现场如无法读懂，宜用合理化原则中的取非读法：**but** 之前的分句说的是其论点对美国黑人的种族歧视时较为管用，转折后的内容就应该说其理论对华人和犹太人相对无用。

意群训练：His thesis <u>works</u> relatively well when <u>applied</u> to <u>discrimination</u> against Blacks in the United States, but his definition of racial prejudice as "racially-based <u>negative</u> prejudgments against a group generally accepted as a race in any given region of ethnic competition," can be interpreted as also including hostility toward such ethnic groups as the Chinese in California and the Jews in medieval Europe.

序号：010

> Such variations in size, shape, chemistry, conduction speed, excitation threshold, and the like as had been demonstrated in nerve cells remained negligible in significance for any possible correlation with the manifold dimensions of mental experience.

难句类型： 复杂修饰　　**难度：** 5

标志： **Such** variations (in size, shape, chemistry, conduction speed, excitation threshold, and the like) (**as** had been demonstrated in nerve cells) remained negligible /in significance/ / for any possible **correlation with** the manifold dimensions of mental experience.　/

译文：（神经细胞中所显示出的）（在诸如大小、形状、化学构成、传导速度、兴奋阈值及其他类似方面的）差异，对于解释建立大脑体验的诸多方面与神经细胞的可能的联系来说，意义仍然微不足道。

解释： 即使是初练难句的人其实也很熟悉 **such** thing **as** something 这样的语言方式，可是当中间的小东西 thing 居然变成了一个长达十二个单词的大东西的时候，实在令人搞不清后面的 as 及其后的 something 到底为哪方神圣。再加上以 such as 为中心的长主语距离系动词 remain 太远，更增加了本句的难度。请读者反复阅读，直到读出这样的感觉：顺序阅读原文时，原文似乎就是几大块，就好像是Such things as A remain negligible in a certain sense.

意群训练： Such variations in size, shape, chemistry, conduction speed, excitation threshold, and the like as had been demonstrated in nerve cells remained negligible in significance for any possible correlation with the manifold dimensions of mental experience.

序号：**011**

> It was possible to demonstrate by other methods refined structural differences among neuron types; however, proof was lacking that the quality of the impulse or its condition was influenced by these differences, which seemed instead to influence the developmental patterning of the neural circuits.

难句类型：复杂修饰＋倒装　　**难度：**5

标志：It was possible to demonstrate /by other methods/ refined structural differences (among neuron types); **however,** proof was lacking [that the quality (of the impulse) or its condition was influenced /by these differences/, (which **seemed** instead **to** influence the developmental patterning of the neural circuits)].

译文：有可能/通过其他方法/来证明（神经元种类间的）细微的结构差异；可是，这样的证据是缺乏的，［即（神经冲动的）性质或状态是/受这些差异/所影响的，（而 这些差异 看起来却能影响神经网络的发育模式）］。

解释：与很多人的印象相反，lack 从来就不能做形容词：它只有动词或名词的词性。其形容词的形式是 lacking，意思是缺乏的，不足的。

本句的在 however 之前和之后的两个分句，是两个倒装结构，前一个是小倒装，正常语序是：to demonstrate　refined structural differences（among neuron types）/by other methods/；however 后面是个大倒装，lacking 之后的 that 引导的同位语从句是修饰主语 proof 的，但是因为它太长，所以为了避免头重脚轻，被放到了 lacking 之后。正常的语序应该是 proof that the quality of...was lacking。

意群训练：It was possible to demonstrate by other methods refined structural differences among neuron types; however, proof was lacking that the quality of the impulse or its condition was influenced by these differences, which seemed instead to influence the developmental patterning of the neural circuits.

序号：012

> Although qualitative variance among nerve energies was never rigidly disproved, the doctrine was generally abandoned in favor of the opposing view, namely, that nerve impulses are essentially homogeneous in quality and are transmitted as "common currency" throughout the nervous system.

难句类型：复杂修饰 + 双重否定　　**难度**：4

请思考：*如果 but 引导的分句难以看懂，是否可用<u>合理化原则</u>推理出其意思？*

标志：**Although** qualitative variance （among nerve energies） <u>was never rigidly disproved</u>, ***but*** the doctrine <u>was generally abandoned</u> /in favor of the opposing view, （namely, that nerve impulses are essentially homogeneous in quality and are transmitted as "common currency" throughout the nervous system.）/

译文：尽管（在神经能量上存在着）<u>质的不同这一点</u><u>从来都没有在严格的意义上被反对过</u>，*但是<u>以上教条</u>通常被抛弃掉*，/而转向相反的观点，（即：神经冲动从根本上本质相同，而且被当作"一种普通流"在整个神经系统中传播）/。

解释：a. 前半个分句中有一个双重否定，<u>was never rigidly disproved</u>，这种表示法用中文说出来还是比较好懂的，原因是我们熟悉中文的这种表示法；但是在英文中出现，因为在以前的学习中见得少，所以感觉上很别扭。因此，同学们的任务，就是通过反复阅读此类句子来熟悉这样的英语。其实在英文表达中，很多双重否定与中文表达是一样的，表示肯定：如 not unlimited 就等于 limited。但是值得提请读者注意的是，在 GRE 和 GMAT 这两种对考生的逻辑有苛刻要求的考试中，如果这种双重否定中所涉及的概念不是 dichotomous（即二分法的词汇，比如上面例子中的 limited 和 unlimited），则双重否定不一定表示肯定：比如本例中的 not disprove，不能理解为 agree。不反对者中，的确有人会同意，但通常以心存疑虑、随大流者居多。不但如此，在双重否定中加上限定词以后，在否定的范围上也有所变化，如本句的 be never rigidly disproved，没有完全被反对，不能理解为从来都是被严格支持的，而应该理解成从来都可能有人支持的。综上所述，对于双重否定的句子，简单地把其置换为肯定，不是最精确的理解。而最好的方法，就是通过多读、多练来熟悉其语言表达以及逻辑方式，按照其字面的表达理解成"没有完全被否"，然后大脑中反映出其目前的生存状态是一个仍未消失的状态：这种理解才是在考试现场既快速又精确的理解。

b. 运用前面所说的用合理化原则中的取非读法，可以很容易的读出作者在后半个分句中想说前面的那种观点被反对了。但是初学者会对这个分句中的 something be abandoned **in favor of** something else 这种语言表达感到突然，如果理解成"因为喜爱后者所以抛弃了前者"，虽然也能说得通，但是其实原文本来没有这种因果关系，in favor of 强调的是这两种动作的同时性：抛弃了前者，而转向后者；namely 之后的内容是前面的 opposing view 的同位语。

意群训练：Although qualitative variance among nerve energies was never rigidly disproved, the doctrine was generally abandoned in favor of the opposing view, namely, that nerve impulses are essentially homogeneous in quality and are transmitted as "common currency" throughout the nervous system.

序号：013

> Other experiments revealed slight variations in the size, number, arrangement, and interconnection of the nerve cells, but as far as psychoneural correlations were concerned, the obvious similarities of these sensory fields to each other seemed much more remarkable than any of the minute differences.

难句类型：复杂修饰＋插入语　　**难度**：4⁻

标志：*Although* other experiments revealed slight variations (in the size, number, arrangement, and interconnection of the nerve cells), **but** /as far as psychoneural correlations were concerned/, the obvious similarities (of these sensory fields to each other) seemed much **more** remarkable /**than** any of the minute differences/.

译文：尽管其他实验显示（在神经细胞的大小、数量、排列和相互连接上）有一些小的差异，但是/就心理－神经的关系而言/，（这些感官区域彼此间的）明显的相似性看起来远远要/比其微小的差异/更为令人注目。

解释：在前后两个分句之间有一个插入语/as far as psychoneural correlations were concerned /。在后面的分句中，主语 the obvious similarities 之后的、修饰主语的成分较长，以致于有很多读者看到相隔很远的 more remarkable than 时一下子反应不过来是什么比后者更明显。其简化形式应为：similarities seemed more remarkable than differences。

意群训练：Other experiments revealed slight variations in the size, number, arrangement, and interconnection of the nerve cells, but as far as psychoneural correlations were concerned, the obvious similarities of these sensory fields to each other seemed much more remarkable than any of the minute differences.

序号：014

> Although some experiments show that, as an object becomes familiar, its internal representation becomes more holistic and the recognition process correspondingly more parallel, the weight of evidence seems to support the serial hypothesis, at least for objects that are not notably simple and familiar.

难句类型：复杂修饰＋插入语＋省略　　　　难度：4$^+$

请思考：如果 Although 引导的分句中的 holistic 不认识，是否可用合理化原则推理出其意思？

标志：**Although** some experiments show that, /as an object becomes familiar, / its internal representation becomes more holistic **and** *that* the recognition process correspondingly *becomes* more parallel, **but** the weight of evidence seems to support the serial hypothesis, /at least for objects (that are not notably simple and familiar) /.

译文：虽然有些实验显示/当一个物体变得熟悉的时候，/它在内心中的形象变得更为完整，而且对它的辨认过程也变得更加并行，*但是证据的天平似乎更倾斜于支持*（那个辨认过程是一）系列的假说，/至少对（那些不是特别简单的或熟悉的）物体来说/。

解释：在 Although 引导的分句中，谓语 shows 后面跟着一个长长的宾语从句，从句中先出现一个插入语 as an object becomes familiar，之后的内容是由 **and** 连接的两套并列的主谓宾。其实 and 前后就是两个句子，只不过作者省略了后面的句子中与前面相同的引导词 that 和谓语 become。

句子中有一个生词 holistic，其实即使不认识，也能用合理化原则猜出它是后面 serial 的反义词、parallel 的同义词，大约是统一、完整或同时的意思；其实只要能理解到其是与 serial 相反的意思即可。

意群训练：Although some experiments show that, as an object becomes familiar, its internal representation becomes more holistic and the recognition process correspondingly more parallel, the weight of evidence seems to support the serial hypothesis, at least for objects that are not notably simple and familiar.

序号：015

> In large part as a consequence of the feminist movement, historians have focused a great deal of attention in recent years on determining more accurately the status of women in various periods.

难句类型：倒装　　**难度**：3⁺

标志：/In large part as a consequence of the feminist movement, /historians have **focused** a great deal of attention /in recent years/ **on** determining /more accurately/ the status of women in various periods.

解释：focus A（attention/effort 等）on B，指把 A 集中于 B 上。本句中介词 on 的宾语 determining /more accurately/ the status of women in various periods 中有一个小倒装，正

常语序应该是 determining the status of women in various periods more accurately.

译文：/很大程度上作为妇女运动的一个结果/，历史学家们/近年来/把大量的注意力集中于/更为准确地/确定妇女们在不同时期的地位上面。

意群训练： In large part as a consequence of the feminist movement, historians have focused a great deal of attention in recent years on determining more accurately the status of women in various periods.

序号：016

> If one begins by examining why ancients refer to Amazons, it becomes clear that ancient Greek descriptions of such societies were meant not so much to represent observed historical fact—real Amazonian societies—but rather to offer "moral lessons" on the supposed outcome of women's rule in their own society.

难句类型：复杂修饰 + 插入语 + 抽象词　　**难度：**4

标志：/If one begins by examining why ancients refer to Amazons/, it becomes clear that ancient Greek descriptions (of such societies) were **meant not** /so much/ to represent observed historical fact—real Amazonian societies—**but rather to** offer "moral lessons" /on the supposed outcome (of women's rule in their own society) /.

译文：/如果我们先来研究一下为什么古人会提到亚马逊人/，下面的一点就变得清晰了，那就是古希腊（对于这种社会）的描述不是/太多地/被用来表达观察到的历史事实——真正的亚马逊社会的——而是为了/对于（妇女在其社会中的统治）所设想的后果/提供一种"道德教训"。

解释：有两个词汇需要先解释一下："something be meant to represent" 是 "use something to mean" 的被动语态。mean 在这里不是常用的"……的意思是"的意思，

而是表示做某事所表达的目的、意图，其英文释义为：to serve or intend to convey, show, or indicate。句中的结构为：something be meant **not** so much to..., **but rather** to...，实际上是把 **be meant to** 和 **not...rather...**的两个固定搭配套在了一起，意思是：不是为了……而是为了……。

另外，supposed 的意思很抽象，不容易理解。此词既有"据信，被认为"的意思，也有"预期的"意思，还有表示贬义的"假想的，被想当然的"意思。英文释义为：a：held as an opinion：BELIEVED；also：mistakenly believed：IMAGINED ＜the sight which makes supposed terror true—Shakespeare＞ b：considered probable or certain：EXPECTED ＜it was not supposed that everybody could master the technical aspects—J. C. Murra＞。

本句的 supposed 用法极其特殊，在此处的意思，用以上任何一个释义来理解居然都可以成立，既是在说一个预期的社会状态，又是在说一个虚构出来的、本来不存在的社会状态；其用法类似于中文中的"一语双关"，是文章作者自以为文笔精妙（**supposed** refinement in his style of writing）之处。

意群训练： If one begins by examining why ancients refer to Amazons, it becomes clear that ancient Greek descriptions of such societies were meant not so much to represent observed historical fact—real Amazonian societies—but rather to offer "moral lessons" on the supposed outcome of women's rule in their own society.

序号：017

> Thus, for instance, it may come as a shock to mathematicians to learn that the *Schrodinger* equation for the hydrogen atom is not a literally correct description of this atom, but only an approximation to a somewhat more correct equation taking account of spin, magnetic dipole, and relativistic effects; and that this corrected equation is itself only an imperfect approximation to an infinite set of quantum field-theoretical equations.

难句类型： 复杂修饰＋插入语＋省略　　**难度：** 5

请思考： 如果本句中大量的物理名词看不懂，对句子理解到什么程度就可以达到考试的要求？

标志： Thus, for instance, it may come as a shock /to mathematicians/ to learn that the *Schrodinger*, equation for the hydrogen atom is not a literally correct description of this atom, **but** *it is* only an approximation [to a somewhat more correct equation (taking account of spin, magnetic dipole, and relativistic effects)]; **and** that this corrected equation is itself only an imperfect approximation (to an infinite set of quantum field-theoretical equations).

译文： 所以，我们可以举一个例子，/对于数学家们而言/，得知以下的两种情况会令他们震惊不已：1.氢原子的薛定鄂方程并不是对这种原子的一个精确的、正确的描述，而它只是［对于一个在某种程度上更为正确的方程式的］一个近似表述，（该更为正确的方程式 是描述自选、磁双偶极子以及相对论效应的）。2.后面所说的这个更为正确的方程式自己也仅是（对于无限序列的量子场论方程式的）一个不完美的近似表述。

解释： 读到此句时，数学家不见得震惊，晕倒的考生恐怕不在少数。不但句子结构复杂，而且罗列了大量的专有名词。对于不是理科的同学来讲，在阅读这篇文章的现场清楚地明白应该读到什么程度远比研究这些生僻的专有名词更重要。其实是否知道薛定鄂方程对读者来说并不见得重要，GRE 考试的出题者也不见得知道它；关键是要读懂句子的主要意思：数学家不能理解不精确和近似值的伟大意义。不过在本书中，出现的句子均以阅读训练为目的，所以读者仍要把句子的结构读清楚。

主句中的主语 it 是一个形式主语，其具体的内容应该是从 to learn 开始一直到句子结束的长达八行的不定式，但是此不定式实在太长，如果放在句首则句子无法均衡。Learn 后面带着两个以 that 引导的宾语从句，中间以分号和 "and" 分开，可以把分号以后的句子看成是 and *it may come as a shock to mathematicians to learn* that 的省略形式。

意群训练： Thus, for instance, it may come as a shock to mathematicians to learn that the *Schrodinger* equation for the hydrogen atom is not a literally correct description of this atom, but only an approximation to a somewhat more correct equation taking account of spin, magnetic dipole, and relativistic effects; and that this corrected equation is itself only an imperfect approximation to an infinite set of quantum field-theoretical equations.

序号：**018**

> The physicist rightly dreads precise argument, since an argument that is convincing only if it is precise loses all its force if the assumptions on which it is based are slightly changed, whereas an argument that is convincing though imprecise may well be stable under small perturbations of its underlying assumptions.

难句类型：复杂修饰　　**难度：**5⁺

请思考： 本句子中的主句加上从句加在一起一共有几个？

标志： The physicist rightly <u>dreads</u> precise argument, **since** an argument（that is convincing /only if it is precise/）<u>loses all its force</u> /if the assumptions（on which it is based）<u>are slightly changed</u>, / **whereas** an argument（that is convincing though imprecise）<u>may well be stable</u> /under small perturbations（of its underlying assumptions）. /

译文： 物理学家正确地<u>不敢做精确的论证</u>，因为一个（/只有当它是精确的时候/才令人信服的/<u>论证</u>，/（如果作为它的基础的）假设<u>发生了一点点变化</u>/<u>就失去了其全部说服力</u>；而（一个尽管不很精确但是却令人信服的）论证，/（当作为它的基础的假设）稍有变动时，/<u>仍有可能是稳定的</u>。

解释： 本句在文章中就是一个自然段。虽然长度比不上前面第一章中所举的那个长达10行的例子，但是难度绝不在那句话之下。本句堪称句子的大杂烩，连主句带从句居然一共有八个！从大往小说，由 **whereas** 连接了两个大句子，whereas 后面的句子中的主语 an argument 之后又跟了一个定语从句 that is convincing though imprecise，修饰 argument。whereas 前面共有六个句子：由 the physicist 作主语的主句；由 since 的原因状语从句；修饰 since 从句中主语 an argument 的由 that 引导的定语从句；此定语从句中的条件状语从句 only if it is precise；since 从句中的条件状语从句 if the assumptions on which it is based are slightly changed；以及修饰此从句中的主语 assumptions 的定语从句 on which it is based，一共八个句子，从句套从句。

　　然而，在考试现场去数句子的数目，是只有呆子才会去干的事情。读者们惟一要干的事情，就是反复阅读这句话，什么时候练到不必去想其语法结构就能按原文顺序读懂，才算初步掌握；再进一步把它读顺，直到你看不出这个句子有什么特别的地方，看上去还挺舒服，就算训练成功。

意群训练： The physicist rightly dreads precise argument, since an argument that is convincing only if it is precise loses all its force if the assumptions on which it is based are slightly changed, whereas an argument that is convincing though imprecise may well be stable under small perturbations of its underlying assumptions.

序号：019

> However, as they gained cohesion, the Bluestockings came to regard themselves as a women's group and to possess a sense of female solidarity lacking in the *salonnieres*, who remained isolated from one another by the primacy each held in her own salon.

难句类型： 复杂修饰　　　　　　　　　　**难度：** 4⁻

标志： **However**, /as they gained cohesion/, the Bluestockings came to regard themselves /as a women's group/ **and** *came* to possess a sense of female solidarity { lacking in the *salonnieres*, [who remained isolated from one another by the primacy (*that* each *salonniere* held in her own salon.)] }

译文： 然而，/随着她们获得凝聚力/，"蓝袜女"们开始把自己视/为一个妇女的团体/，并抱有一个女性团结的意识；{ 此种意识是"沙龙女"们所缺乏的，[她们仍然彼此之间互不来往，这是由于（每个"沙龙女"在自己沙龙中的）老大地位造成的。] }

解释： 本句读到表示并列的连词 **and** 开始变难。and 之后的不定式与前面的不定式是并列的，to 的前面省略了一个与前面一样的谓语 came。分词短语 lacking in... 作定语修饰 a sense of female solidarity；其后的由 who 引导的定语从句又修饰逗号前的 salonnieres；此从句中又有一个定语从句 *that* each（*salonniere*）held in her own salon 修饰其前的 primacy，但是由于引导词 that 在从句中作宾语，因此被省略。

意群训练： However, as they gained cohesion, the Bluestockings came to regard themselves as a women's group and to possess a sense of female solidarity lacking in the *salonnieres*, who remained isolated from one another by the primacy each held in her own salon.

序号：020

As my own studies have advanced, I have been increasingly impressed with the functional similarities between insect and vertebrate societies and less so with the structural differences that seem, at first glance, to constitute such an immense gulf between them.

难句类型： 复杂修饰＋插入语＋省略　　**难度：** 5

标志： ／As my own studies have advanced，／ I have been increasingly impressed ／with the functional similarities（**between** insect *societies* **and** vertebrate societies）／ **and** less so （less so ＝*I have been increasingly less impressed* 的省略形式）／with the structural differences（ that seem，at first glance，to constitute such an immense gulf between them. ）／

译文： ／随着我自己的研究不断推进，／我越来越留下深刻的印象／于后面两者之间的功能上的相似性，（这两者是在昆虫*社会*和脊椎动物的社会之间）；并且就越来越感觉不／到它们之间的结构上的差异，（ 此差异乍看上去似乎构成了二者之间的巨大鸿沟。）

解释： 本句子的中间一段（impressed with the functional similarities between insect and vertebrate societies and less so with the structural differences）容易令人看晕，其中的 insect and vertebrate societies and less so with 由两个 and 连接了三个部分，然而它们其实不是同一层次的并列，第一个 and 实际上是 **between** insect*societies* **and** vertebrate societies 的一部分，insect 后面省略了与后面一样的 *societies*；第二个 and 表示其后的所有内容与前面整个的句子是并列的，而 and 之后的 less so with 其实是对于一个完整的表达方式 *I have been increasingly* less *impressed* with 的省略形式，去掉了与前面重复的成分。

后面修饰 structural differences 的定语从句（that seem, at first glance, to constitute such an immense gulf between them.）中，又出现了一个别扭的插入语 at first glance，把应该连在一起的 seem to 粗暴地分开，令不熟悉此类难句的人倍感不适。

意群训练：<u>As my own studies have advanced, I have been increasingly impressed with the functional similarities between insect and vertebrate societies and less so with the structural differences that seem, at first glance, to constitute such an immense gulf between them.</u>

序号：021

> Although fiction assuredly springs from political circumstances, its authors react to those circumstances in ways other than ideological, and talking about novels and stories primarily as instruments of ideology circumvents much of the fictional enterprise.

难句类型：复杂修饰　　　　**难度：**4

标志：Although fiction assuredly <u>springs</u> /from political circumstances/ **, but** its authors <u>react</u>（to those circumstances）/in ways other than ideological /, **and** talking about novels and stories /primarily as instruments of ideology/ <u>circumvents</u> much of the <u>fictional enterprise</u>.

译文：尽管小说确实都是<u>来自</u>/于政治氛围之下的/，**但是**<u>其作者</u>（对这些环境的）<u>反应</u>/却与意识形态无关/，**而且**/主要以意识形态为工具来/讨论小说和故事，则在很大程度上<u>限制（或陷害）了小说事业</u>。

解释：本句从句子的结构上来讲，惟一的难度在于 **and** 之后的句子的主语 talking about novels and stories /primarily as instruments of ideology/太长，以至于看到谓语 circumvent 的时候已经搞不清楚主谓了。

更大的难度恐怕还在于对两个词汇的理解：circumvent 和 enterprise。我们以前所背过的 circumvent 有两个词义，一是规避，一是以计谋战胜，但是这两种意思放到此处都显然不通；其实 circumvent 有一个我们没有背过的最常用的意思是包围，限制或陷害：Merriam-Webster 字典的第一条释义：circumvent：to hem in（to surround in a restrictive manner；confine）；Webster's New World Dictionary 字典第二条释义：circumvent：surround or encircle with evils, enmity, etc.; entrap 。至于 enterprise，常用的词义是企业，但在此处指事业。

意群训练： Although fiction assuredly springs from political circumstances, its authors react to those circumstances in ways other than ideological, and talking about novels and stories primarily as instruments of ideology circumvents much of the fictional enterprise.

序号：022

> Is this a defect, or are the authors working out of, or trying to forge, a different kind of aesthetic?

难句类型： 插入语　　**难度：** 3

标志： Is this a defect, **or** are the authors working out of, **or** trying to forge, a different kind of aesthetic?

译文： 这到底是个欠缺，还是作者想要按照一种不同的美学来创作，抑或是试图创造一种不同的美学呢？

解释： 本句的句子既短，意思也不难理解，但插入语（or trying to forge）的干扰作用却极强。

意群训练： Is this a defect, or are the authors working out of, or trying to forge, a different kind of aesthetic?

序号：023

> In addition, the style of some Black novels, like Jean Toomer's *Cane*, verges on expressionism or surrealism; does this technique provide a counterpoint to the prevalent theme that portrays the fate against which Black heroes are pitted, a theme usually conveyed by more naturalistic modes of expression?

难句类型： 复杂修饰＋插入语　　　**难度：** 5

标志： ／In addition／, the style of some Black novels, like Jean Toomer's *Cane*, **verges on** expressionism or surrealism; does this technique provide a counterpoint ｛to the prevalent theme ［ that portrays the fate （against which Black heroes are pitted）］, （a theme usually conveyed by more naturalistic modes of expression）｝?

译文： ／不但如此／，有些黑人小说（比如 JT 的《甘蔗》）的风格接近于表现主义或超现实主义；这种技巧是否 ｛为流行的主题｝ 提供了一个和谐的对应呢？ 这种主题 ［刻画了（黑人主人公与 之 相抗争的）命运，（这是一个通常用更为自然主义的表现手法所表达的主题）。

解释： 在本句中有三个词需要先解释一番：verge on 这个词组是"接近于，濒于"的意思；hero 在文学作品中是主人公的意思；pit 做动词时，除了"挖坑，窖藏"之外，还有"使⋯⋯竞争，使⋯⋯斗争"的意思，其英文释义为：（**A**）to set（as gamecocks）into or as if into a pit to fight（**B**）to set into opposition or rivalry—usually used with against。在此用的是（**B**）词义的被动语态：fate against which Black heros are pitted，如果用主动语态则是：pit black heros against fate。

另外，本句的结构复杂。分号之后是一个一般疑问句，但是由于修饰成分过多、过长，使得读者看不清楚这个句子在问什么。其实如果没有最后的那个 prevalent theme 的同位语 a theme usually conveyed by more naturalistic modes of expression，本句会易懂得多。

意群训练： In addition, the style of some Black novels, like Jean Toomer's *Cane*, verges on expressionism or surrealism; does this technique provide a counterpoint to the prevalent theme that portrays the fate against which Black heroes are pitted, a theme usually conveyed by more naturalistic modes of expression?

序号：024

> Black Fiction surveys a wide variety of novels, bringing to our attention in the process some fascinating and little-known works like James Weldon Johnson's *Autobiography of an Ex-Colored Man*.

难句类型：倒装　　　　　　　　　**难度：4**

标志： Black Fiction surveys a wide variety of novels, / **bringing to** our attention /in the process some fascinating and little-known works（like James Weldon Johnson's *Autobiography of an Ex-Colored Man* ）/.

译文：《黑人小说》考察了很广泛的范围内的小说，/ 把一些很迷人的、但鲜为人知的作品（比如 James Weldon Johnson 的《一个曾经是有色人种的人的自传》）/在此过程中/带到了我们的视野之中/。

解释： 在以 bringing 开头的作状语的分词中出现了倒装，bring A to B 被倒装成了 bring to B A，其倒装的原因仍是为了避免头重脚轻。正常的语序应该如下：**bringing** some fascinating and little-known works like James Weldon Johnson's *Autobiography of an Ex-Colored Man* /**to** our attention in the process. /

意群训练： Black Fiction surveys a wide variety of novels, bringing to our attentionin the process some fascinating and little-known works like James Weldon Johnson's *Autobiography of an Ex-Colored Man*.

序号：025

> Although these molecules allow radiation at visible wavelengths, where most of the energy of sunlight is concentrated, to pass through, they absorb some of the longer-wavelength, infrared emissions radiated from the Earth's surface, radiation that would otherwise be transmitted back into space.

难句类型：复杂修饰＋插入语　　**难度**：4

标志：**Although** these molecules <u>allow</u> radiation at visible wavelengths，where most of the energy of sunlight is concentrated，/**to** pass through，/**but** they <u>absorb</u> some of the longer-wavelength, infrared emissions（radiated from the Earth's surface，）（radiation that would otherwise be transmitted back into space）.

译文：尽管这些分子<u>允许</u>（大多数太阳能集中于此的）可见光波长的辐射<u>通过</u>，*可是*它们却<u>吸收了</u>（从地球表面反射出来的）更长波长的红外线辐射，（如果没有二氧化碳分子这种辐射将会被传送回太空）。

解释：前面的分句中有一个不算是很长的插入语，但是因为它插入的位置正好在固定搭配 **allow** something **to** do something 中间，将 allow 和 to 分得很远，所以读起来让人感觉很不舒服。

后面的分句中的最后的一行 radiation that would otherwise be transmitted back into space 是其前面的 infrared emissions 的同位语。其中的 otherwise 词作状语，表示如果后面的分句所说的 they absorb some of the longer-wavelength, infrared emissions 不发生时的后果。

意群训练：Although these molecules <u>allow</u> radiation at visible wavelengths，where most of the energy of sunlight is concentrated，to pass through，they absorb some of the longer-wavelength, infrared emissions radiated from the Earth's surface，radiation that would otherwise be transmitted back into space.

序号：**026**

> The role those anthropologists ascribe to evolution is not of dictating the details of human behavior but one of imposing constraints—ways of feeling, thinking, and acting that "come naturally" in archetypal situations in any culture.

难句类型：复杂修饰＋省略　　**难度**：4

标志： The role（ *that* those anthropologists ascribe to evolution）is not *the role* of dictating the details of human behavior **but** *is* one *role* of imposing constraints ［—ways of feeling, thinking, and acting（that "come naturally" in archetypal situations in any culture）］.

译文：（那些人类学家们归诸进化的）角色不是规定人类行为的细节，而是一个建立某种行为上的限制［——即确定（在任何文化的原型场景下都会"自然而然地产生的"）感觉、思考和行动的方式］的角色。

解释： 尽管我们很熟悉 the role of something 这种表达，但本句中 the role of 被作者用得很活。首先，在 role 后面有一个省略了引导词 that 的定语从句（因为 role 在从句中作 ascribe 的宾语），这样就把 role 和系动词 is 隔得很远。其次，**but** 前面的句子的主要结构 The role is not of doing something 其实是 The role is not *the role* of doing something 的省略形式，因为后面的 the role 与前面的完全重复，如果不把它省略掉，谁看到都要觉得罗嗦。因为同样的道理，**but** 之后的 one of imposing constraints 上是 *is* one *role* of imposing constraints 的省略形式。

意群训练： The role those anthropologists ascribe to evolution is not of dictating the details of human behavior but one of imposing constraints—ways of feeling, thinking, and acting that "come naturally" in archetypal situations in any culture.

序号：027

Q26 Which of the following most probably provides an appropriate analogy from human morphology for the "details" versus "constraints" distinction made in the passage in relation to human behavior?

难句类型： 复杂修饰 + 抽象词　　　　**难度：5**

标志： Which of the following most probably provides an appropriate **analogy**/from human morphology/ **for** the（ "details" versus "constraints"）distinction（made in the passage /in relation to human behavior/）?

译文：以下哪一个选项最有可能为（文章中所谈到的/与人类行为有关的/）（"人类行为的细节"相对"人类行为上的限制"）之间的差异/从人类形态的**角度上**/<u>提供了一个合适的类比</u>？

解释：本句子在所有的 GRE/GMAT 阅读题的题干中是最难读懂的题干之一。本句不但结构复杂，而且用词抽象，使得读者如果想根据语义来搞清楚谁修饰谁，也变得极为困难。分析如下：

本句的主干是：Which of the following provides an analogy for the "details" versus "constraints" distinction? Versus 是一个介词，等于 against，即体育比赛中的 VS。其他的所有成分均是一些修饰成分。其中一个对答题最重要的限制条件是/from human morphology/，指此类比的比较双方所比的必须是人类形态上的特征。

意群训练：<u>Which of the following</u> <u>most probably</u> <u>provides an appropriate analogy</u> <u>from human morphology</u> <u>for the</u> "details" <u>versus</u> "constraints" <u>distinction made in the passage</u> <u>in relation to human behavior?</u>

序号：028

> A low number of algal cells in the presence of a high number of grazers suggested, but did not prove, that the grazers had removed most of the algae.

难句类型：插入语　　　　　**难度**：3⁺

标志：<u>A low number of algal cells</u> / in the presence of a high number of grazers / <u>suggested</u>, but did not prove, │that│ the grazers had removed most of the algae.

译文：/在食草动物的数量很大时/仅有<u>少量的水藻细胞</u>这一点暗示着（<u>但却不能证明</u>）是食草动物除去了大多数水藻。

解释：本句主语很长，而且谓语 suggested 与 that 引导的宾语从句间被插入语 but

did not prove 隔开，造成阅读障碍。当 suggest 与 but did not prove 连在一起使用的时候，其意思不是建议，而是指一种基于主观臆测的推理，中文翻译成"暗示"。其英文释义为：to call to mind by thought or association ＜ the explosion... suggested sabotage—F. L. Paxson ＞。在 GRE、GMAT 以及 LSAT 文章中，常用 suggest，but do not prove 来描述一种没有真凭实据的、可能有问题的理论，然后在后面的叙述中把它否掉。

意群训练：A low number of algal cells in the presence of a high number of grazers suggested, but did not prove, that the grazers had removed most of the algae.

序号：029

Perhaps the fact that many of these first studies considered only algae of a size that could be collected in a net (net phytoplankton), a practice that over-looked the smaller phytoplankton (nannoplankton) that we now know grazers are most likely to feed on, led to a de-emphasis of the role of grazers in subsequent research.

难句类型：复杂修饰 + 插入语　　　　**难度：**5

标志：/Perhaps/ the fact { that many of these first studies considered /only/ algae [of a size (that could be collected /in a net)] (net phytoplankton) }, a practice [that over-looked the smaller phytoplankton (nannoplanktont) (that we now know grazers are most likely to feed on) } , led /to a de-emphasis of the role of grazers in subsequent research/.

译文：/可能/这样一个事实，{ 那就是 很多这样的最初的研究/只/考虑了 [（那些能够/用网/捞起来的）尺寸的] 水藻（net phytoplankton)}，这样一个 [忽视了（我们现在知道是食草浮游动物最有可能吃的）更小的浮游植物（nannoplankton）] 的做法，导致/了在接下来的研究中对于食草浮游动物的作用的贬低/。

解释：句子的结构繁杂。句子的主语令人吃惊得长，在最后一个逗号后的 led 以前，全是主语！其实句子的主干简单，就是 the fact led to a de-emphasis of the role of grazers。但是本句的主语 the fact 后面的修饰成分长的吓人，先是个定语从句；定语从句中又套了一个定语从句。然后逗号后面的 a practice 引导的部分是前面的主语的同位语兼作插入语，practice 后面的修饰它一大堆东西又是定语从句套着定语从句。本句是典型的层层修饰的结构。

意群训练： Perhaps the fact that many of these first studies considered only algae of a size that could be collected in a net（net phytoplankton），a practice that overlooked the smaller phytoplankton（nannoplankton）that we now know grazers are most likely to feed on, led to a de-emphasis of the role of grazers in subsequent research.

序号：030

> Studies by Hargrave and Geen estimated natural community grazing rates by measuring feeding rates of individual zooplankton species in the laboratory and then computing community grazing rates for field conditions using the known population density of grazers.

难句类型：复杂修饰　　　难度：5

标志： Studies（by Hargrave and Geen）estimated natural community grazing rates / by measuring feeding rates of individual zooplankton species in the laboratory/ **and then** /by computing community grazing rates for field conditions / using the known population density of grazers. //

译文：（Hargrave 和 Geen 所做的研究）估计了自然群体的捕食速率，/是通过首先测量了实验室中的浮游动物品种的个体的捕食速率/，然后//再用已知的捕食者的种群密度/计算出其野外的群体捕食速率。/

解释： 本句对阅读者的阅读能力提出了很高的要求，不但要求读者读清楚句子的复杂的结构，而且对读者的词汇能力也提出了较高的要求。

by 以前结构无需解释，by 以后有两个作介词宾语的动名词结构，measuring 和后面表示并列和顺接的 **and then** 之后的 computing，说的是计算方法：前一个 measuring 所的是先算出实验室中的浮游动物品种的单位捕食速率, 后面的 computing 前其实省略了一个 by, 而且在这个动名词结构中还包括了一个分词结构 using the known population density of grazers, 用已知的捕食者的种群密度计算出其野外的群体捕食速率。整个的 by 以后的计算过程说简单了就是:

$$实验室单位速率 \times 野外密度 = 野外群体速率$$

另外本句中的词汇也颇有迷惑性: 虽然没有太难的单词, 但是很多单词都是同义词和反义词, 容易让人读混: (斜线分隔同义词, 冒号分隔反义词)

estimate / measure / compute

feeding rates / grazing rates

zooplankton / grazers

natural / field : laboratory

community : individual

意群训练: Studies by Hargrave and Geen estimated natural community grazing rates by measuring feeding rates of individual zooplankton species in the laboratory and then computing community grazing rates for field conditions using the known population density of grazers.

序号: 031

In the periods of peak zooplankton abundance, that is, in the late spring and in the summer, Haney recorded maximum daily community grazing rates, for nutrient-poor lakes and bog lakes, respectively, of 6. 6 percent and 114 percent of daily phytoplankton production.

难句类型: 插入语　　　　**难度**: 3[+]

标志: /In the periods of peak zooplankton abundance, that is, in the late spring and in the summer, / Haney recorded maximum daily community grazing **rates**, for nutrient-poor lakes and bog lakes, respectively, **of** 6. 6 percent and 114 percent of daily phytoplankton production.

译文：/在浮游动物最多的季节，也就是在晚春和夏天，/Haney 记录下了最高的群体捕食<u>速率</u>，对于贫养湖和沼泽湖来讲，各自是 6.6% 和 114% 的浮游植物的日产量。

解释： 句中有两组插入语，每组两个插入语。尤其是第二组，把 **rate of** 从中间劈开。不过因为句义尚好理解，所以本句只是有一点别扭，但不算太难。

意群训练： In the periods of peak zooplankton abundance, that is, in the late spring and in the summer, Haney recorded maximum daily community grazing rates, for nutrient-poor lakes and bog lakes, respectively, of 6.6 percent and 114 percent of daily phytoplankton production.

序号：032

> The hydrologic cycle, a major topic in this science, is the complete cycle of phenomena through which water passes, beginning as atmospheric water vapor, passing into liquid and solid form as precipitation, thence along and into the ground surface, and finally again returning to the form of atmospheric water vapor by means of evaporation and transpiration.

难句类型： 复杂修饰 ＋ 插入语＋省略　　　　**难度：** 4

标志： The hydrologic cycle, a major topic in this science, is the complete cycle of phenomena（through which water passes），/beginning as atmospheric water vapor, passing into liquid and solid form as precipitation, **thence** passing along and entering into the ground surface, **and** finally again returning to the form of atmospheric water vapor by means of evaporation and transpiration. /

译文： 水文循环，水利科学中的主要课题，是一个（水需要经历的）完整的循环过程，循环在开始时作为大气中的水蒸气，再进入液体和固体状态作为降雨或降雪，然后流过并进入地表，并最终通过蒸发和气化作用重返气态的水蒸气的形式。

解释：beginning 开始的一系列分词都是修饰主语The hydrologic cycle的，分别是 beginning / passing /*passing* / returning 。值得注意的是，**thence** along and into the ground surface 是 **thence** *passing* along and *entering* into the ground surface 的省略形式，但是看上去意思却很清楚。类似这样的省略，是出题者合理地利用了省略来达到改编学术论文时压缩文章篇幅的目的。

意群训练：The hydrologic cycle, a major topic in this science, is the complete cycle of phenomena through which water passes, beginning as atmospheric water vapor, passing into liquid and solid form as precipitation, thence along and into the ground surface, and finally again returning to the form of atmospheric water vapor by means of evaporation and transpiration.

序号：033

Only when a system possesses natural or artificial boundaries that associate the water within it with the hydrologic cycle may the entire system properly be termed hydrogeologic.

难句类型：复杂修饰 + 倒装　　　　**难度：4**

标志：Only /**when** a system possesses（natural or artificial）boundaries［that **associate** the water（within it）**with** the hydrologic cycle］/ **may** the entire system properly be termed hydrogeologic.

译文：只有当一个系统拥有（自然的或人工形成的）边界［来把（边界中的）水与水文循环联系起来的时候］，才有可能把整个的系统恰当地称为水文地质学系统。

解释：only 放在句首时，主句的情态动词 may 倒装，这是我们高中就已经学过的东西。然而句首的 only 与倒装的 may 距离如此之远，这在以前却没有见过，所以读上去让人不习惯。

另外一个难点在于，在前面的由 when 所引导的时间状语从句中，宾语 boundaries 后面跟了一个定语从句，that associate the water within it with the hydrologic cycle，

而且从句中的 **associate with** 又被 water within it 所分开，读者有要分神去考虑 it 指的是什么（就是指前面的 boundaries），所以读到后面倒装的 may 的时候，难免不知所云。

意群训练： Only when a system possesses natural or artificial boundaries that associate the water within it with the hydrologic cycle may the entire system properly be termed hydrogeologic.

序号：034

The historian Frederick J. Turner wrote in the 1890's that the agrarian discontent that had been developing steadily in the United States since about 1870 had been precipitated by the closing of the internal frontier—that is, the depletion of available new land needed for further expansion of the American farming system.

难句类型： 复杂修饰 **难度：** 4

标志： The historian Frederick J. Turner wrote /in the 1890's / that the agrarian discontent（that had been developing steadily in the United States since about 1870）had been precipitated /by the closing of the internal frontier— [that is, the depletion of available new land（needed for further expansion of the American farming system）] /.

译文： 历史学家 FJT/在 19 世纪 90 年代/写道，（自从 1870 年开始就在美国持续发展的）农民的不满是被内部边疆的消失所加剧的，[而内部边疆的消失即指（所需进一步扩展美国农业系统的）可资利用的新土地的枯竭。]

解释： 典型的句子套句子。主句是 Frederick J. Turner wrote that，宾语从句中主干是 the agrarian discontent had been precipitated /by the closing of the internal frontier，在从句的主语 the agrarian discontent 后面又来了一个定语从句。

意群训练： The historian Frederick J. Turner wrote in the 1890's that the agrarian discontent that had been developing steadily in the United States since about 1870 had been precipitated by the closing of the internal frontier—that is, the depletion of available new land needed for further expansion of the American farming system.

序号：035

> In the early 1950's, historians who studied preindustrial Europe (which we may define here as Europe in the period from roughly 1300 to 1800) began, for the first time in large numbers, to investigate more of the preindustrial European population than the 2 or 3 percent who comprised the political and social elite: the kings, generals, judges, nobles, bishops, and local magnates who had hitherto usually filled history books.

难句类型： 复杂修饰 + 插入语　　　　**难度：** 4

标志： /In the early 1950's, / historians [who studied preindustrial Europe (which we may define here as Europe in the period from roughly 1300 to 1800)] **began**, /for the first time in large numbers/, **to** investigate **more of** the preindustrial European population **than** the 2 or 3 percent [(who comprised the political and social elite: the kings, generals, judges, nobles, bishops, and local magnates) (who had hitherto usually filled history books)].

译文： /在 20 世纪 50 年代的早期，/ [研究欧洲工业化以前的（我们在此把这个时间段模糊定位于公元 1300 年至 1800 年）] 历史学家们开始/第一次以大量的数据/来调查那些在占工业化以前的欧洲人口 2% 到 3% 的包括政治和社会精英以外的人口，[而那 2% 到 3% 精英们（是到目前为止都一直充斥着历史教科书的）（国王、将军、贵族、主教以及地方上的达官显贵们。）]

解释： 句中有两个插入语，一个是跟在 preindustrial Europe 之后的 which we may define here as Europe in the period from roughly 1300 to 1800，这个插入语的直接作用是解释前面的 preindustrail Europe 的年代，而起到的客观作用则是把主句中的主语和谓语分割得很远；第二个插入语 for the first time in large numbers，是在 **began**, **to** investigate 中间，把一个好好的 **began to** 斩为两段。

这句话另外一个难以理解的地方是 **more of** the preindustrial European population **than** the 2 or 3 percent，表示的是在工业化以前的欧洲人口中超过了那 2% 到 3% 的人，亦即占 97% 到 98% 的人民群众。

意群训练：In the early 1950's, historians who studied preindustrial Europe（which we may define here as Europe in the period from roughly 1300 to 1800）began, for the first time in large numbers, to investigate more of the preindustrial European population than the 2 or 3 percent who comprised the political and social elite: the kings, generals, judges, nobles, bishops, and local magnates who had hitherto usually filled history books.

序号：036

> Historians such as Le Roy Ladurie have used the documents to extract case histories, which have illuminated the attitudes of different social groups（these attitudes include, but are not confined to, attitudes toward crime and the law）and have revealed how the authorities administered justice.

难句类型：复杂修饰 + 插入语　　　　**难度：**3⁺

标志：Historians（such as Le Roy Ladurie）have used the documents / to extract case histories, / 〔which have illuminated the attitudes of different social groups（these attitudes include, but are not confined to, attitudes toward crime and the law）**and** have revealed how the authorities administered justice〕.

译文：（像 Le Roy Ladurie 这样的）历史学家们使用这些记录／来提取出个案史／，〔这些个案史说明了不同社会团体的态度（这些态度说明了，但是又不局限于，对犯罪和法律的态度），并且也说明了当权者是怎样管辖司法的〕。

解释：逗号以后的内容都是修饰逗号前的 case history 的。在 which 引导的非限定性定语从句中有一个插入语（these attitudes include, but are not confined to, attitudes toward crime and the law），我们可以看到这个插入语中又套了一个插入语 but not confined to。

意群训练：Historians such as Le Roy Ladurie have used the documents to extract case histories，which have illuminated the attitudes of different social groups（these attitudes include，but are not confined to，attitudes toward crime and the law）and have revealed how the authorities administered justice.

序号：037

It can be inferred from the passage that a historian who wished to compare crime rates per thousand in a European city in one decade of the fifteenth century with crime rates in another decade of that century would probably be most aided by better information about which of the following?

难句类型：复杂修饰　　**难度：5**

标志：It can be inferred /from the passage/ that a historian ［who wished to **compare** crime rates（per thousand in a European city）（in one decade of the fifteenth century）/**with** crime rates（*per thousand in a European city*）（in another decade of that century）/］would probably be most aided / by better information about which of the following/?

译文：从文章当中可以推断出来，一个［希望比较（15 世纪的某个十年的）（某个欧洲城市中的每千人）犯罪率/与（另外一个十年中的）（城市中每千人）犯罪率/的］历史学家将会/被以下哪种信息的提高/所最好地帮助？

解释：句首的 it 是形式主语，其具体内容是从 that 开始到句子结束的全部内容。that 从句中，主语 a historian 之后修饰它的超长的定语从句是这个句子难以读懂的原因。**compare** crime rates **with** crime rates 中间被修饰第一个 crime rates 的两个修饰成分（per thousand in a European city）（in one decade of the fifteenth century）分隔得很远。在 with 之后的第二个 crime rates 后面，省略了与前面重复的（*per thousand in a European city*）。

意群训练：It can be inferred from the passage that a historian who wished to compare crime rates per thousand in a European city in one decade of the fifteenth century with crime rates in another decade of that century would probably be most aided by better information about which of the following?

序号：038

> My point is that its central consciousness—its profound understanding of class and gender as shaping influences on people's lives—owes much to that earlier literary heritage, a heritage that, in general, has not been sufficiently valued by most contemporary literary critics.

难句类型：复杂修饰＋插入语　　　　**难度：**4

标志： My point is that its central consciousness—its profound **understanding** of class and gender **as** shaping influences on people's lives—owes much to that earlier literary heritage, a heritage that, in general, has not been sufficiently valued by most contemporary literary critics.

译文：我的观点是，其中心的意识——即其深刻的把阶级和性别理解（understanding）成（as）对人们的生活起到一个塑造性的影响的作用——很大程度上是得益于那个更早的文化遗产，一个总体而言没有被当代的文学评论家所足够重视的遗产。

解释：宾语从句中的主语和谓语被长插入语分开，造成阅读障碍。插入语中一个固定搭配 understanding of A as B，是把 A 理解成 B 的意思。不过本句子中 as 的宾语不容易理解：shaping influences on people's lives 可以理解成"形成了对人们生活的影响"也可以理解成"对人们生活的塑造性（决定性）影响"。当然后面的理解是正确的，然而在阅读现场想要在瞬间做出正确判断，还有赖于考生的阅读理解力和词汇功底的深浅。

插入语后面还有一个固定搭配：A owes much to B，指前者有很多东西是来自于后者、得益于后者的。

意群训练：My point is that its central consciousness—its profound understanding of class and gender <u>as shaping influences</u> on people's lives—owes much to that earlier literary heritage, a heritage that, <u>in general</u>, has not been sufficiently valued by most contemporary literary critics.

序号：039

Even the requirement that biomaterials processed from these materials be nontoxic to host tissue can be met by techniques derived from studying the reactions of tissue cultures to biomaterials or from short-term implants.

难句类型：复杂修饰 + 省略 + 专有名词 + 固定搭配　　　　**难度**：5

标　志：Even the requirement [that biomaterials (processed from these materials) *should* be nontoxic to host tissue] can be met /by techniques [**derived from** studying the **reactions** (of tissue cultures **to** biomaterials) **or** *derived* **from** studying short-term implants] /.

译　文：即使是这样的要求，[即 （从这些材料中加工出来的）生物材料应该对受移植者的组织无害]，也能够/通过 [从研究（组织培养对生物材料的）反应而来的，或从研究短期移植*而来的*] 技术/来满足。

解　释：主语 the requirement 后面带着一个长长的修饰主语的同位语；由于 requirement 的同位语中要求使用虚拟语气，所以其中的系动词成了原型（should be 省略了 should）。如此之长的修饰成分过后，谓语 can be met 与主语的关系已经很难理清了。从 by 开始的状语的结构更为复杂：修饰 techniques 的后置的定语 [**derived from** studying the **reaction**s (of tissue cultures **to** biomaterials **or** *derived* **from** studying short-term implants)] 实际上是由 **or** 所连接的两个 derive from；但是这两个 derive from 又都极其难懂：第一个 derive from 中还套了另外一个固定搭配 the **reaction**s (of tissue cultures **to** biomaterials)；第二个 derive from 则干脆把 derive 给省略了。此外，上本句的专有名词奇多，这使得阅读的难度非常高。

意群训练：Even the requirement that biomaterials processed from these materials be nontoxic to host tissue can be met by techniques derived from studying the reactions of tissue cultures to biomaterials or from short-term implants.

序号：040

But achieving necessary matches in physical properties across interfaces between living and non-living matter requires knowledge of which molecules control the bonding of cells to each other—an area that we have not yet explored thoroughly.

难句类型： 复杂修饰　　　　**难度：** 4

标志：But achieving necessary matches / in physical properties across interfaces **between** living **and** nonliving matter / requires knowledge（of which molecules control the bonding of cells to each other—an area that we have not yet explored thoroughly）.

译文： 但是，/ 想要在活的与无生命的物质之间在物理性质上 / 达到必要的匹配，需要这样的知识，（那就是到底是什么分子控制细胞彼此连接——这是一个我们到目前为止尚未透彻研究的领域）。

解释： 本句这样的复杂修饰和插入语的作用差不多：主语 achieving necessary matches 之后的修饰成分 / in physical properties across interfaces **between** living **and** nonliving matter / 把主语和谓语 requires 分开。值得注意的是修饰宾语的 of which molecules 中的 which 在此不是定语从句的引导词，而是一个形容词，意思是：哪个。

意群训练： But achieving necessary matches in physical properties across interfaces between living and nonliving matter requires knowledge of which molecules control the bonding of cells to each other—an area that we have not yet explored thoroughly.

序号：**041**

> Islamic law is a phenomenon so different from all other forms of law—notwithstanding, of course, a considerable and inevitable number of coincidences with one or the other of them as far as subject matter and positive enactment are concerned—that its study is indispensable in order to appreciate adequately the full range of possible legal phenomena.

难句类型：复杂修饰 + 插入语 + 抽象词　　　　**难度**：5

请思考：如果四行长的插入语看不懂，是否可用合理化原则推理出其意思？

标志：Islamic law is a phenomenon **so** different from all other forms of law—**notwithstanding**, of course, *it has* a considerable and inevitable number of coincidences with one or the other of them /**as far as** subject matter and positive enactment are concerned/—**that** its study is indispensable in order to appreciate adequately the full range of possible legal phenomena.

译文：伊斯兰法是一个与其他所有形式的法律都如此之不同的法律现象——尽管，当然，/从其涉及的内容和实际实施的角度来看/，伊斯兰法与其他的某些法律存在着大量的和必然的一致之处——以至于对于它的研究是不可缺少的，这样才能充分地理解所有可能的法律现象的全部范围。

解释：这是一个被 GRE 考生尊称为 No. 题三大难文章之一的《伊斯兰法》中的臭名昭著的句子。本句插入语前后都不难，关键是如何对待这段插入语。

首先，插入语很长，在原文中有四行。笔者在前面不只一次提醒读者，三行以上的插入语必须跳过，看懂前后的内容再回头来看插入语。插入语难懂的第一个原因是其中混有大量的抽象词和法律术语；还有一个重要原因，那就是它是一个由 notwithstanding... 构成的介词短语。notwithstanding 作为介词，相当于 in spite of，对此我们不够熟悉。

不管从哪个角度上来看，这句话中的那个插入语都极像是 ETS 布下的一个陷阱：

首先，插入语的内容对理解文章毫无作用；其次，考试中对插入语也没有出题；第三，其实这句话中的插入语根本不必读，也可以根据插入语前后的内容用<u>合理化原则</u>的取非读法猜出其意思：插入语前后的内容是伊斯兰法与其他法律不同，插入部分以 notwithstanding 开头，又有 of course，可见插入部分一定是让步语气，因此可以对前后的内容取非，猜出插入部分一定是在说伊斯兰法与其他法律有相同之处。

句末的 in order to appreciate adequately the full range of possible legal phenomena 中，包含一个倒装：正常语序的 appreciate the full range of possible legal phenomena adequately 中的副词 adequately 被提到 apperciate 的宾语之前。

意群训练：Islamic law <u>is</u> a phenomenon so different from all other forms of law—<u>notwithstanding</u>, of course, a considerable and <u>inevitable</u> number of coincidences <u>with</u> one or <u>the</u> other <u>of</u> them as far as subject matter and <u>positive enactment are concerned</u>—that its study is indispensable in order to appreciate adequately the full range of possible legal phenomena.

序号：042

> *Both Jewish law and canon law are more uniform than Islamic law.* Though historically there is a discernible break between Jewish law of the sovereign state of ancient Israel and of the Diaspora (the dispersion of Jewish people after the conquest of Israel), the spirit of the legal matter in later parts of the Old Testament is very close to that of the Talmud, one of the primary codifications of Jewish law in the Diaspora.

请思考：如果第二句话看不懂，是否可用<u>合理化原则</u>根据用斜体字标出的第一句话推理出其意思？

难句类型：复杂修饰 + 插入语 + 省略 + 专有名词　　**难度**：5

标志：*Both Jewish law and canon law are more uniform than Islamic law.* **Though** historically there <u>is</u> a discernible <u>break</u> **between** Jewish law of the sovereign state of ancient Israel **and** *Jewish law* of the Diaspora (the dispersion of Jewish people after the conquest of Israel),

but the spirit（of the legal matter in later parts of the Old Testament）is very close to that of the Talmud, one of the primary codifications of Jewish law in the Diaspora.

译文：*犹太法和天主教法都比伊斯兰法更为完整。尽管在历史上在古以色列的独立国家的犹太法和 Diaspora 时期（即以色列在被征服后犹太人被驱逐的时期）的犹太法之间有一个明确的断裂，但*（旧约全书中后半部分中的法律事务的）精神与 Talmud（指犹太法在 Diaspora 时期的主要法典）是极为一致的。

解释：本句与上面的句子来自于同一篇文章。本文的主题是伊斯兰法，但作者反复地用犹太法来吓唬读者。同样，ETS 也未就此句话出题。

这句话难读原因有二：第一，作者在 **between** Jewish law of the sovereign state of ancient Israel **and** of the Diaspora 一句中的 and 之后省略了 Jewish law，使人看到 of the Diaspora 时搞不清楚在什么与什么之间；第二个难懂的原因是文中出现了大量的专有名词、法律术语和历史背景。其实读者除了 Israel 和 Jewish 两个单词有必要也有可能认识之外，其他单词既不需要了解也无法了解。像什么 Diaspora（大流散时期）、Old Testament（旧约全书）、Talmud（犹太教法典）等名词，在非宗教国家的考生（如中国考生）的大脑中，对其概念并不是很清楚，更不要说其英语的表达了。那么 ETS 的出题者在阅读文章中搞出这种东西来，不是有违背公平出题原则之嫌了么？

笔者之所以用斜体字列出前面的一句话，是因为后面这句极难读懂的话，出题者其实并没有逼着读者必须读懂，完全可以根据前面那句话的内容把它的意思推出来。前面那句话是一个判断句，说犹太法和伊斯兰法一致，后面这句话是对上面一句话的解释，因此肯定也在说它一致。再看第二句话的结构，上来就是一个用 though 表示的让步语气，我们可以看出有一个 break between，那么逗号后就应该是省略了 but 的转折语气，该说没有 break between。果然我们看到了 very close to 的字样。我们也知道，既有让步又有转折时，作者强调的是转折之后的内容。所以这句话仍是在说犹太法一致。

意群训练：Though historically there is a discernible break between Jewish law of the sovereign state of ancient Israel and of the Diaspora (the dispersion of Jewish people after the conquest of Israel), the spirit of the legal matter in later parts of the Old Testament is very close to that of the Talmud, one of the primary codifications of Jewish law in the Diaspora.

序号：**043**

> Islam, on the other hand, represented a radical breakaway from the Arab paganism that preceded it; Islamic law is the result of an examination, from a religious angle, of legal subject matter that was far from uniform, comprising as it did the various components of the laws of pre-Islamic Arabia and numerous legal elements taken over from the non-Arab peoples of the conquered territories.

难句类型：复杂修饰 + 插入语　　　**难度：**4

标志：Islam, on the other hand, represented a radical breakaway〔from the Arab paganism（that preceded it）〕; Islamic law is the result｛of an **examination**, from a religious angle,〔**of** legal subject matter（that was far from uniform）〕｝, ╱comprising as it did the various components（of the laws of pre-Islamic Arabia）**and** numerous legal elements（taken over from the non-Arab peoples of the conquered territories）╱.

译文：伊斯兰，在另一方面，代表着〔与（伊斯兰法以前的）阿拉伯异教的〕决然断裂；伊斯兰法是一种从宗教的角度｛检查的｝结果，｛检查的对象〔（是远远谈不上统一的）主体事物〕｝；╱它包括了伊斯兰教出现以前的阿拉伯法律的种种成分，并包含了（很多从被征服的非阿拉伯地区那里拿来的）法律因素╱。

解释：本句是接着上面那句话写下来的，是在说伊斯兰法的不一致。句中有三个插入语，都起到了一定的干扰作用。第一个是 on the other hand，隔开了主语与谓语。第二个是 from a religious angle，分开了 **examination of**；第三个 as it did，根本就是句废话，分断了动词 comprise 和动词的宾语 the various components。

有一点请读者注意，本句子的难度明显低于前面那句说犹太法的话，其原理何在？因为文章的主题就是伊斯兰法。这是出题者必须考虑的一点。

意群训练：Islam, on the other hand, represented a radical breakaway from the Arab paganism that preceded it; Islamic law is the result of an examination, from a religious angle, of legal subject matter that was far from uniform, comprising as it did the various components of the laws of pre-Islamic Arabia and numerous legal elements taken over from the non-Arab peoples of the conquered territories.

序号：**044**

> One such novel idea is that of inserting into the chromosomes of plants discrete genes that are not a part of the plants' natural constitution: specifically, the idea of inserting into nonleguminous plants the genes, if they can be identified and isolated, that fit the leguminous plants to be hosts for nitrogen-fixing bacteria. Hence, the intensified research on legumes.

难句类型：复杂修饰 + 插入语 + 倒装 + 省略　　　　**难度**：5

标志：One such novel idea is that *idea* [of **inserting** /into the chromosomes of plants/ discrete genes (that are not a part of the plants' natural constitution)]: specifically, the idea [of **inserting** /into nonleguminous plants /the genes, if they can be identified and isolated, (that fit the leguminous plants to be hosts for nitrogen-fixing bacteria)]. Hence, *there is* the intensified research on legumes.

译文：一个这样的全新的想法，是把（非此植物的自然组成部分的）不相关的基因插入/到植物的染色体中；具体说来就是这么一个想法：把一些使得豆科植物能够成为固氮菌的寄主的基因（如果它们能够被找到并分离出来的话）插入/到非豆科植物的基因中去/。因此才出现了对豆科植物的深入研究。

解释：本句的难度以倒装为主，复杂为辅；然而二者相互借力，难度更大。而且本句中有两个省略，就更令读者头痛。

句子一开始的 One such novel idea is that of 之中的 that of，是 that *idea* of 的省略形式。此处容易理解，后面开始变难。**inserting into** the chromosomes of plants discrete genes（that are not a part of the plants' natural constitution）看上去不舒服的原因，是作者在此用了一个倒装；正常语序应该是：**inserting** discrete genes（that are not a part of the plants' natural constitution）**into** the chromosomes of plants，即把非此植物的 genes 插入到

该植物中。之所以倒装，是因为 discrete genes 加上复杂修饰的成分以后太长之故。同样，后面的 the idea of **inserting** /**into** nonleguminous plants /the genes, if they can be identified and isolated, that fit the leguminous plants to be hosts for nitrogen-fixing bacteria 一句，正常的语序也是 the idea of **inserting** the genes, if they can be identified and isolated, that fit the leguminous plants to be hosts for nitrogen-fixing bacteria /**into** nonleguminous plants /, 即把使得豆科植物成为固氮菌的寄主的基因（如果它们能够被找到并分离出来的话）插入/到非豆科植物的基因中去/。这一回，genes 之后不但有定语从句的复杂修饰，而且在 genes 和 that 从句之间还有一个不短的插入语，增加了阅读难度。

最后的一句话，Hence, the intensified research on legumes，其实也不是一句话，只是一个词：research。作者省略了 there is。其实此处即使看不清语法结构，作者的意思还是可以懂的。因此，笔者在前面强调的"如果可以看懂意思，不必去分析语法"，在实战的应用中有其意义：GRE 和 GMAT 中很多表达其实不严格遵守语法，或者有考生不懂的语法，读者处心积虑去研究它们，不但没有实战的意义，而且还令读者徒增烦恼。

本句是 GRE 和 GMAT 考试中集各种语言现象之大成者，包括了几乎所有的难句类型。希望读者一定把这句话读熟；有心者最好能把它背熟，一定对提高你的阅读能力有好处。

意群训练：One such novel idea is that of inserting into the chromosomes of plants discrete genes that are not a part of the plants' natural constitution：specifically, the idea of inserting into nonleguminous plants the genes, if they can be identified and isolated, that fit the leguminous plants to be hosts for nitrogen-fixing bacteria. Hence, the intensified research on legumes.

序号：045

> It is one of nature's great ironies that the availability of nitrogen in the soil frequently sets an upper limit on plant growth even though the plants' leaves are bathed in a sea of nitrogen gas.

难句类型：复杂修饰　　　　**难度：**3$^+$

标志: It is one of nature's great ironies that the availability of nitrogen (in the soil) frequently sets an upper limit /on plant growth/ **even though** the plants' leaves are bathed /in a sea of nitrogen gas/.

译文: 这真是自然界的一个巨大的讽刺:(土壤中的氮的供给之少)经常/给植物的生长/设立一个上限, 尽管植物的叶子被沉浸于/氮气的海洋中/。

解释: It 是形式主语, 其真正的内容是 that 之后的由 even though 连接的两个句子。其实本句的真正难度倒不在于句子的结构, 而是对于其意思的理解。尤其是文科学生, 可能缺乏必要的背景知识, 就更不容易读懂。句中的 set an upper limit on plant growth 直译为 "给植物的生长设立一个上限", 其真正的意思是 "限制了植物的生长"; 因此 the availability of nitrogen in the soil frequently sets an upper limit on plant growth 之中的 availability 一定指的是氮的供给之少。整句话的意思是, 土壤中的氮植物能够利用, 却太少; 而空气中虽有大量的氮, 植物却不能利用, 这岂不是自然界所开的一个大玩笑?

意群训练: It is one of nature's great ironies that the availability of nitrogen in the soil frequently sets an upper limit on plant growth even though the plants' leaves are bathed in a sea of nitrogen gas.

序号: **046**

> Unless they succeed, the yield gains of the Green Revolution will be largely lost even if the genes in legumes that equip those plants to enter into a symbiosis with nitrogen fixers are identified and isolated, and even if the transfer of those gene complexes, once they are found, becomes possible.

难句类型: 复杂修饰 + 插入语   **难度**: 4

标志: Unless they succeed, the yield gains (of the Green Revolution) will be largely lost /even if the genes (in legumes) (that equip those plants to enter into a symbiosis with nitrogen fixers) are identified and isolated, **and** /even if the transfer of those gene complexes, once they are found, becomes possible/.

译文： 除非他们（指基因生物学家）成功，否则/即使（使得豆科植物与固氮菌形成共生关系的）基因能够被找到和分离出来，而且即使基因综合体在被发现之后的转基因成为可能，/ 绿色革命所带来的产量上的获得将很大程度上被丧失掉。

解释： 主句比较简单，而后面跟着的由 **and** 连接的两个表示让步的条件状语从句就相对复杂。第一个从句是用一个修饰主语的定语从句 that equip those plants to enter into a symbiosis with nitrogen fixers 把主谓隔开；第二个从句则动用了插入语 once they are found 把主谓隔开。

意群训练： Unless they succeed, the yield gains of the Green Revolution will be largely lost even if the genes in legumes that equip those plants to enter into a symbiosis with nitrogen fixers are identified and isolated, and even if the transfer of those gene complexes, once they are found, becomes possible.

序号：047

> Its subject (to use Maynard Mack's categories) is "life-as-spectacle," for readers, diverted by its various incidents, observe its hero Odysseus primarily from without; the tragic *Iliad*, however, presents "life-as-experience": readers are asked to identify with the mind of Achilles, whose motivations render him a not particularly likable hero.

难句类型： 复杂修饰 + 插入语 + 抽象词 + 熟词僻义   **难度：5**

请思考： 如果看不懂分号前的 without 的意思，是否可用合理化原则根据分号后的那句话推理出其意思？

标志： Its subject (to use Maynard Mack's categories) is "life-as-spectacle," for readers, diverted / by its various incidents, / observe its hero Odysseus /primarily from without/; the tragic *Iliad*, **however**, presents "life-as-experience": readers are asked to identify / with the mind [of Achilles, (whose motivations render him a not particularly likable hero)] /.

译文： 其主题（如果使用 Maynard Mack 的分类法）是"把生活作为景象"，因为读者，由于被/其不同的事件/转移了注意力，/主要从外部的角度来/ 观察其主人公 Odysseus；然而悲剧 I，却表现了一种"把生活当作经历"：读者们被要求去认同/Achilles［的内心世界，（而 Achilles 的动机使得他成为一个不是特别有吸引力的主人公）］/ 。

解释： 本句中尽管也存在一些复杂修饰和插入的内容，但是本句话之所以难懂，与其说是因为这些东西的影响，倒不如说是因为用词的抽象和语义的难以理解。作为一篇文学评论型的文章，文章中充斥着一些很抽象的词汇；在本句话中就有 subject／category／spectacle／divert／incident／hero／primarily／without／present／identify／motivation／particularly／likable 等等。背过这些单词的中文释义，并不意味着在阅读中能够清楚地理解其真正含义。对于抽象词的训练方法，请参见附录中的《阅读抽象词提速法》。这里仅解释几个对于这句话最重要的单词：

hero：在此不是指英雄。在文学评论型的文章当中，此单词的意思是主人公。
without：在此处是一个熟词僻义，意思是外部，等于 outside
likable：不可望文生义，它不是像什么东西的意思，而是有吸引力的意思，其同义词有 pleasant 或 attractive。

本句中，对于理解全句起到最大影响的，就是能否正确地理解 without 这个单词。然而问题在于，如果不认识 without 的这个熟词僻义，是否可用合理化原则根据分号后的那句话推理出其意思？根据紧跟着分号的 **however**，我们可以推断出分号前后的两句话所说的内容截然相反，因此可以从 Iliad 戏剧的描述中推出，without 的意思应该是不去认同其主人公的内心世界。

意群训练： Its subject（to use Maynard Mack's categories）is "life-as-spectacle," for readers, diverted by its various incidents, observe its hero Odysseus primarily from without; the tragic *Iliad*, however, presents "life-as-experience": readers are asked to identify with the mind of Achilles, whose motivations render him a not particularly likable hero.

序号：048

> Most striking among the many asymmetries evident in an adult flatfish is eye placement: before maturity one eye migrates, so that in an adult flatfish both eyes are on the same side of the head.

难句类型： 倒装 + 省略　　　　　**难度：** 3⁺

标志：Most striking /among the many asymmetries evident in an adult flatfish/ **is** eye placement: before maturity one eye migrates, **so that** in an adult flatfish both eyes are on the same side of the head.

译文： /在很多的成年比目鱼所表现出来的不对称中/，眼睛的位置是最引人注目的：在成熟以前一个眼睛迁移了，以至于在一个成年鱼的身上，两只眼睛都在身体的同一侧。

解释： 本句的倒装本质上与我们早就学习过的一种倒装结构是一样的，即形容词放在句首时，主语和谓语倒装。本句的主干的正常语序应该是：Eye placement is most striking；倒装后成了：Most striking is eye placement。但是这种倒装在 GRE 考试中出现，又有了新的特色：被提到句首的 Most striking 被长长的状语 among the many asymmetries evident in an adult flatfish 与后面的主语和表语分开，造成阅读困难。

意群训练： Most striking among the many asymmetries evident in an adult flatfish is eye placement: before maturity one eye migrates, so that in an adult flatfish both eyes are on the same side of the head.

序号：049

> A critique of the Handlins' interpretation of why legal slavery did not appear until the 1660's suggests that assumptions about the relation between slavery and racial prejudice should be reexamined, and that explanations for the different treatment of Black slaves in North and South America should be expanded.

难句类型：复杂修饰 + 省略　　　**难度**：4

标志：A critique〔of the Handlins' interpretation（of why legal slavery did not appear until the 1660's）〕suggests that assumptions〔about the relation（between slavery and racial prejudice）〕should be reexamined, **and** *suggests* that explanations｛for the different treatment〔of Black slaves（in North and South America）〕should be expanded｝.

译文：一个〔对于 Handlins 的（关于为何法律上的奴隶制没有在 17 世纪 60 年代以前出现的原因）所做解释的〕批评显示，〔（关于奴隶制和种族偏见之间的）关系的〕假说应当被重新检查，而且显示出，｛对于〔（在北美和南美之间的）对黑奴的〕不同处理的｝解释应当被扩展。

解释：句子的主干清楚：A critique suggests that…, **and** suggests that…。但是因为句子的结构复杂、修饰成分多，再加上后面的 and 之后的 suggests 被省略，所以句子的结构很难被读出来。

　　本句中的 suggest 不再是 "暗示"，而是 "显示，说明" 的意思，其同义词为：point, indicate, imply。

　　本句的两个 suggest 之后的宾语从句都根据语法的要求使用了虚拟语气。

意群训练：A critique of the Handlins' interpretation of why legal slavery did not appear until the 1660's suggests that assumptions about the relation between slavery and racial prejudice should be reexamined, and that explanations for the different treatment of Black slaves in North and South America should be expanded.

序号：050

The best evidence for the layered mantle thesis is the well-established fact that volcanic rocks found on oceanic islands, islands believed to result from mantle plumes arising from the lower mantle, are composed of material fundamentally different from that of the midocean ridge system, whose source, most geologists contend, is the upper mantle.

难句类型： 复杂修饰 + 插入语　　　　**难度：** 5¯

标志： The best evidence /for the layered mantle thesis/ is the well-established fact {that volcanic rocks (found on oceanic islands, islands believed to result from mantle plumes arising from the lower mantle), are composed /of material [fundamentally different from that of the midocean ridge system, (whose source, most geologists contend, is the upper mantle)]}.

译文： /对于地幔分层论来说，/最好的证据就是这样的一个确凿的事实，{即（在海洋上的岛屿——即人们相信是产生于从下层地幔中升起来的地幔柱的那些岛屿——上发现的）火山岩石是形成/于一些这样的材料，[此材料从根本上不同于构成中部海脊的材料，（而中部海脊的来源，很多地质学家论辩道，是上层地幔）]}。

解释： 本句前面的主干并不算难，即 the evidence is the fact that，难就难在 fact 之后说明 fact 的同位语从句。此从句中既有大段插入语，又有从句，较为难读。同位语从句的主语是 volcanic rocks，主语后面的 found on oceanic islands 是分词修饰 volcanic rocks 的；islands 后面又有一个说明 islands 的同位语 islands believed to result from mantle plumes arising from the lower mantle，此同位语实际起到了一个分隔主谓的同位语的作用。其后是谓语动词 are composed /of 以及 of 的宾语 material，然后是修饰 material 并包含了一个定语从句的长长的定语 [fundamentally different from that of the midocean ridge system, (whose source, most geologists contend, is the upper mantle.)]。

句中有一些专有词汇。如果抛开文章不说，单看这一个句子，则句首的 layered mantle thesis 就难以理解。但是如果读者能够读懂句子的大致意思，看到 layered mantle thesis 的最有力证据就是其材料 fundamentally different from... the upper mantle，这应该可以推测出，既然不同于上层地幔，则这个理论一定是在说地幔有不同的层面。

意群训练： The best evidence for the layered mantle thesis is the well-established fact that volcanic rocks found on oceanic islands, islands believed to result from mantle plumes arising from the lower mantle, are composed of material fundamentally different from that of the midocean ridge system, whose source, most geologists contend, is the upper mantle.

序号：051

> Some geologists, however, on the basis of observations concerning mantle xenoliths, argue that the mantle is not layered, but that heterogeneity is created by fluids rich in "incompatible elements" (elements tending toward liquid rather than solid state) percolating upward and transforming portions of the upper mantle irregularly, according to the vagaries of the fluids' pathways.

难句类型：复杂修饰 + 插入语　　　**难度：**4[+]

标志：Some geologists, however, on the basis of observations concerning mantle xenoliths, argue [that] the mantle is not layered, **but** that heterogeneity is created /by fluids [rich in "incompatible elements" (elements tending toward liquid rather than solid state) (percolating upward and transforming portions of the upper mantle irregularly), /according to the vagaries of the fluids' pathways/] /.

译文：但是，一些地质学家（基于关于地幔捕虏岩的观察）认为，地幔不是分层的，而其不同的成分是/由一些流体造成的，这些流体［富含"不相容成分"（即那些趋向于作为液体而非固体而存在的成分），（这些物质向上渗透，并/依照这些流体所经过的随机路径/不规则地改变了上地幔的某些部分）］/。

解释：本句的主句中有一个长插入语however, on the basis of observations concerning mantle xenoliths，割裂了主谓。但句子的主要难度还是在 that 引导的宾语从句中。从句中有由 **but** 所连接的两个句子，第二个句子that heterogeneity is created /by fluids 之后出现了大段的对 fluids 的修饰成分，一直延续到句末。首先是 rich in "incompatible elements" 修饰 fluids；后面又有一个同位语和一个分词结构，都是修饰 "incompatible elements" 的；最后还有一个状语来修饰那个分词结构，层层修饰，比较复杂。

意群训练：Some geologists, however, on the basis of observations concerning mantle xenoliths, argue that the mantle is not layered, but that heterogeneity is created by fluids rich in "incompatible elements" (elements tending toward liquid rather than solid state) percolating upward and transforming portions of the upper mantle irregularly, according to the vagaries of the fluids' pathways.

序号：052

> Fallois proposed that Proust had tried to begin a novel in 1908, abandoned it for what was to be a long demonstration of Saint-Beuve's blindness to the real nature of great writing, found the essay giving rise to personal memories and fictional developments, and allowed these to take over in a steadily developing novel.

难句类型： 复杂修饰 + 抽象词　　　　难度：5⁻

标志： Fallois proposed that Proust had tried to begin a novel in 1908, abandoned it / for what was to be a long demonstration [of Saint-Beuve's blindness (to the real nature of great writing)] /, found the essay giving rise to personal memories and fictional developments, **and** allowed these to take over in a steadily developing novel.

译文： Fallois 认为，Proust 在 1908 年试图开始写一部小说，又/为了写一部批判 [S-B 的（对伟大作品的真正本质的）视而不见] 的长篇的证明/而放弃了这部小说，其后又发现这一论文又勾起了其个人记忆及小说情节的萌生，使得后者取而代之形成了一部稳定展开的小说。

解释： 本句来自历来被 GRE 考生尊称为所有 GRE 文科文章中难度第一的"布鲁斯特的追忆似水年华"，这篇文章的难度远远高于计算机考试的题目。布鲁斯特是公认的意识流小说的先驱，据笔者推测，本文的原作者必定是研究布鲁斯特的大家，因此其文章必然带有思维的跳跃、不连贯性、时空颠倒等意识流手法；经过 ETS 的改编后，虽然可读性略有增加，然积重难返、无法救药，于是堕落成了一篇流水账文章。从本句的结构来看，也可以表现作者的这种叙事风格：

本句从 that 引导的宾语从句开始，实际上是以布鲁斯特的意识流向为线索，以列举的方式描述其动机的变化，从一开始的写别的小说，到为了批 S-B 放弃它，再到从批 S-B 的文章中得到启发，最后形成《追忆似水年华》，其英文为 Proust <u>had tried</u> <u>to...</u>, <u>abandoned...</u>, <u>found...</u>, and <u>allowed...</u>。但是因为 abandoned 之后的状语/for···/ 的结构复杂、用词抽象，所以这个结构不太容易被看出来。

blindness 在此不是指真盲，而是指缺乏辨认能力（difficult to discern, make out, or discover），视而不见。give rise to 词组的意思是"引起，使发生"。

意群训练： <u>Fallois proposed that</u> Proust had <u>tried to begin a novel in 1908</u>, <u>abandoned it</u> <u>for</u> <u>what was to be a long demonstration of Saint-Beuve's</u> <u>blindness to the real nature of great</u> <u>writing</u>, <u>found the essay giving rise to</u>personal memories <u>and fictional developments</u>, <u>and allowed these to take over in a steadily developing novel</u>.

序号：053

> The very richness and complexity of the meaningful relationships that kept presenting and rearranging themselves on all levels, from abstract intelligence to profound dreamy feelings, made it difficult for Proust to set them out coherently.

难句类型： 复杂修饰 + 插入语 + 抽象词　　　　**难度：**5

标志： The very richness and complexity [of the meaningful relationships（that kept presenting and rearranging themselves /on all levels, from abstract intelligence to profound dreamy feelings/），] made it /difficult for Proust to set them out coherently/.

译文： 正是这种 [（/在不同层面——从抽象的智力层面到深层的梦幻般的感情 ——上/不断重新出现和重新排列的）有意义的关联] 丰富性和复杂性，使得布罗斯特/难以把它们（*此处指有意义的关联*）和谐一致地展现出来/。

解释： 请原谅笔者在此处所做中文翻译的艰涩难懂；为了让读者能够更好地理解句子的结构，本书尽量把中文翻译与英文原文的语序相对应，而且尽可能的不用意译。为了达到这个目的，可以说绞尽脑汁。但本句之难懂也全非笔者之故，原文作者使用了大量的抽象词。

本句仍然来自于上面说过的这篇关于布鲁斯特的文章。句中的主语是 The very richness and complexity，其后的修饰成分长达三行：［of the meaningful relationships（that kept presenting and rearranging themselves／on all levels, from abstract intelligence to profound dreamy feelings／），］，其中还夹杂着插入语，有效地分开了主语和谓语。其实本句虽然结构也比较复杂，但是不见得比前面的句子复杂很多，其真正的难点，还在于句中大量的抽象词的使用。由于笔者在附录中所提到的原因，抽象词可以严重的占据大脑资源，因此带有大量的抽象词的结构复杂的句子就更为难懂，比如本句就是一个很好的例子：复杂修饰与抽象词狼狈为奸，句意令人难以理解。

意群训练： The very richness and complexity of the meaningful relationships that kept presenting and rearranging themselves on all levels, from abstrat intelligence to profound dreamy feelings, made it difficult for Proust to set them out coherently.

序号：054

> But those of us who hoped, with Kolb, that Kolb's newly published complete edition of Proust's correspondence for 1909 would document the process in greater detail are disappointed.

难句类型： 复杂修饰 + 插入语　　　**难度：** 4

标　志： **But** those of us ［who hoped, with Kolb, that（Kolb's newly published）complete edition（of Proust's correspondence for 1909）would document the process／in greater detail／］are disappointed.

译　文： 但是我们当中的［那些希望（也算上 K 本人）（K 新出版的）（布鲁斯特 1909 年书信的）全集能够／更加详细地／记录下这一过程的人］都大失所望。

解　释： 本句中从句套从句，致使主语 those of us 与谓语的距离极远，而且中间的成分又极多，使得句子很难读懂。修饰主语those of us的定语从句 who hoped 之中又套了一个宾语从句；宾语从句的主语complete edition又被一前一后的两个定语所修饰，之后才依次是宾语从句的谓语、宾语；主句的系动词、表语。

意群训练：But those of us who hoped, with Kolb, that Kolb's newly published complete edition of Proust's correspondence for 1909 would document the process in greater detail are disappointed.

序号：055

> Now we must also examine the culture as we Mexican Americans have experienced it, passing from a sovereign people to compatriots with newly arriving settlers to, finally, a conquered people—a charter minority on our own land.

难句类型：　复杂修饰 ＋ 插入语 ＋ 固定搭配　　　**难度**：5ˉ

标志：/Now/ we must also examine the culture /as we Mexican Americans have experienced it/, /passing **from** a sovereign people **to** compatriots with newly arriving settlers **to**, finally, a conquered people—a charter minority on our own land/.

译文：/现在/我们必须也/按照我们墨西哥裔的美国人的经历/来审视这个文化，/我们的经历是从一个主权的民族变成了新来的定居者的同胞再最终沦落成为一个被征服的民族——在我们自己的土地上的宪章规定的少数民族/。

解释：主句中的/as we Mexican Americans have experienced it/是 examine 的状语，说明审视的角度；后面直到句尾的分词结构又是 experience 的状语，详述了经历的具体过程。就是这个分词有些难懂，因为我们熟知的结构是 from... to...，没有见过、也没有想到过后面居然还有一个 to，因此看到这个套了一个插入语的 newly arriving settlers to, finally, a conquered people 的时候头脑发生混乱，不明所以、不知所措。这里的 to 还是与前面的 from 搭配的，也就是说，原文的结构是：**from... to... to...**。

意群训练：Now we must also examine the culture as we Mexican Americans have experienced it, passing from a sovereign people to compatriots with newly arriving settlers to, finally, a conquered people—a charter minority on our own land.

序号：056

> It is possible to make specific complementary DNA's (cDNA's) that can serve as molecular probes to seek out the messenger RNA's (mRNA's) of the peptide hormones. If brain cells are making the hormones, the cells will contain these mRNA's. If the products the brain cells make resemble the hormones but are not identical to them, then the cDNA's should still bind to these mRNA's, but should not bind as tightly as they would to mRNA's for the true hormones.

难句类型： 易混词   **难度：** 4⁺

解释： 与其他难句不同的是，以上的英文不止一句。笔者之所以在本句中不设标志和翻译，是因为这三句话从结构上和意思上来说并不难。然而很少有人能够真正的一次把这段话读清楚，原因在于两个容易混淆的单词 cDNA's 和 mRNA's 在文中交替出现，而且相互作用；再加上 brain cell 和 hormones 从中捣乱，更难读清楚原文的意思。

原文的主要意思如下：可以用 cDNA's 来探测 mRNA's。如果脑细胞产生了荷尔蒙（hormones），则其中必有 mRNA's（意味着可用 cDNA's 探测荷尔蒙）。如果脑细胞造的不是真荷尔蒙，则可以用 cDNA's 与其中的 mRNA's 附着的情况来确定此荷尔蒙的真假。

意群训练： It is possible to make specific complementary DNA's (cDNA's) that can serve as molecular probes to seek out the messenger RNA's (mRNA's) of the peptide hormones. If brain cells are making the hormones, the cells will contain these mRNA's. If the products the brain cells make resemble the hormones but are not identical to them, then the cDNA's should still bind to these mRNA's, but should not bind as tightly as they would to mRNA's forthe true hormones.

序号：057

> The molecular approach to detecting peptide hormones using cDNA probes should also be much faster than the immunological method because it can take years of tedious purifications to isolate peptide hormones and then develop antiserums to them.

难句类型： 复杂修饰 ＋ 易混指代　　　　**难度：** 4

标志： The molecular approach （to detecting peptide hormones ／using cDNA probes／ should also be ／much faster than the immunological method ／ ／because it can take years of tedious purifications ／to isolate peptide hormones **and** then develop antiserums to them. ／／

译文： （／采用 cDNA 探子／来探测 p 荷尔蒙）这样一种分子生物学手段也应该／比免疫学方法要快得多／，／因为后者要花上几年的时间做枯燥的提纯工作，／来分离 p 荷尔蒙并培养出其抗血清／／。

解释： 主语后的修饰成分同样隔开了主语和谓语。但本句的难度主要在 because 从句中。按照一般的习惯，作为从句主语的 it 应该指主句的主语，但本句的主句是一个比较结构，A should be faster than B because it...，此处 it 也可以指 B。但是因为这种指代不符和我们以前所形成的习惯，所以阅读现场不得不边读边根据句意来判断，这就增加了阅读理解的难度。

现场阅读时，类似 antiserums 的这种专有名词不必理会，仅需从词头 anti- 推出这是一个反 p 荷尔蒙的东西即可。

意群训练： The molecular approach to detecting peptide hormones using cDNA probes should also be much faster than the immunological method because it can take years of tedious purifications to isolate peptide hormones and then develop antiserums to them.

序号：058

> Nevertheless, researchers of the Pleistocene epoch have developed all sorts of more or less fanciful model schemes of how they would have arranged the Ice Age had they been in charge of events.

难句类型：复杂修饰 + 倒装 + 修辞　　　　**难度：**3⁺

标志：Nevertheless, researchers（of the Pleistocene epoch）have developed（all sorts of）（more or less fanciful）model schemes（of how they **would have** arranged the Ice Age **had** they been in charge of events.

译文：然而，（研究 P 时代的）研究者发展出了（各种各样的）（或多或少有些奇思怪想的）模型系统，（*用来显示*如果由他们来决定地质事件的话他们将会如何安排冰川纪。

解释：句末的由 how 引导的名词性从句中包括了双重的倒装，正常的语序本来是：If they had been in charge of events, they would have arranged the Ice Age in certain model schemes。本句中由于 arrange 的方式被提前，就造成了 arrange 的动作执行者也要提前，前面的 if they had been 则必须后置；这样一来又造成了 if 被省略，成为 had they been 的倒装结构。

另外，作者为了表达其对于这些研究者的模型的负态度，并炫耀其幽默感，在本句中使用了虚拟语气，并使用了 fanciful 这个词以表示这些研究的不负责任、异想天开和幼童心理。

意群训练：Nevertheless, researchers of the Pleistocene epoch have developed all sorts of more or less fanciful model schemes of how they would have arranged the Ice Age had they been in charge of events.

序号：059

> This succession was based primarily on a series of deposits and events not directly related to glacial and interglacial periods, rather than on the more usual modern method of studying biological remains found in interglacial beds themselves interstratified within glacial deposits.

难句类型：复杂修饰 + 省略 + 易混指代　　　　**难度**：4

标志：This succession was based primarily / on（a series of）deposits and events（not directly related to glacial and interglacial periods）/，**rather than** *being based* / on the more usual modern method［of studying biological remains（found in interglacial beds）**themselves** interstratified within glacial deposits）］.

译文：这一序列主要是基/于（一系列的）（与冰川期和间冰期并不直接相关的）沉积物和事件做出的，而不是基/于更为通常使用的现代方法/，［去研究（间冰期的地层中的）生物遗迹，（这些遗迹位于冰川沉积物的各个层面之间）］。

解释：句子中 rather than 之后省略了与前面重复的 *being based*，直接加上了介词 on。Modern method 后面的部分都是修饰 method 的。其中的 remains 既可以作动词，也可以作名词，此处是名词的用法，biological remains 指的是类似于动物化石之类的遗迹。读到这里我们看到了句子的难点，themselves 即可以指前面离得很远的的 modern method（当然，在语法上来讲单复数不一致），也可以指前面离得较远的 biological remains，亦可以指紧挨着的 interglacial beds，到底是指代哪一个，只有通过理解句意，才能确定在此处指 biological remains。

意群训练：This succession was based primarily on a series of deposits and events not directly related to glacial and interglacial periods, rather than on the more usual modern method of studying biological remains found in interglacial beds themselves interstratified within glacial deposits.

序号：**060**

> There have been attempts to explain these taboos in terms of inappropriate social relationships either between those who are involved and those who are not simultaneously involved in the satisfaction of a bodily need, or between those already satiated and those who appear to be shamelessly gorging.

难句类型：复杂修饰 ＋ 省略　　　　**难度：**5

标志： There <u>have been</u> <u>attempts</u> [to explain these taboos / in terms of inappropriate social relationships (**either between** those who are involved *in the satisfaction of a bodily need* **and** those who are not simultaneously involved in the satisfaction of a bodily need, **or between** those already satiated **and** those who appear to be shamelessly gorging) /].

译文： 有<u>一些试图</u> [／使用不合适的社会关系／去解释这些禁忌，（这些社会关系或者是在那些正在经历一种身体需要得到满足的人和此时身体需要得不到满足的人之间的，或者是在那些已经吃饱的人和那些看起来正在不知羞耻地狼吞虎咽的人之间的）]。

解释： 前面的主架构 There <u>have been</u> <u>attempts</u> [to explain these taboos 很简单，从 in terms of inappropriate social relationships 开始句子变难，relationship 后面跟着一个一直延续到句末的长长的修饰成分，其中有两个固定搭配：**either... or...**；和 **between... and...**。不但如此，原文把这两个搭配又套在一起，变成了 either between... and...，or between... and...；再加上每一个 between... and 之后都是 those who 这样的结构，就愈发令人眼花缭乱了。

意群训练： <u>There</u> <u>have been</u> <u>attempts to explain these taboos</u> in terms of <u>inappropriate so-cial relationships</u> either between those <u>who are involved</u> and those <u>who are not</u> <u>simultaneously</u> <u>involved in</u> the satisfaction of <u>a bodily need</u>, <u>or between those</u> <u>already satiated</u> and those <u>who</u> <u>appear to be</u> <u>shamelessly gorging</u>.

序号：061

Many critics of Emily Bronte's novel *Wuthering Heights* see its second part as a counterpoint that comments on, if it does not reverse, the first part, where a "romantic" reading receives more confirmation.

难句类型： 复杂修饰 + 插入语　　　　**难度：** 5

标志： Many critics（of Emily Bronte's novel *Wuthering Heights*）see its second part／as a counterpoint［that comments／on, if it does not reverse, the first part,（where a "romantic" reading receives more confirmation）］／.

译文： 很多（对于艾米丽·勃朗蒂的小说《呼啸山庄》的）评论家把小说的第二部分看／成［如果不是反对小说第一部分的，则是评论小说第一部分的］一个和谐的对应物（而在第一部分中一种浪漫主义的解读得到了更多的确认）／。

解释： 上面的翻译中为了符合中文习惯不得不把修饰 the first part 的 where 引导的定语从句翻译到中括号以外。

本句主要难在两个地方：一个是插入语 if it does not reverse 如何理解，另一个是 counterpoint 的意思是什么。首先，插入语的位置比较讨厌，把 comments on the first part 这样一个连贯的说法割成两段，增加了阅读的难度。而且它的意思容易理解错：if 既可以理解成"如果"的意思，也可以理解成"即使"的意思。如果理解成"即使"的意思，上下文的意思则要理解成"即使不反对第一部分，也要给予第一部分一个负面的评论"。然而此处不能这样理解，因为 that 之前的 counterpoint 的意思不是相反、对立，而是指和谐的组成部分的意思。这个词来源于一个音乐术语，指音乐中的对位法、旋律配合，引伸为形容两个不同的东西彼此和谐一致，同义词是 harmony。因此文中的 if it does not reverse 的意思是"假如不反对第一部分，则是与第一部分和谐一致的评论"的意思。这种情况下，插入语纯属废话。

意群训练： Many critics of Emily Bronte's novel *Wuthering Heights* see its second part as a counterpoint that comments on, if it does not reverse, the first part, where a "romantic" reading receives more confirmation.

序号：062

> Granted that the presence of these elements need not argue an authorial awareness of novelistic construction comparable to that of Henry James, their presence does encourage attempts to unify the novel's heterogeneous parts.

难句类型： 复杂修饰＋抽象词   **难度：** 4$^+$

标志： **Granted that** the presence of these elements need not argue（an authorial）awareness（of novelistic construction）（comparable to that of Henry James），***but*** their presence does encourage attempts（to unify the novel's heterogeneous parts）.

译文： 当然这些因素的出现并不一定意味着（作者）（对于小说结构的）意识（能与 HJ 的意识相比），*但是*它们的出现确实可以鼓励一些（把小说的不同部分统一到一起的）尝试。

解释： 本句的结构固然复杂，但造成最大的阅读难度的，主要还是对一些抽象词汇的理解。下面是对一些关键词汇的解释：

Granted that 出现在句首，其意思是"大家都同意，当然"，实际上是一种让步语气，等于 admitted，of course。

need not argue 中的 argue 在此不是表示常用的那个辩论、争论的意思，而是表示意味着或证实的意思，其同义词是 maintain 或 prove。

Comparable 的词义有两个，除了读者熟悉的 ***adj.*** that can be compared 之外，还有一个意思是 ***adj.*** worthy of comparison，其同义词是 as good as。本文中用的是后面的这个意思。对于这个词义的理解，后面的第 18 题考到了。

意群训练： Granted that the presence of these elements need not argue an authorial awareness of novelistic construction comparable to that of Henry James, their presence does encourage attempts to unify the novel's heterogeneous parts.

序号：063

> This is not because such an interpretation necessarily stiffens into a thesis (although rigidity in any interpretation of this or of any novel is always a danger), but because *Wuthering Heights* has recalcitrant elements of undeniable power that, ultimately, resist inclusion in an all-encompassing interpretation.

难句类型： 复杂修饰＋插入语＋抽象词　　　**难度：5**

标志： This is **not** | because | such an interpretation necessarily stiffens /into a thesis/（although rigidity in any interpretation of this or of any novel is always a danger）, **but** | because | *Wuthering Heights* has recalcitrant elements [of undeniable power（that, ultimately, resist inclusion in an all-encompassing interpretation）].

译文： 这倒不是 | 因为 | 这样一种解释一定会僵化/到一个论点上/（尽管对这部小说或者任何小说的任何僵化的解释永远是一个危险），而是 | 因为 | 《呼啸山庄》中有（一些具有不可否认的力量的）顽固因素，（这些因素，最终，拒绝被囊括在一个包罗万象的解释当中）。

解释： 本句的两个插入语虽然也有一些干扰性，但是最为主要的难点在于成批出现的抽象词，如：interpretation / necessarily / stiffen / thesis / rigidity / recalcitrant / element / undeniable / power / ultimately / resist / inclusion / all-encompassing 等。据笔者估测，对于初学 GRE 或 GMAT 的学习者而言，在一句话中出现了三个以上的抽象词就会使阅读理解产生障碍，而这句话中出现了十三个这样的单词，读不懂也不足为怪。

意群训练： This is not because such an interpretation necessarily stiffens into a thesis (although rigidity in any interpretation of this or of any novel is always a danger), but because *Wuthering Heights* has recalcitrant elements of undeniable power that, ultimately, resist inclusion in an all-encompassing interpretation.

序号：064

> The isotopic composition of lead often varies from one source of common copper ore to another, with variations exceeding the measurement error; and preliminary studies indicate virtually uniform isotopic composition of the lead from a single copper-ore source.

请思考：What can be inferred from the above sentence?

难句类型：复杂修饰＋插入语＋专业抽象词　　　　**难度：4**

标志： The isotopic composition of lead often varies /**from** one source of common copper ore **to** another/, /with variations exceeding the measurement error; / **and** preliminary studies indicate virtually uniform isotopic composition (of the lead) /from a single copper-ore source/.

译文：铅的同位素的成分经常/在一个普通的铜矿石的挖掘地与另外一个挖掘地之间/有所不同/，/其差异超过了测量误差/；而且初步的研究显示，/从同一个铜矿的挖掘地所得的/（铅的）同位素成分几乎完全一致。

解释：本句是一个怪异的现象的典型例子：句子结构谈不上复杂，所用单词也不难，但是除非读者有理工科的科研（最好是材料科学的科研）背景，否则句子虽然能够顺利得读下来，但是却搞不清句子说的是什么意思。

首先，句子中出现的一些词汇虽然也都比较常见，但是在理科文章中出现，就有了专有名词的意味，同时还带有很抽象的学术含义，笔者称之为"专业抽象词"。如 isotopic composition；source；variation；measurement error；preliminary study 等。认识这些单词，并不意味着懂得它们在文章中的意义和作用。比如说 measurement error，大家都可以望文生义的理解成测量错误、测量误差，但是在对文章的阅读中这种字面上的理解是远远不够的。其实此处强调的并不是测量中出现的错误和毛病，而是指那些每次测量都会发生的、永远也无法避免的、在测量值和实际值之间的正常的差异。

因此，本句话的真实含义也难以理解。句子只是罗列了一堆事实，而作者真正想说的意思是什么呢？其实 variations exceeding the measurement error 的言外之意是这些不同（variations）是真正有意义的不同，而不是试验的误差；那么，不同矿源的铜矿的铅同位素成分真的不同，相同的矿源的铅同位素几乎相同，就意味着我们可以通过测量铅同位素的成分来确定铜矿的矿源（挖掘地）。

意群训练： The isotopic composition of lead often varies from one source of common copper ore to another, with variations exceeding the measurement error; and preliminary studies indicate virtually uniform isotopic composition of the lead from a single copper-ore source.

序号：065

> More probable is bird transport, either externally, by accidental attachment of the seeds to feathers, or internally, by the swallowing of fruit and subsequent excretion of the seeds.

难句类型： 复杂修饰＋插入语＋倒装　　　**难度：** 3⁺

标志： More probable is bird transport, **either** externally, /by accidental **attachment** of the seeds **to** feathers/, **or** internally, /by the swallowing of fruit and subsequent excretion of the seeds. /

译文： 鸟类传播是更为可能的方式，既可能是体外携带，/通过偶然的把种子附着在羽毛上/，也可能是体内携带，/通过吞下果实后来又将种子排泄出去的方式/。

解释： 句首有一个倒装，正常语序是 bird transport is more probable。后面的句子中由于插入部分的频繁出现使句子显得十分凌乱。

意群训练： More probable is bird transport, either externally, by accidental attachment of the seeds to feathers, or internally, by the swallowing of fruit and subsequent excretion of the seeds.

序号：**066**

> A long-held view of the history of the English colonies that became the United States has been that England's policy toward these colonies before 1763 was dictated by commercial interests and that a change to a more imperial policy, dominated by expansionist militarist objectives, generated the tensions that ultimately led to the American Revolution.

难句类型：复杂修饰＋插入语　　　**难度**：4⁺

标志：A long-held view ｛of the history ［of the English colonies （ that became the United States ）］｝ has been that England's policy （toward these colonies before 1763 ） was dictated by commercial interests **and** *has been* that a change （to a more imperial policy）, dominated by expansionist militarist objectives, generated the tensions （ that ultimately led to the American Revolution）.

译文：一个 ｛对于 ［（后来成了美国的）英国殖民地］ 的历史的｝ 长久以来的观点，认为英国（在 1763 年以前对于这些殖民地的）政策被经济利益所支配，而且认为一种（向着更大程度的帝国制度的政策上的）转变——为扩张主义的军事目标所左右——产生了（最终导致美国革命的）紧张气氛。

解释：主架构简单，可是主语和表语从句都不让人省心。句子的主干其实就是：A long-held view has been that...。但是主语 A long-held view 之后却是修饰它的一个三层的定语：｛of the history ［of the English colonies （that became the United States）］｝。系动词 has been 之后所接的表语从句其实不止一个，其实原句是用了 **and** 来连接两个并列的表语从句：has been that... **and** has been that...。后面的 has been 照例被省略。

意群训练：A long-held view of the history of the English colonies that became the United States has been that England's policy toward these colonies before 1763 was dictated by commercial interests and that a change to a more imperial policy, dominated by expansionist milita-rist objectives, generated the tensions that ultimately led to the American Revolution.

序号：067

It is not known how rare this resemblance is, or whether it is most often seen in inclusions of silicates such as garnet, whose crystallography is generally somewhat similar to that of diamond; but when present, the resemblance is regarded as compelling evidence that the diamonds and inclusions are truly cogenetic.

难句类型：复杂修饰＋插入语　　　　**难度**：4

标志：It is not known how rare this resemblance is, or whether it is most often seen in inclusions of silicates such as garnet, (whose crystallography is generally somewhat similar to that of diamond；) **but** / when it is present, / the resemblance is regarded /as compelling evidence (that the diamonds and inclusions are truly cogenetic) /.

译文：现在还不知道这种相似稀少到什么程度，也不知道它是否最常见于像 g（石榴石）那样的硅酸岩的内含物（杂质）中；（g 的晶体结构通常有点类似于钻石的结构）；但是当这种类似出现的时候，这种类似就被视/为（钻石和内含物确实同源的）有力证据。/

解释：本句的句子既长，专有名词又多，从句层出不穷，故而难读。在本句中出现的专有名词中，除了 silicates（硅酸盐）这个单词常常出现于理科文章中，需要记忆之外，其他单词阅读现场简单处理一番即可：inclusions 可以猜出是被包含的物质；gar-net 作首字母提炼叫 g；crystallography 只要能从词头推出这个单词与晶体有关即可。

另外，这篇文章的结构极为特殊，请读者注意阅读时不可不看内容而全凭套路感。

意群训练：It is not known how rare this resemblance is, or whether it is most often seen in inclusions of silicates such as garnet, whose crystallography is generally somewhat similar to that of diamond; but when present, the resemblance is regarded as compelling evidence that the diamonds and inclusions are truly cogenetic.

序号：068

> Even the "radical" critiques of this mainstream research model, such as the critique developed in *Divided Society*, attach the issue of ethnic assimilation too mechanically to factors of economic and social mobility and are thus unable to illuminate the cultural subordination of Puerto Ricans as a colonial minority.

难句类型： 复杂修饰＋插入语＋省略＋抽象词 **难度：** 4⁺

标志： **Even** the "radical" critiques （of this mainstream research model,）（such as the critique developed in *Divided Society*,）**attach** the issue of ethnic assimilation too mechanically **to** factors of economic and social mobility **and** *they* are thus unable （to illuminate the cultural subordination of Puerto Ricans as a colonial minority）.

译文： 甚至连（对这种主流研究模式的）"激进"批评，（比如在《分裂的社会》一书中的批评），也把民族被同化的问题机械地与经济和社会流动性的因素联系到一起，这样这些批评就无法（把 PR 人作为殖民地的少数民族来说明其文化上的次等地位）。

解释： 本句实际上是由 and 连接的两个句子。阅读的一个难度在于，and 之后省略了主语 *they*（此处指前面的主语 the "radical" critiques），而 are thus unable to 又与前面离得太远，使读者难以找到主语。

另外，句中的固定搭配 attach A to B 当中的 A、B 既长又抽象，理解起来较为困难。

意群训练： Even the "radical" critiques of this mainstream research model, such as the critique developed in *Divided Society*, attach the issue of ethnic assimilation too mechanically to factors of economic and social mobility and are thus unable to illuminate the cultural subordination of Puerto Ricans as a colonial minority.

序号：069

> They are called virtual particles in order to distinguish them from real particles, whose lifetimes are not constrained in the same way, and which can be detected.

难句类型：复杂修饰 + 插入语　　　**难度**：3

标志：They are called virtual particles /in order to distinguish them from real particles, (whose lifetimes are not constrained in the same way,) **and** (which can be detected) /.

译文：它们被称之为"虚粒子"/以用来与"实粒子"相区分，（后者的生命期不以同样的方式受到制约），而且（能够被探测到）/。

解释：本句的怪异之处在于，real particles 后面跟着两个定语从句，都是同时修饰 real particles 的。而且两个从句之间还用逗号隔开，却又加上 and 连接，令人一眼看上去极不习惯。

意群训练：They are called virtual particles in order to distinguish them from real particles, whose lifetimes are not constrained in the same way, and which can be detected.

序号：070

> Open acknowledgement of the existence of women's oppression was too radical for the United States in the fifties, and Beauvoir's conclusion, that change in women's economic condition, though insufficient by itself, "remains the basic factor" in improving women's situation, was particularly unacceptable.

难句类型：复杂修饰＋插入语　　　　**难度**：4⁺

标志：Open acknowledgement ［of the existence（of women's oppression）］ was too radical /for the United States in the fifties/，**and** Beauvoir's conclusion，［ that change（in women's economic condition），though insufficient by itself，**but** "remains the basic factor"（in improving women's situation）］，was particularly unacceptable.

译文：公开［对（妇女压迫的）存在的］承认/对于50年代的美国而言/有些过分激进，而且B的结论，［即（妇女经济状况的）变化，尽管它本身不是一个充分的因素，但是"仍然是（提高妇女地位的）根本因素"的观点，是尤其无法令人接受的。

解释：本句是由 and 所连接的两个分句。前一个分句的主语虽然有一些修饰成分，但整体而言还算好读；后面的分句中的修饰成分就比较难读：主语Beauvoir's conclusion 后面被加上了同位语从句 that change in...，而且在从句的主语和谓语之间还加了一个插入语；当我们好不容易把同位语从句中的成分补齐，后面又看到系表结构was particularly unacceptable 的时候，想不起来主语是谁，不禁心中茫然；如果是没有练习过难句的人，也只好黯然神伤。

意群训练：Open acknowledgement of the existence of women's oppression was too radical for the United States in the fifties，and Beauvoir's conclusion，that change in women's economic condition，though insufficient by itself，"remains the basic factor" in improving women's situation，was particularly unacceptable.

序号：071

Other theorists propose that the Moon was ripped out of the Earth's rocky mantle by the Earth's collision with another large celestial body after much of the Earth's iron fell to its core.

难句类型：复杂修饰　　　　**难度**：4

标志： Other theorists propose that the Moon was ripped/out of the Earth's rocky mantle// by the Earth's collision with another large celestial body//after much of the Earth's iron fell to its core. /

译文： 其他的理论学家们认为，月亮/是在地球的大部分铁落入地核后//由于与其他大型天体的碰撞/而被/从地球的岩石状地幔中/撕裂出来的。

解释： 这个句子虽然还算短，但结构却不简单：句中共有三个介词结构作状语。结构的复杂在本句中给读者带来了真正的阅读困难：月亮、地球、大型天体之间的关系如何？三个事件之间的先后顺序怎样？

另外的一个难点在于，在 the Moon was ripped out of the Earth's rocky mantle 这段话中，be ripped out of something 可以作两种理解。rip 既有撕开的意思，又有剥去的意思，而此处的 be ripped out of something 很容易被读者理解成"被剥夺走某物"的意思。实际上，根据对上下文的理解，这里应该理解成"从某物中撕裂出来"的意思。

意群训练： Other theorists propose that the Moon was ripped out of the Earth's rocky mantle by the Earth's collision with another large celestial body after much of the Earth's iron fell to its core.

序号：072

> However, recent scholarship has strongly suggested that those aspects of early New England culture that seem to have been most distinctly Puritan, such as the strong religious orientation and the communal impulse, were not even typical of New England as a whole, but were largely confined to the two colonies of Massachusetts and Connecticut.

难句类型： 复杂修饰 + 插入语　　　**难度：** 4

标志： **However**, recent scholarship has strongly suggested that those aspects [of early

New England culture (that seem to have been most distinctly Puritan)], such as the strong religious orientation and the communal impulse, were **not** even typical of New England /as a whole/, **but** were largely confined [to the two colonies (of Massachusetts and Connecticut)].

译文：然而，近来的学术研究强烈地显示那些 [（看来最为明确的清教徒的）早期新英格兰文化的] 一些方面，比如强烈的宗教导向和团体意识，/整体而言/却不是新英格兰的典型特征，而是在很大程度上只局限 [于（马萨诸塞和康涅狄格）两个州]。

解释：宾语从句的主语those aspects后面跟着长长的修饰成分 [of early New England culture (that seem to have been most distinctly Puritan)]。不但如此，主语和表语之间又被长长的插入语 such as... 分开，而且表语也不是一个，而是were **not**..., **but** were... 的结构，使得句子十分难读。

意群训练：However, recent scholarship has strongly suggested that those aspects of early New England culture that seem to have been most distinctly Puritan, such as the strong religious orientation and the communal impulse, were not even typical of New England as a whole, but were largely confined to the two colonies of Massachusetts and Connecticut.

序号：073

Thus, what in contrast to the Puritan colonies appears to Davis to be peculiarly Southern—acquisitiveness, a strong interest in politics and the law, and a tendency to cultivate metropolitan cultural models—was not only more typically English than the cultural patterns exhibited by Puritan Massachusetts and Connecticut, but also almost certainly characteristic of most other early modern British colonies from Barbados north to Rhode Island and New Hampshire.

难句类型：复杂修饰＋插入语　　　**难度**：4

标志：**Thus**, what/in contrast to the Puritan colonies/ appears /to Davis/ to be peculiarly Southern—acquisitiveness, a strong interest in politics and the law, and a tendency to cultivate metropolitan cultural models—was **not only more** typically English **than** the cultural patterns exhibited by Puritan Massachusetts and Connecticut, **but also** *was* almost certainly characteristic of most other early modern British colonies from Barbados north **to** Rhode Island and New Hampshire.

译 文： 因 此，/与清教徒的殖民地形成了强烈的对比的//在戴维斯/看来是特别有南方色彩的特征——如：进取心、对政治及法律的强烈兴趣和培养大都市文化的欲望——不仅仅比由清教的马萨诸塞州和康涅狄格州所展现出来的文化模式/更具有典型的英国特征，而且/几乎一定/就是（大多数其他早期现代英国殖民地的）典型特征，（这些殖民地的范围从巴巴多斯以北到新罕布什尔州）。

解释： 这个颇长的句子是由一个 what 从句做主语，此主语what/in contrast to the Puritan colonies/ appears /to Davis/ to be peculiarly Southern中有又一些插入的修饰成分，其实主干很简单，就是 what appears to be Southern。Southern 后的两个破折号之间的内容是主语的同位语，实际起到了一个插入语的作用。一直到句子写了五行之后，谓语动词 was 才姗然出现，难怪读者看得不舒服。**but also** 之后，省略了与前面一样的 was。

笔者在此再次提醒读者，笔者之所以对此类句子做语法分析，是为了让读者熟悉这些语法结构，而不是希望读者在现场阅读时也去分析其语法。正确的方法是通过熟读本书中的种种难句，使大脑习惯这些语言结构；实战的现场阅读时把注意力集中在句子的意思上。比如这句话，只要读出"与 D 的观念相反，南方的州与清教的殖民地一样，都是有着英国风格的"的意思即可。

意群训练： Thus, what in contrast to the Puritan colonies appears to Davis to be peculiarly Southern—acquisitiveness, a strong interest in politics and the law, and a tendency to cultivate metropolitan cultural models—was not only more typically English than the cultural patterns exhibited by Puritan Massachusetts and Connecticut, but also almost certainly characteristic of most other early modern British colonies from Barbados north to Rhode Island and New Hampshire.

序号：074

> Portrayals of the folk of Mecklenburg County, North Carolina, whom he remembers from early childhood, of the jazz musicians and tenement roofs of his Harlem days, of Pittsburgh steelworkers, and his reconstruction of classical Greek myths in the guise of the ancient Black kingdom of Benin, attest to this.

难句类型：复杂修饰　　　**难度：5**

标志： Portrayals ｛〔of the folk of Mecklenburg County, North Carolina, （whom he remembers from early childhood）〕, （of the jazz musicians and tenement roofs of his Harlem days）, （of Pittsburgh steelworkers）｝, **and** his reconstruction （of classical Greek myths）/**in the guise of** the ancient Black kingdom of Benin/, attest /to this/.

译文： 一些描述, ｛〔关于（他从小就记得的）北卡罗来纳的 M 县的人民〕、（关于他在 H 的日子里的爵士乐手和公寓的房顶）、（关于匹兹堡的钢铁工人）｝ 的描述, 和（他的）/假借古代贝宁王国/（对古希腊神话的）重塑, 都表现/了这一点/。

解释： 本句主语之长、主语的长度与谓语长度的比例之大，都是极为罕见的。在最后的三个单词 attest /to this/之前的所有内容，全是主语；主语和谓语的比例达到了 46 比 3。不熟悉 GRE 和 GMAT 句式的人是很难把这句话读懂的。

句子的主语实际上是一个由 **and** 连接的并列的结构，而真正的主语只有两个：Portrayals 和 his reconstruction。Portrayals 后面长度惊人的修饰成分以三个大列举的方式说出了其描述的对象，其中第一个列举中又包含了一个定语从句，修饰前面的 folk（人，人们，人民，民族）。第二个主语的修饰成分中使用了一个抽象词组：**in the guise of**, 相当于一个介词，其意思是"假借，在……的幌子下，假装"。

意群训练： Portrayals of the folk of Mecklenburg County, North Carolina, whom he remembers from early childhood, of the jazz musicians and tenement roofs of his Harlem days, of Pittsburgh steelworkers, and his reconstruction of classical Greek myths in the guise of the ancient Black kingdom of Benin, attest to this.

序号：075

A very specialized feeding adaptation in zooplankton is that of the tadpolelike appendicularian who lives in a walnut-sized（or smaller）balloon of mucus equipped with filters that capture and concentrate phytoplankton.

难句类型： 复杂修饰　　　**难度：** 4

标志：（A very specialized feeding）adaptation（in zooplankton）is that of the tadpolelike appendicularian｛who lives in a walnut-sized（or smaller）balloon of mucus［equipped with filters（that capture and concentrate phytoplankton）］｝.

译文：（在浮游动物中出现的）（一种很具体化的用来捕食的）适应，就是 TA 这种动物的适应；｛它生存于一个核桃大小（或更小）的 M 的球状物中，［M 球装备了一些（能够捕捉并聚拢浮游植物的）过滤装置］｝。

解释： GRE 和 GMAT 考试中比较有特色的一个语言现象就是 that（those）of 的频繁出现。that（those）of 的作用是省略掉与前面一样的名词性成分，从而起到简化句子的结构、缩短句子的长度的作用。然而对于初学 GRE 和 GMAT 的人来说，由于以前较少遇到这种结构，而且即使遇到也是在比较简单的句子中间遇到的，所以在复杂句式中一旦遇到，往往一下子搞不清楚这个 that（或 those）指的是前面众多名词性成分中间的哪一个。解决这个问题的办法，就是多读、反复读这样的句子，熟能生巧。

意群训练： A very specialized feeding adaptation in zooplankton is that of the tadpolelike appendicularian who lives in a walnut-sized（or smaller）balloon of mucus equipped with filters that capture and concentrate phytoplankton.

序号：076

These historians, however, have analyzed less fully the development of specifically feminist ideas and activities during the same period.

难句类型：倒装　　　　**难度：**3⁺

标志：These historians, **however**, have analyzed /less fully/ the development of specifically feminist ideas and activities /during the same period/.

译文：然而这些历史学家们却/不曾对/ /同一时期的/具体的妇女思潮和妇女运动做出/充分的/分析。

解释：本句看着别扭的原因是句子的语序颠倒，正常的语序应该是：However, these historians have analyzed the development of specifically feminist ideas and activities during the same period less fully。但是这种语序仍然令人费解：为什么作者不说 these historians haven't fully analyzed the development of feminist ideas？既明确又好懂，何乐而不为？

其实这里倒不见得是 ETS 故意作梗，不让读者读懂，而是因为以上的两种说法之间存在着细微差别：前者强调的是有分析，但与文中的其他研究相比不够完整；后者则是强调没有怎么去研究。GRE 和 GMAT 中使用的英语属于中高级英语，其中的细微之处请读者细心体会。

意群训练：These historians, however, have analyzed less fully the development of specifically feminist ideas and activities during the same period.

序号：077

> Apparently most massive stars manage to lose sufficient material that their masses drop below the critical value of 1.4 M$_\odot$ before they exhaust their nuclear fuel.

难句类型：特殊省略＋固定搭配　　　　**难度：**5

标志：Apparently most massive stars manage to lose sufficient material *so that* their masses drop below the critical value of 1.4 M$_\odot$/before they exhaust their nuclear fuel. /

译文：显然，大多数的巨星能够失去足够多的物质以致于/在燃尽其核燃料以前/

它们的质量下降到关键值 1. 4 M⊙ 以下。

解释： 我们中国考生容易习惯性的把 that 以及其后的内容看成了一个定语从句来修饰 material，但是这样读下来发现意思不通，于是发生思维混乱，大脑拒绝工作，以致当场晕厥。

原文相当于在 **that** 之前省略了 *so*，引导一个表目的的状语从句。事实上 that 本身有这种做连接词的用法，相当于 so that 或 in order that。例如：Speak loud that everybody may hear what you say。

意群训练： Apparently most massive stars manage to lose sufficient material that their masses drop below the critical value of 1. 4 M⊙ before they exhaust their nuclear fuel.

序号：078

> This is so even though the armed forces operate in an ethos of institutional change oriented toward occupational equality and under the federal sanction of equal pay for equal work.

难句类型： 倒装 + 省略   **难度：**5

标志： This is so **even though** the armed forces operate /in an ethos of institutional change（oriented toward occupational equality）/ **and *even though*** *the armed forces operate* /under the federal sanction（of equal pay for equal work）/.

译文： 即使当武装部队/是在一种（趋向职业平等的）制度变化的风气中/运作的时候，而且*即使部队*/是在联邦政府的（同工同酬的）约束下/运行 的时候，情况仍然是这样。

解释： 不论笔者把这句话算成倒装还是省略，其实都有些牵强。阅读能力较高的读者应该可以看出，文中的语序和表达都是完全符合英文规则的；但问题在于它极其不符合汉语习惯！按照中文的习惯，even though 之后的长长的从句应当放在句首，而 This is so 则应该放到最后来说。而且，如果要用 and 来连接这么长的两个状语，也应该在其中补充上主语和谓语才能让人看懂。

但是这就是考试中的英语，也是英语国家的高级知识分子们天天用来做学问的英语；既然他们可以看懂，并能写出来，我们也一定可以看懂，需要的时候也一定能够写出来。

意群训练： This is so even though the armed forces operate in an ethos of institutional change oriented toward occupational equality and under the federal sanction of equal pay for equal work.

序号：079

> An impact capable of ejecting a fragment of the Martian surface into an Earth-intersecting orbit is even less probable than such an event on the Moon, in view of the Moon's smaller size and closer proximity to Earth.

难句类型： 复杂修饰＋省略＋易混指代　　　　**难度：** 5

标志: An impact *on Mars* （capable of **eject**ing a fragment of the Martian surface **into** an Earth-intersecting orbit) is **even less** probable ／**than such an event** on the Moon／, ／**in view of** the Moon's smaller size and closer proximity to Earth／.

译文： 一个（能够把火星表面的碎片射入地球交叉轨道的）碰撞发生的可能甚至小／于这种事件在月亮上发生的可能性／，／考虑到月亮的更小的尺寸及其与地球接近的程度／。

解释： in view of 的意思是考虑到，由于，等于 because of。本句粗看上去十分简单，可是你看完之后会发现本句十分难懂。这句话的意思很容易被理解成：如果考虑到月亮的尺寸和与地球的距离的话，火星碎片被撞击所发射到地球上的几率，要小于发射到月亮上的几率。有点常识的人就会知道这是不可能的：月亮比地球小得多，而且与火星的距离也与地球类似，碎片射到月亮上的几率怎么会反而高呢？这里的关键在于 **such an event** 在文章中指什么，如果是指把火星碎片射到月亮上，那么本句的意思当然是荒谬的；可是如果是指把月亮的碎片发射到地球上，那么本句的意思就对了。实际上句首的 An impact 之后被省略了一个 *on Mars*，所以原文的

such an event on moon，指的是 An impact（on moon）（capable of ejecting a fragment of the lunar surface into an Earth-intersecting orbit），因此如果把原文补全，则句子就变成了下面的样子：

An impact（capable of ejecting a fragment of the Martian surface into an Earth-intersecting orbit）is even **less** probable **than** an impact（on moon）（capable of ejecting a fragment of the lunar surface into an Earth-intersecting orbit），in view of the Moon's smaller size and closer proximity to Earth.

这个意思是可以理解的。

意群训练：An impact capable of ejecting a fragment of the Martian surface into an Earth-intersecting orbit is even less probable than such an event on the Moon，in view of the Moon's smaller size and closer proximity to Earth.

序号：080

Not only are liver transplants never rejected，but they even induce a state of donor-specific unresponsiveness in which subsequent transplants of other organs，such as skin，from that donor are accepted permanently.

难句类型：复杂修饰 + 插入语 + 倒装　　　　**难度：4**

标志：Not only are liver transplants never rejected, **but** they even induce a state of donor-specific unresponsiveness（in which subsequent **transplants** of other organs, such as skin, ／ **from** that donor／ are accepted permanently.）

译文：不仅肝的移植从来没有被排斥，而且这些移植还诱导了一种对供应移植器官者特定的无反应状态，（在此状态中接下来/从那个供应者得来的/其他器官如皮肤，会被永久地接受）。

解释：Not only 放在句首时谓语被提前，这种倒装对我们的读者来讲不算什么新鲜事。干扰度比较大的是在修饰 unresponsiveness 的定语从句（in which **transplants of other organs**, such as ~~skin~~, /**from** that donor/ ~~are accepted~~ permanently）中，插入语 such as skin 和与前面的 **transplants** 搭配的 **from** that donor 共同作用，反复地打断读者的思路，使得从句中主语和谓语不能连贯。

意群训练：Not only are liver transplants never rejected, but they even induce a state of donor-specific unresponsiveness in which subsequent transplants of other organs, such as skin, from that donor are accepted permanently.

序号：081

> As rock interfaces are crossed, the elastic characteristics encountered generally change abruptly, which causes part of the energy to be reflected back to the surface, where it is recorded by seismic instruments.

难句类型：复杂修饰 + 省略 + 过去分词与谓语易混　　　　**难度**：4

标志：/As rock interfaces are crossed/, the elastic characteristics（encountered *by seismic waves*）generally change abruptly, [which causes part of the energy to be reflected back to the surface,（where it is recorded by seismic instruments.）]

译文：/当岩石界面被穿过的时候/，（震波所遇到的）弹性性质通常会发生突然的变化，[这 就使得一部分能量被反射回地面，（在地面反射回来的波被震波记录仪所记录下来）。]

解释：绝大多数人读到 the elastic characteristics encountered generally change abruptly 这一句的时候，第一反应都是把 encountered 看成了谓语动词，再看到 change abruptly 的时候又搞不懂怎么会跑出来两个动词，反复看上 n 遍才看清楚这句话的结构。本句难就难在主语 the elastic characteristics 后面的表示被动的过去分词 encountered 的动作发出者在句子中根本就没有出现过，相当于原文在 encountered 后面省略了一个 *by seismic waves*，但是读者却没有心理准备，同时也不熟悉这种分词修饰的方式，因此难以读懂。

另外，这里的 which 引导的定语从句修饰的是前面整个的句子，即"弹性性质通常会发生突然的变化"的整个事件，使得一部分能量被反射回来。

意群训练： As rock interfaces are crossed, the elastic characteristics encountered generally change abruptly, which causes part of the energy to be reflected back to the surface, where it is recorded by seismic instruments.

序号：082

While the new doctrine seems almost certainly correct, the one papyrus fragment raises the specter that another may be unearthed, showing, for instance, that it was a posthumous production of the Danaid tetralogy which bested Sophocles, and throwing the date once more into utter confusion.

难句类型： 复杂修饰＋插入语   **难度：4**

标志: **While** the new doctrine seems almost certainly correct, ***but*** the one papyrus fragment raises the specter(that another may be unearthed, ∕showing, for instance, that it was a posthumous production of the Danaid tetralogy which bested Sophocles∕, **and**∕throwing the date once more into utter confusion∕).

译文： 尽管这个新学说看起来几乎一定正确，可是这个沙草纸的残片却引起了这样的恐惧，（那就是另外一个残片可能会被挖掘出来，∕显示出，比如说，是属于 D 四部曲的一个作者死后发表的遗作击败了 S∕，这样就∕重新把作品的年代置于极度的混乱之中∕）。

解释: specter 之后的 that 从句是 specter 的同位语。从句中有两个分词作状语，中间由 and 连接。其中以第一个分词结构（showing that it was a posthumous production of the Danaid tetralogy which bested Sophocles）的意思较为难懂，有两个地方要解释一下：

首先，best 在这里的用法我们以前很少见到，用作及物动词，是击败后者的意思，等于 defeat，overcome，或 outdo。

其次，a posthumous production of the Danaid tetralogy 这种说法不符合我们的常规想法。我们看到 a posthumous production of 的时候，根据中文的语言习惯，惯性的到 of 之后去找人名，但是看到后面跟着的是作品名，就想不通了。与中文不同的是，英文中的"遗作"后面不一定只能接人名，接作品名的时候指的是作品在作者死前未发表的那一部分。比如本文的四部曲，可能作者死前全部写好，但只发表了三部，但是死后发表的遗作第四部击败了 S。

意群训练：While the new doctrine seems almost certainly correct, the one papyrus fragment raises the specter that another may be unearthed, showing, for instance, that it was a posthumous production of the Danaid tetralogy which bested Sophocles, and throwing the date once more into utter confusion.

序号：083

> The methods that a community devises to perpetuate itself come into being to preserve aspects of the cultural legacy that that community perceives as essential.

难句类型：复杂修饰　　　**难度：**3 +

标志：The methods（that a community devises to perpetuate itself）come into being/to preserve aspects of the cultural legacy（that that community perceives as essential）/.

译文：（一个社会设计出来保存自己的）方法得以形成/来保持（那个社会认为是最重要的）文化遗产的一些方面/。

解释：本句是前面所举的复杂修饰类难句的例句，已经有所详述。

意群训练：The methods that a community devises to perpetuate itself come into being to preserve aspects of the cultural legacy that that community perceives as essential.

序号：**084**

> Traditionally, pollination by wind has been viewed as a reproductive process marked by random events in which the vagaries of the wind are compensated for by the generation of vast quantities of pollen, so that the ultimate production of new seeds is assured at the expense of producing much more pollen than is actually used.

难句类型：复杂修饰　　　　**难度**：4

标志：/Traditionally/, pollination by wind has been viewed as a reproductive process [marked by random events (in which the vagaries of the wind are compensated for /by the generation of vast quantities of pollen/)], **so that** the ultimate production (of new seeds) is assured /at the expense of producing much more pollen than is actually used/.

译文：/传统上/，风媒传粉被看成是一个这样的繁殖过程：[其特征就是有一些随机事件的发生，（在这些随机事件里，风的反复无常/被大量地产生的花粉/所补偿）]，以致于（新种子的）最终产生被保证了，/其代价是产生远远多于实际使用量的花粉/。

解释：笔者曾经遇到过一个同学，下课以后来找我，说这篇文章读得不好，因为首段的两句话看不懂。这篇文章的首段很长，但仅由两句话构成，不但讲述了老观点的内容，而且解释了这篇文章的主题（subject）的所在，从这里我们可以看出在现场迅速读懂难句的重要性。

marked by 之后的内容是修饰 reproductive process 的。其后的 random events 后面又跟着一个定语从句来修饰它。从句中的被动语态 the vagaries of the wind are compensated for /by the generation of vast quantities of pollen/ 有些特殊，因为文中不是按照中文的习惯说 are compensated，而是说 compensated for，这是由于主语 the vagaries of the wind 并不是被补偿的对象，而是补偿的原因。后面的 at the expense of 是"以……为代价"的意思。

意群训练：Traditionally, pollination by wind has been viewed as a reproductive process marked by random events in which the vagaries of the wind are compensated for by the generation of vast quantities of pollen，so that the ultimate production of new seeds is assured at the expense of producing much more pollen than is actually used.

序号：085

> Because the potential hazards pollen grains are subject to as they are transported over long distances are enormous, wind pollinated plants have, in the view above, compensated for the ensuing loss of pollen through happenstance by virtue of producing an amount of pollen that is one to three orders of magnitude greater than the amount produced by species pollinated by insects.

难句类型：复杂修饰＋插入语＋省略　　　　**难度**：5

标志：**Because** the potential hazards *that* pollen grains are subject to /as they are transported over long distances/）are enormous，wind pollinated plants have，in the view above，compensated for the ensuing loss of pollen（through happenstance）/by virtue［of producing an amount of pollen（that is one to three **orders of magnitude** greater than the amount produced by species pollinated by insects）］.

译文：由于（花粉颗粒/在远距离传播时/所受到的）潜在危险是巨大的，因此，在以上观点中，风媒植物补偿了随之而来的（由于偶然性所带来的）花粉浪费，通过［产生的花粉数量（比由虫媒植物所产生的花粉的数量高一到三个数量级的）］本领。

解释：本句就是上面所说的构成本篇文章首段的第二句话，而且本句的难度超过上一句。本句一上来就不好读：**Because** the potential hazards（*that* pollen grains are subject to /as they are transported over long distances/）are enormous，其中主语后的 pollen grains are subject to 本来是一个定语从句，但是由于主语 the potential hazards 在从句中作介词 to 的宾语，所以引导词 that 被省略，这就显得句子的结构模糊不清，再加上 as 引导的状语从句，隔开了主语和谓语，给读者造成了较大的阅读困难。后面的分句中，句子的结构更为复杂：插入语、定语和状语层层相套。

有两个词组需要解释一下：**orders of magnitude** 指的是数量级，其中 order 是等级、级别的意思，而 magnitude 在此不是指重要、星球的光亮度，指的是尺寸大小或数量多少的程度，同义词是 size，quantity，number。后面的 species pollinated by insects 特指虫媒植物。

意群训练： Because <u>the potential hazards</u> <u>pollen grains</u> <u>are subject to</u> <u>as they are transported</u> <u>over long distances</u> <u>are enormous</u>, <u>wind pollinated plants</u> <u>have</u>, <u>in the view above</u>, <u>compensated for</u> <u>the ensuing</u> <u>loss of pollen</u> <u>through happenstance</u> <u>by virtue of</u> <u>producing an amount of pollen</u> <u>that is one to three</u> <u>orders of magnitude</u> <u>greater than</u> <u>the amount produced by</u> <u>species</u> <u>pollinated by insects</u>.

序号：086

> For example, the spiral arrangement of scale-bract complexes on ovule-bearing pine cones, where the female reproductive organs of conifers are located, is important to the production of airflow patterns that spiral over the cone's surfaces, thereby passing airborne pollen from one scale to the next.

难句类型： 复杂修饰＋插入语＋专有名词　　　　**难度：** 5

标志： For example, the spiral arrangement（of scale-bract complexes）［on ovule-bearing pine cones,（ where the female reproductive organs of conifers are located,）］is important ［to the production of airflow patterns（that spiral over the cone's surfaces）］, **thereby** passing airborne pollen **from** one scale **to** the next.

译文： 比如说，［（针叶树的雌性生殖器官所在的）o-b 的松果上的］（s-b c 的）螺旋状安排，［对于产生（在松果表面盘旋的）气流来讲］是重要的，这样才能把空气传播的花粉从一个 s 传播到另一个 s。

解释： 本句的两大难点中，一是结构复杂，二是专有名词较多。在主语 the spiral arrangement 之后，出现了长长的定语，其中套了三层修饰，这样读者就难以把主语和谓语联系到一块。另外，句中的大量生词也明显干扰了我们的理解：spiral arrangement（螺旋状安排）、scale-bract complexes（鳞苞综合体）、ovule-bearing（携带胚珠的）、pine cones（松果）、female reproductive organ（雌性生殖器官）、airflow pattern（气流模式）等。其中只有后面的三个单词我们有可能根据常识大概猜出其含义。那么现场阅读时遇到这种东西又该如何处理呢？

可以肯定的是，ETS 的出题者并没有期望读者都是生物学家或者是物理学家，而且从众多文章的出题的情况来看，也根本不可能考到任何必须对专有名词作精确理解的内容。读到这种东西的时候，读者的首要任务是从联系文章主题的角度，读出这句话与文章主题有关的意思，从而理解它在文章中的作用。比如这个句子，读者只要能够读出 the arrangement of female reproductive organs of conifers are important to reduce the pollen waste 这个意思即可。

意群训练： For example, the spiral arrangement of scale-bract complexes on ovule-bearing pine cones, where the female reproductive organs of conifers are located, is important to the production of airflow patterns that spiral over the cone's surfaces, thereby passing airborne pollen from one scale to the next.

序号：087

> Friedrich Engels, however, predicted that women would be liberated from the "social, legal, and economic subordination" of the family by technological developments that made possible the recruitment of "the whole female sex into public industry".

难句类型： 复杂修饰＋倒装　　　　　**难度：** 3⁺

标志： Friedrich Engels, however, predicted that women would be liberated /from the "social, legal, and economic subordination" of the family/ /by technological developments（that **made** /**possible**/ the recruitment of "the whole female sex into public industry）/".

译文： FE, 却预测妇女们将被/从家庭的"社会、法律和经济压迫"中/解放出来, /这是通过（使得征召"整个女性阶层进入到公共的工业中去"/成为可能/的）

技术进步的方式做到的／。

解释：本句前半部分简单，后面的宾语从句中的第二个状语 by technological developments 后面跟着的定语从句中出现了倒装：⟨that⟩ **made** ／**possible**／ the recruitment of "the whole female sex into public industry." 的正常语序应该是：⟨that⟩ **made** the recruitment of "the whole female sex into public industry" ／**possible**／，固定搭配 make... possible 中的形容词 possible 被倒装到了前面。

意群训练：Friedrich Engels，however，predicted that women would be liberated from the "social，legal，and economic subordination" of the family by technological developments that made possible the recruitment of "the whole female sex into public industry."

序号：088

> It was not the change in office technology, but rather the separation of secretarial work, previously seen as an apprenticeship for beginning managers, from administrative work that in the 1880s created a new class of "dead-end" jobs, thenceforth considered "women's work".

难句类型：复杂修饰＋插入语　　　**难度**：5

标志：It was { **not** the change in office technology, **but rather** the **separation** [of secretarial work, (previously seen as an apprenticeship for beginning managers,) ／**from** administrative work] } ⟨that⟩ in the 1880's created a new class of "dead-end" jobs, (thenceforth considered "women's work".)

译文：⟨倒不是办公室技术的进步，而是 [（原来被视为见习经理的职位的）秘书工作／与管理工作的/] 分离，⟩ 在 19 世纪 80 年代产生了一种新的 "死胡同" 工作，（这种工作从那以后就被认为是 "妇女的工作"）。

解释：这句话的结构是 It was something that...，It 是形式主语，其真正的内容是

was 之后、that 以前的 something 的内容。本句的"something"结构复杂、长度惊人，并且包含了一个较长的插入语，把固定搭配 **separation from** 分开，造成了极大的阅读困难。其实这个句子说得简单就是 It was the separation of secretarial work from administrative work 〔that〕 created a new class of jobs。

意群训练：It was not the change in office technology，but rather the separation of secretarial work，previously seen as an apprenticeship for beginning managers，from administrative work that in the 1880's created a new class of "dead-end" jobs，thenceforth considered "women's work".

序号：089

> The increase in the numbers of married women employed outside the home in the twentieth century had less to do with the mechanization of housework and an increase in leisure time for these women than it did with their own economic necessity and with high marriage rates that shrank the available pool of single women workers, previously, in many cases, the only women employers would hire.

难句类型：复杂修饰＋插入语　　　　**难度**：5

标志：The increase ［in the numbers of married women（employed outside the home）／in the twentieth century／］had **less** to do with the mechanization of housework **and** an increase in leisure time for these women **than** it did with their own economic necessity **and** with high marriage rates（that shrank the available pool of single women workers，（previously，in many cases），the only women employers would hire.）

译文：［／20世纪初／（在家庭以外被雇用的）已婚妇女的人数上的］增加与其说是与家务劳动的机械化及这些妇女闲暇时间的增加有关，倒不如说是与以下的两种东西有关：她们自己的经济需要及（减少了单身女工的劳动力资源的）高结婚率，而单身女工（是原来在大多数情况下雇主愿意雇用的惟一的一种女性）。

解释：主语The increase之后照例来了一堆修饰成分。后面的 had less to do with... than do with... 的意思是与前面的东西的关系不如与后面的关系那么重要，相当于中文的与其说……还不如说……。但是本句的比较双方都是又臭又长的由 and 所连接的两个名词性短语，令读者阅读时的思维难以连贯。

the pool of 如果后面跟着一种人群，则这个词组指劳动力资源。

意群训练：The increase in the numbers of married women employed outside the home in the twentieth century had less to do with the mechanization of housework and an increase in leisure time for these women than it did with their own economic necessity and with high marriage rates that shrank the available pool of single women workers, previously, in many cases, the only women employers would hire.

序号：090

> For one thing, no population can be driven entirely by density-independent factors all the time.

请思考：如果文中说这句话的前提是 all population are driven by two (and only two) categories of growth parameters, one is density-dependent factors, and the other is density-independent factors, **那么作者说上面的** no population can be driven entirely by density-independent factors all the time **的用意何在？**

难句类型：正话反说　　难度：5

标志： For one thing, no population can be driven /entirely by density-independent factors/ /all the time/.

译文：首先，没有任何种群能够/在所有的时间内//完全地被 d-i 因素/所控制。

解释：本句虽然貌不惊人，但本书既然将其收录进来、并标出难度5，就意味着其中有怪异之处。值得一提的是，本文前面曾把控制种群密度的因素分为两种，一种叫做 density-dependent factors（这里简称 d-d 因素），另一种叫做 density-independent factors（简称 d-i 因素）。

固定搭配 too... to... 是太怎么样以致不能如何的意思，其后的 specify 后面的内容实际上是一个宾语从句。文章的作者把从句中的宾语提到主语和谓语之前，并省略引导词 that，使得句子非常难以读懂。最后的 let alone 的意思是表示递进的"更不要说，何况"。

意群训练： Human genes contain too little information even to specify which hemisphere of the brain each of a human's 10^{11} neurons should occupy, let alone the hundreds of connections that each neuron makes.

序号：107

For the woman who is a practitioner of feminist literary criticism, the subjectivity versus objectivity, or critic-as-artist-or-scientist, debate has special significance; for her, the question is not only academic, but political as well, and her definition will court special risks whichever side of the issue it favors.

请思考： 句末的 it 指的是什么？

难句类型： 复杂修饰＋插入语＋倒装＋省略＋抽象词＋易混指代　　**难度：5**

标志：/For the woman（who is a practitioner of feminist literary criticism），/ the subjectivity **versus** objectivity，（or critic-as-artist **or** *critic-as* -scientist），debate has special significance；for her，the question is **not only** academic，**but** political **as well**，and her definition will court special risks /whichever side of the issue it favors/.

译文：/对于一个（从事于女权主义文学评论的）妇女来说/，主观性还是客观性（或者说评论家应该作艺术家、还是作科学家）的争论有着特殊的重要性；对她来说，此问题不仅仅是学术上的，而且还是政治上的，并且她所给出的定义，/不管有利于问题的哪一方/，都会招致特殊的风险。

解释： 首先解释一下几个词汇：

versus：在这里不是前面讲过的 against 的意思，它和后面的 or 都是"是……还是……"的意思，其英文释义为：in contrast to or as the alternative of ＜ free trade versus protection ＞。

court：招致（风险、失败）；英文释义：to act as to invite or provoke 〈courts disaster〉

分号前面的句子的主语被插入语"or critic-as-artist-or-scientist"分开，正常情况下应该是 the subjectivity **versus** objectivity debate。这种名词修饰名词的情况在 GRE 和 GMAT 考试中是常见的，如前面讲过的句子中出现的"mind-body problem"。

最后的条件状语从句 whichever side of the issue it favors 看上去不难，但却不好理解。首先是 whichever 被提前的表示方法，相当于 no matter it favors which side of the issue 的倒装，no matter 被省略，which 提前并改成了 whichever；后面的 side of the issue 也被提前到主谓 it favors。issue 在此之前面的主要问题，即主观性还是客观性的问题，而 it 前面的名词太多，一下子不好辨别。其实就是指本句的主语 her definition。

意群训练： For the woman who is a practitioner of feminist literary criticism, the subjectivity versus objectivity, or critic-as-artist-or-scientist, debate has special significance; for her, the question is not only academic, but political as well, and her definition will court special risks whichever side of the issue it favors.

序号：108

> If she defines feminist criticism as objective and scientific—a valid, verifiable, intellectual method that anyone, whether man or woman, can perform——the definition not only precludes the critic-as-artist approach, but may also impede accomplishment of the utilitarian political objectives of those who seek to change the academic establishment and its thinking, especially about sex roles.

难句类型： 复杂修饰＋插入语＋抽象词　　　**难度：** 4

标志：If she <u>defines</u> feminist criticism **as** objective and scientific （—a valid，verifiable，intellectual method that anyone，whether man or woman，can perform—）***then*** the definition **not only** precludes the critic-as-artist approach，**but** may **also** <u>impede</u> <u>accomplishment</u> ｛of the utilitarian political objectives of those ［who seek to change the academic establishment and its thinking，（especially about sex roles）.］｝

译文：假如<u>她</u>把女权主义文学评论<u>定义为</u>客观的和科学性的（——一个有效的、可证实的、理性的、无论男女都可以使用的方法——）*那么，这个定义不仅*将排挤掉把批评家作为艺术家的方法，而且可能会<u>阻碍</u> ｛［那些寻求去改变学术界的现状及其思维（特别是有关性别角色的思维）的人们的］实用主义的政治目标的｝ <u>成就</u>。

解释：这句话在原文中紧接着上例的难句。句中的插入语虽然长，但是并不打断正常的语义，因此不算难懂；但是 but also 之后的分句中的宾语 accomplishment 的修饰成分实在太复杂，而且充斥着各色的极端抽象的词汇，没有一定的词汇功底，这句话的意思是不容易看懂的。

意群训练：If she <u>defines</u> feminist criticism as <u>objective</u> and <u>scientific</u>—a valid，verifia-<u>ble</u>，intellectual method <u>that</u> <u>anyone</u>，<u>whether man or woman</u>，<u>can perform</u> —the definition <u>not only</u> <u>precludes</u> the <u>critic-as-artist approach</u>，<u>but</u> <u>may also</u> <u>impede</u> <u>accomplishment</u> of the <u>u</u>-<u>tilitarian political objectives</u> <u>of those who seek to change</u> <u>the academic establishment</u> <u>and its</u> <u>thinking</u>，<u>especially about</u> <u>sex roles</u>.

序号：109

These questions are political in the sense that the debate over them will inevitably be less an exploration of abstract matters in a spirit of disinterested inquiry than an academic power struggle in which the careers and professional fortunes of many women scholars—only now entering the academic profession in substantial numbers—will be at stake, and with them the chances for a distinctive contribution to humanistic understanding, a contribution that might be an important influence against sexism in our society.

难句类型：复杂修饰＋插入语＋省略＋抽象词　　　　　**难度**：5+

标志：These questions are political /in the sense[that the debate (over them) will inevitably be **less** an exploration of abstract matters (in a spirit of disinterested inquiry) **than** an academic power struggle (in which the careers and professional fortunes of many women scholars— only now entering the academic profession in substantial numbers—will be at stake) , **and**/with them/ the chances for a distinctive contribution to humanistic understanding, (a contribution that might be an important influence against sexism in our society)/.

译文：这些问题有政治意味，/因为（对于这些问题的）争论将不可避免地成为，与其说是（在一种公平探讨的精神下）对抽象的事物的一种探索，还不如说是一场学术权力的斗争，（在此斗争中很多女性学者——只是现在才大量地进入到学术界——的饭碗和职业命运都将会处于危机之中）；同时她们对人文学科的理解做出独特的贡献的机会也会受到威胁，（这种贡献有可能对于反对我们社会中的性别歧视做出重大的影响）。/

解释：相信有不少同学在阅读现场看到这个长达10行、不算标点就有81个单词的庞然大句的时候，不禁心为之颤、色为之变、气为之短、胆为之寒。曾经有人把GRE戏称为God Read English，我们果然在这个句子中看到了"天书"的风采。

经笔者认真的统计，本句是一切英语考试中所出现过的最长的句子。而值得一提的是，笔者自己当初在模考中读到此处的时候，却根本没有感觉到这个句子的长短，只是在模考结束以后回头看文章的时候，才发觉这篇文章中的第三段整个就是一句话。其原因在于笔者当时已经对GRE考试中出现的阅读难句做过认真的、系统的训练，而经过难句训练的人在读文章的时候，既不看句子的长短，也不想的句子结构，只看句子的意思。其道理在于，他（她）读过太多遍的长句子，以致于对句子的长度早已麻木；而且也太熟悉这些句子的语法结构，不用想就知道这些结构所表达的含义。这才是我们训练难句的终极目的。

本句的主句极短，难就难在从 in the sense that 开始到整句话结束为止的状语上。that 引导的从句作 sense 的同位语。从句中的主架构还是前面曾经讲过的 less...than... 的结构，译成"与其说是……还不如说是……"。**and** 后面的 chances 与前面的 the careers and professional forture 并列。

意群训练：These questions are political in the sense that the debate over them will inevitably be less an exploration of abstract matters in a spirit of disinterested inquiry than an academic power struggle in which the careers and professional fortunes of many women scholars—only now entering the academic profession in substantial numbers—will be at stake, and with them the chances for a distinctive contribution to humanistic understanding, a contribution that might be an important influence against sexism in our society.

序号：110

> Perhaps he believed that he could not criticize American foreign policy without endangering the support for civil rights that he had won from the federal government.

难句类型：复杂修饰＋正话反说（双重否定）　　　**难度：**4⁻

标志：Perhaps he believed that he could not criticize American foreign policy / without endangering the support for civil rights（ that he had won from the federal government）/.

译文：他有可能相信，他不能够既批评美国的对外政策，/同时又不危及到（他从联邦政府那里已经获得的）对民权运动的支持/。

解释：单从语言上来讲，这句话并不难。但是我们可以发觉作者在句子中拐弯抹角的、双重否定的表达，想说的一定不是字面上的意思。

这是一个标准的正话反说："他有可能相信，他不能够既批评美国的对外政策，/同时又不危及到（他从联邦政府那里已经获得的）对民权运动的支持/"的实际意思就是：他可能相信，如果他批评美国的对外政策，就有可能会危及到（他从联邦政府那里已经获得的）对民权运动的支持。

其实这是一个较为简单的思维转换，也是 GRE 和 GMAT 的阅读和逻辑中经常出现的表达方法。希望读者通过反复地训练，迅速习惯这种语言方式。

意群训练：Perhaps he believed that he could not criticize American foreign policy without endangering the support for civil rights that he had won from the federal government.

序号: **111**

> However, some broods possess a few snails of the oppo-
> sing hand, and in predominantly sinistral broods, the in-
> cidence of dextrality is surprisingly high.

请思考: 如果本句话的前提是: 所有的 **snail** 的 **hand** 只能有两种: **sinistral versus dextral**, 那么作者真正想说的是什么?

难句类型: 正话反说(或暗含的强对比)   **难度**: 5

标志: However, some broods possess a few snails of the opposing hand, **and** in predominantly sinistral broods, / the incidence of dextrality is surprisingly high.

译文: 可是, 一些窝中会有一些相反旋向的蜗牛; 而且/在主要是左旋的窝当中/, 出现右旋的几率是令人惊奇地高。

解释: 本句貌不惊人, 实无难句之伟岸雄姿, 然而不知在考试中难倒了多少英雄好汉。原文的表面意思简单至极: 一些窝中会有一些相反旋向的蜗牛; 在左旋为主的窝当中, 出现右旋的几率是令人惊奇地高。关键是作者只是单纯地想说左旋窝的右旋几率么? 什么是高, 是绝对值还是相对值? 如果是相对值, 那么是与什么相比呢?

这么一提示, 读者可能会发现作者的言外之意。作者的真实意图, 是想将两种窝的情况做一个对比, 把句子补全就是: 在左旋窝中会出现右旋, 右旋窝中有左旋; 而左旋窝中的右旋数量要远远高于右旋窝中的左旋数量。这篇文章对这句话出了一道题, 答案就是——右旋窝中的左旋数量少于左旋窝中的右旋数量。

ETS 的出题者的语言表述常常象初恋中的腼腆少女, 言语间闪烁其辞、留有余味, 让我们的考生自己去猜想, 恐怕不是出于羞涩; 其真实用心和真确含义, 关乎读者的考试成败, 不可不察。

意群训练: However, some broods possess a few snails of the opposing hand, and in predominantly sinistral broods, the incidence of dextrality is surprisingly high.

序号：112

> In experiments，an injection of cytoplasm from dextral eggs changes the pattern of sinistral eggs，but an injection from sinistral eggs does not influence dextral eggs.

难句类型：省略＋易混词　　　　**难度：4⁺**

标志：/In experiments/，an injection of cytoplasm（from dextral eggs）changes the pattern of sinistral eggs/to dextral/，**but** an injection of cytoplasm（from sinistral eggs）does not influence the pattern of dextral eggs.

译文：/在实验当中/，一个（来自于右旋蛋的）蛋白质的注射把左旋蛋的模式改变/成了右旋蛋/，而一个（来自于左旋蛋的）细胞质的注射却并不影响右旋蛋的模式。

解释：本句与上一句来自于同一篇文章：蜗牛的左旋与右旋。在阅读这篇文章的过程当中，所有同学都在竭尽全力的分清左、右的区别，然而读到这里的时候，ETS 的出题者终于突破了读者的心理底线，彻底地搞混了左右之间的关系。

其实在这里之所以左右容易搞混，还有一个人为的重要原因，就是这句话使用了大量的省略：文中的 changes the pattern of sinistral eggs 后面，实际上省略了一个 to dextral，而最后的分句 an injection from sinistral eggs does not influence dextral eggs，则是 an injection of cytoplasm from sinistral eggs does not influence the pattern of dextral eggs 的省略形式。

意群训练：In experiments，an injection of cytoplasm from dextral eggs changes the pattern of sinistral eggs，but an injection from sinistral eggs does not influence dextral eggs.

序号：113

> Recently some scientists have concluded that meteorites found on Earth and long believed to have a Martian origin might actually have been blasted free of Mars's gravity by the impact on Mars of other meteorites.

难句类型：复杂修饰　　　**难度：4 +**

标志： /Recently/ some scientists have concluded that meteorites (found on Earth) **and** (long believed to have a Martian origin) might actually have been blasted /free of Mars's gravity/ /by the **impact** on Mars **of** other meteorites/.

译文： /近来/一些科学家得出结论，（地球上发现的）并（一直被认为是来自于火星的）陨石有可能实际上是/在其他的陨石对火星的冲击下/被炸/离了火星的引力/。

解释： 这个句子难就难在以 that 引导的宾语从句。从句中的主语是 meteorites，修饰它的成分有两个，一个是（found on Earth），另一个是（long believed to have a Martian origin），两个并列的成分之间以 **and** 相连接。注意，这里不能把原句理解成是 meteorites（found on Earth）**and** meteorites（long believed to have a Martian origin）的省略形式：这个表达是说有两种陨石，一种是地球上发现的，另一种是来自火星的；原文所指的是同一批陨石的两个特征：发现于地球，来自于火星。

句子最后的 by the **impact** on Mars **of** other meteorites 读上去令人感到不舒服的原因，是 the **impact of** other meteorites 中的 impact of 被修饰 impact 的 on Mars 分隔开了。

意群训练： Recently some scientists have concluded that meteorites found on Earth and long believed to have a Martian origin might actually have been blasted free of Mars's gravity by the impact on Mars of other meteorites.

序号：114

> Under the force of this view, it was perhaps inevitable that the art of rhetoric should pass from the status of being regarded as of questionable worth (because although it might be both a source of pleasure and a means to urge people to right action, it might also be a means to distort truth and a source of misguided action) to the status of being wholly condemned.

请思考：对于本句中的插入语，阅读现场应如何处理？

难句类型：插入语　　难度：4

标志：/Under the force of this view/, it was perhaps inevitable that the art of rhetoric should pass/**from** the status [of being regarded as of questionable worth (because although it might be both a source of pleasure and a means to urge people to right action, it might also be a means to distort truth and a source of misguided action) **to** the status (of being wholly condemned.)

译文：/在这种观点的作用下/，有一件事情看起来不可避免，那就是修辞的艺术应该从［被认为是有问题的价值（因为尽管它既有可能是一个快乐的源泉和推动人们去做正确的事情的手段，也有可能成为一种歪曲事实和误导人们的力量。）堕落到（完全被贬低的）价值］。

解释：本句的插入语堪称 GRE 和 GMAT 考试中最长的插入语之一。笔者曾在本书前面的讲解中强调过，这种插入语（三行以上）一定要在阅读时毫不犹豫地跳过，读完整个的句子后回头再来读它。否则不但句意无法衔接，而且类似于本句中的 **from...to...** 的这种固定搭配，也会在插入语的干扰下远隔千山万水，在读者的大脑中永无聚首之日。

意群训练：Under the force of this view, it was perhaps inevitable that the art of rhetoric should pass from the status of being regarded as of questionable worth (because although it might be both a source of pleasure and a means to urge people to right action, it might also be a means to distort truth and a source of misguided action) to the status of being wholly condemned.

序号：115

None of these translations to screen and stage, however, dramatize the anarchy at the conclusion of *A Connecticut Yankee*, which ends with the violent overthrow of Morgan's three-year-old progressive order and his return to the nineteenth century, where he apparently commits suicide after being labeled a lunatic for his incoherent babblings about drawbridges and battlements.

难句类型：复杂修饰　　　　　难度：4

标志：None of these translations（to screen and stage），however，dramatize the anarchy at the conclusion of *A Connecticut Yankee*，{which ends with the violent overthrow（of Morgan's three-year-old progressive order）**and** *with* his return to the nineteenth century，[where he apparently commits suicide/after being **labeled** a lunatic **for** his incoherent babblings（about drawbridges and battlements/）]}.

译文：然而，没有一个这类（搬上舞台或银幕的）改编能够戏剧性地表现出 ACY 剧结尾处的无政府主义；{A 剧的结尾是（M 的为期三年的进步秩序的）被推翻和 M 的重返 19 世纪，[在这里，/在由于说了一些（关于吊桥和城垛的）不连贯的蠢话而被称为疯子之后/，他显然是以自杀而告终]}。

解释：本句是典型的层层修饰的例子。主句的宾语 anarchy 被修饰得不像话，以致于笔者用光了{[（）]}的三层修饰符号也没有把所有的层次标全（anarchy 与 at the conclusion of 之间未做标记，是后者修饰前者）。其实这种句子无它，惟长而已，多练即可。

意群训练：None of these translations to screen and stage, however, dramatize the anarchy at the conclusion of *A Connecticut Yankee*, which ends with the violent overthrow of Morgan's three-year-old progressive order and his return to the nineteenth century, where he apparently commits suicide after being labeled a lunatic for his incoherent babblings about drawbridges and battlements.

序号：116

Calculations of the density of alloys based on Bernal-type models of the alloys metal component agreed fairly well with the experimentally determined values from measurements on alloys consisting of a noble metal together with a metalloid, such as alloys of palladium and silicon, or alloys consisting of iron, phosphorus, and carbon, although small discrepancies remained.

难句类型：复杂修饰＋插入语　　　　**难度**：5

标志：Calculations（of the density of alloys）（based on Bernal-type models of the alloys metal component）**agreed** fairly well **with** the experimentally determined values /from measurements on alloys（consisting of a noble metal **together with** a metalloid），such as alloys of palladium and silicon，or alloys consisting of iron，phosphorus，and carbon ／ ，**although** small discrepancies remained.

译文：（基于 B 的金属合金成分模型的）（对于合金密度的）计算非常符合通过实验确定的值，/通过测量（包含一种贵金属和一种准金属的）合金的方式，如钯与硅的合金，或铁、磷和碳的合金/；可是仍有一些小的差异存在。

解释：前面的分句中同时有两个成分修饰主语Calculations。宾语the experimentally determined values 之后的、从 from 开始一直到 **although** 之前的内容修饰宾语，说明宾语中 determine 的具体方法。

值得注意的是后面的分句中的 **although**：在由两个分句组成的句子中，although 如果出现在后面的分句的句首，则其不是表示让步，而且一种委婉地表示转折的语气，相当于 but。

意群训练：Calculations of the density of alloys based on Bernal-type models of the alloys metal component agreed fairly well with the experimentally determined values from measurements on alloys consisting of a noble metal together with a metalloid，such as alloys of palladium and silicon，or alloys consisting of iron，phosphorus，and carbon，although small discrepancies remained.

序号：**117**

And Walzer advocates as the means of eliminating this tyranny and of restoring genuine equality " the abolition of the power of money outside its sphere".

难句类型：倒装　　　**难度**：4

标志： And Walzer **advocates** as the means of eliminating this tyranny **and** of restoring genuine equality／"the abolition of the power of money outside its sphere".

译文： 而且W倡议把"在金钱的圈子之外废除金钱的力量"／作为消除这种暴政并且重获真正的平等的方法／。

解释： 本句是典型的倒装。本句的正常语序应该是：And Walzer **advocates** "the abolition of the power of money outside its sphere"／**as** the means of eliminating this tyranny and of restoring genuine equality.／，而句中则把advocates的宾语"the abolition of the power of money outside its sphere"倒装到了句末。

意群训练： And Walzer advocates as the means of eliminating this tyranny and of restoring genuine equality "the abolition of the power of money outside its sphere."

序号：118

> Is it not tyrannical, in Pascal's sense, to insist that those who excel in "sensitivity" or "the ability to express compassion" merit equal wealth with those who excel in qualities (such as "the capacity for hard work") essential in producing wealth?

难句类型： 复杂修饰 + 插入语　　　**难度：** 5

标志： Is it not tyrannical, in Pascal's sense, to insist that those (who excel in "sensitivity" or "the ability to express compassion") merit **equal** wealth／**with** those [who excel in qualities (such as "the capacity for hard work") (essential in producing wealth) \ ]?

译文： 按照P的理解，难道坚持那些（在"敏感性"或"表达同情心的能力"上突出的）人应该与那些［在（对赚钱很重要的）能力（比如"刻苦工作的能力"）上突出的］人得到同样的财富，这种做法就不是暴政吗?

解释： 句首的it是形式主语，其真正的内容在不定式中。insist引导的宾语从句中的谓语 merit 是句子的中心难点。因为我们通常只知道 merit 的名词词义，并不知道它也可以被用作动词，所以此处不容易看懂。其动词的意思是：应该得到……，值得……；英文释义为 to deserve，be worthy of。

另外，句子作为一个疑问句，却结构复杂、冗长不堪，也是本句难以读懂的一个重要原因。

意群训练：Is it not tyrannical, in Pascal's sense, to insist that those who excel in "sensitivity" or "the ability to express compassion" merit equal wealth with those who excel in qualities (such as "the capacity for hard work") essential in producing wealth?

序号：119

Yet Walzer's argument, however deficient, does point to one of the most serious weaknesses of capitalism—namely, that it brings to predominant positions in a society people who, no matter how legitimately they have earned their material rewards, often lack those other qualities that evoke affection or admiration.

难句类型：复杂修饰＋插入语＋倒装　　　　**难度**：5

标志：**Yet** Walzer's argument, however deficient, does point to one of the most serious weaknesses of capitalism—namely, that it **brings**/to predominant positions in a society/ people [who, no matter how legitimately they have earned their material rewards, often lack those other qualities (that evoke affection or admiration)].

译文：然而 W 的论点，不管有什么样的缺陷，也确实指出了资本主义的一个最为严重的弱点——那就是，它(资本主义)把 [那些 不论是如何合法地赚到他们的物质回报的，但是往往缺乏 (那些 能唤起别人的爱戴和崇敬的品质的)] 人带到了/社会上的显要位置/。

解释：第一个插入语 however deficient 中的 however 在此不是转折连词，而是副词，等于 no matter how；但是因为后面出现了 no matter how，而作者又追求语言表述的多样性，所以作者在此使用了 however deficient 这样较为少见的（但在 GRE 考试中多见的）语言。

尽管本句的插入语较多，第二个插入语还很长，但是本句的真正难点在倒装上。破折号后面的部分是主句宾语的同位语从句，此从句中固定搭配 bring A to B 被倒装成了 bring to B A。如果把这句话恢复成正常语序，则是 it **brings** people ［who，no matter how legitimately they have earned their material rewards，often lack those other qualities（that evoke affection or admiration）］/**to** predominant positions in a society/。很明显，这样的语序会显得头重脚轻。

意群训练：Yet Walzer's argument, however deficient, does point to one of the most serious weaknesses of capitalism—namely, that it brings to predominant positions in a society people who, no matter how legitimately they have earned their material rewards, often lack those other qualities that evoke affection or admiration.

序号：120

> The appreciation of traditional oral American Indian literature has been limited, hampered by poor translations and by the difficulty, even in the rare culturally sensitive and aesthetically satisfying translation, of completely conveying the original's verse structure, tone, and syntax.

难句类型：复杂修饰＋插入语　　　　**难度：**4⁻

标志：The appreciation（of traditional oral American Indian literature）has been limited，/hampered by poor translations **and** by the difficulty，even in the[rare（culturally sensitive and aesthetically satisfying）] translation，（of completely conveying the original's verse structure, tone, and syntax）/。

译文：（对于传统的美国印第安的口头文学的）欣赏仍然有限，/这是由于被拙劣的翻译和这样的困难所妨碍：即使在［少见的（具备文化敏感度和在美学上令人满意的）］翻译中，也（无法完全传递原作的韵律结构、语气和句法）／。

解释：本句的插入语不好对付，一来它的长度比较长，而且修饰层次多、内容也不甚好懂；二来这个插入语正好嵌在 difficulty of 的中间，割裂了句义。

意群训练：The appreciation of traditional oral American Indian literature has been limited, hampered by poor translations and by the difficulty, even in the rare culturally sensitive and aesthetically satisfying translation, of completely conveying the original's verse structure, tone, and syntax.

序号：121

> Mores, which embodied each culture's ideal principles for governing every citizen, were developed in the belief that the foundation of a community lies in the cultivation of individual powers to be placed in service to the community.

难句类型：复杂修饰 + 抽象词　　　　**难度**：4⁺

标志：Mores, (which embodied each culture's ideal principles for governing every citizen,) were developed ／in the belief that the foundation of a community lies in the cultivation of individual powers (to be placed in service to the community)／.

译文：道德（——体现了每一个文化管辖每个公民的理想原则——）是发展／于这样的信念之下的，那就是一个社会的基础在于对（那些被定位于要为那个社会做出服务的）个人能力的培养／。

解释：与前面的绝大多数句子相比，本句的结构算不上复杂。但是由于句意抽象，所以读到 the cultivation of individual powers to be placed in service to the community 的时候容易读不懂，因为后面的这个不定式既有可能是修饰 cultivation 的，也有可能是修饰 individual powers 的。这里修饰的是后者。而且这里的 individual powers to be placed in service to the community 不应翻译成"被投入到对社会服务的个人力量",因为如果原文真是为了表达这个意思,则其只需说"individual powers to serve the community"即可。此处是强调这种 individual power 被置于的一种位置、一种定位。当然这种细微的差别不一定会影响答题,但有时会对文章的理解产生影响。

意群训练: <u>Mores</u>, which embodied each <u>culture's ideal principles</u> for governing every citizen, were developed in the belief that the foundation of a community lies in the cultivation of individual powers to be placed in service to the community.

序号:122

Only in the case of the February Revolution do we lack a useful description of participants that might characterize it in the light of what social history has taught us about the process of revolutionary mobilization.

难句类型: 复杂修饰 + 倒装 + 易混指代　　　**难度:** 5

标志: **Only**/in the case of the February Revolution/ <u>do we lack</u> a useful description (of participants) { |that| might characterize **it**/in the light of [|what| social history has taught us (about the process of revolutionary mobilization)] / }.

译文: 只有/在二月革命中/我们才缺乏一种(对于参加者的)有用的描述,{ 此描述 有可能/按照[社会历史教给我们的(关于革命动员过程的)内容]/来描绘出这场革命的特点}。

解释: 句首虽有一个倒装,但是这种简单结构并不能给我们的读者带来大的影响;倒是主句宾语 a useful description (of participants) 之后的定语从句 |that| **might characterize it** 中的两个易混指代及其后的状语 in the light of 给我们的理解造成了巨大的困难。
　　首先,that 从句所修饰的不是 participants,而是 description。紧随其后的 it 指的则是前面的 February Revolution。判断这两点的惟一方法就是通过句子的意思,没有任何其他途径。后面的 in the light of...,是按照……、根据……的意思,其英文解释为 from

the point of view。

　　后面的层层修饰虽然有一定的难度，但是我们已经在前面的句子中司空见惯，在此不多做解释。

　　意群训练：Only in the case of the February Revolution do we lack a useful description of participants that might characterize it in the light of what social history has taught us about the process of revolutionary mobilization.

　　序号：123

> As a consequence, it may prove difficult or impossible to establish for a successful revolution a comprehensive and trustworthy picture of those who participated, or to answer even the most basic questions one might pose concerning the social origins of the insurgents.

　　难句类型：复杂修饰＋倒装＋省略　　　　**难度**：5

　　标志：/As a consequence, /it may prove difficult or impossible to **establish** /**for** a successful revolution/ a comprehensive and trustworthy picture (of those who participated), **or** to answer even the most basic questions (*that* one might pose) (concerning the social origins of the insurgents).

　　译文：/作为一个结果/，有两件事就变得很困难或者根本不可能：1./为一次成功的革命/建立起一个详尽的并可信的（关于参加者的）描述；2. 回答（人们会问的、）（关于起义者的社会背景的）甚至是最为基本的问题。

　　解释：主句的主语 it 是形式主语，其真正内容在后面的两个由 or 连接的并列的不定式中。前一个不定式中出现一个大型倒装，to **establish**/**for** a successful revolution/ a comprehensive and trustworthy picture (of those who participated) 的正常语序是 to **establish** a comprehensive and trustworthy picture (of those who participated) /**for** a successful revolution/。对于类似的结构，读者如果按照笔者的要求认真地过前面的难句，训练到现在应该已经有所感觉。正确的现场感觉是这样：看到 established 之后没有出现宾语，而是

直接出现表示目的的 for，句义不完整，大脑就会根据前面训练得出的经验自动判断可能有倒装的结构；读者本人的反应就是隐隐觉得后面应该有 established 的具体内容。因为有这种预期，读到 a comprehensive and trustworthy picture 的时候，正好可以把它与没有说完的 established 连在一起。

后面的不定式的宾语 even the most basic questions 之后又两个并列的定语，第一个是省略了引导词的定语从句（*that* one might pose），第二个是分词修饰（concerning the social origins of the insurgents）。

意群训练： As a consequence，it may prove difficult or impossible to establish for a successful revolution a comprehensive and trustworthy picture of those who participated，or to answer even the most basic questions one might pose concerning the social origins of the insurgents.

序号：124

> Anthropologists and others are on much firmer ground when they attempt to describe the cultural norms for a small homogeneous tribe or village than when they undertake the formidable task of discovering the norms that exist in a complex modern nation-state composed of many disparate groups.

难句类型： 复杂修饰　　**难度：** 4

标志： Anthropologists and others are on much **firmer** ground / when they attempt to describe the cultural norms (for a small homogeneous tribe or village) **than** / when they undertake the formidable task {of discovering the norms [that exist in a complex modern nation-state (composed of many disparate groups)]} /.

译文： 人类学家们和其他人 / 当试图去描述（一个小的而且同一部落或村庄的）文化标准的时候 /，比起 / 肩负起 {去探寻 [存在于一个（包括很多不同人群的）复杂的现代单一民族国家的] 行为准则的} 艰巨任务来说 /，*前者*是基于一个更为坚实的基础之上的。

解释：句子的结构拉得很长，主要原因是用来比较的两个 when 引导的状语从句都太长。句子的主干是 Anthropologists are on much **firmer** ground/when... / **than**/ when... /。结果 more than 的结构被长长的状语从句分隔得很远。

另外，第二个 when 引导的从句中的宾语也很复杂。解释一个单词：nation-state 指单一民族的国家。此单词的词义不必背下来。

意群训练：Anthropologists and others are on much firmer ground when they attempt to describe the cultural norms for a small homogeneous tribe or village than when they undertake the formidable task of discovering the norms that exist in a complex modern nation-state composed of many disparate groups.

序号：125

> The Italian influence is likely, whatever Valdez' immediate source: the Mexican *carpas* themselves are said to have originated from the theater pieces of a sixteenth-century Spanish writer inspired by encounters with Italian *commedia dell'arte* troupes on tour in Spain.

难句类型：复杂修饰　　　**难度：**4⁺

标志：The Italian influence is likely, /whatever Valdez' immediate source/: the Mexican *carpas* themselves are said to have originated /from the theater pieces of a sixteenth-century Spanish writer inspired by encounters [with Italian *commedia dell'arte* troupes (on tour in Spain)] } /.

译文：/不管 V 的直接来源是什么，/意大利的影响 都 很 有 可 能：墨西哥的 C 戏剧本身就被认为来自/于16 世纪的西班牙某作家的戏剧作品，*而此作家的* ｛灵感就来自于他 \[与（在西班牙巡回演出的）意大利 cd 剧团的 \ ］遭遇｝ /。

解释：本句的冒号以后的分句中的 from 引导的状语的结构又是典型的层层修饰，

再加上主句的内容，整个句子的意思很难理顺。到底是什么来自于什么？

意群训练： The Italian influence is likely, whatever Valdez' immediate source: the Mexicancarpas themselves are said to have originated from the theater pieces of a sixteenth-century Spanish writer inspired by encounters with Italian *commedia dell'arte* troupes on tour in Spain.

序号：126

> It has thus generally been by way of the emphasis on oral literary creativity that these Chicano writers, whose English-language works are sometimes uninspired, developed the powerful and arresting language that characterized their Spanish-language works.

难句类型： 复杂修饰 + 插入语　　　　**难度：** 5

标志： It has thus generally been **/by way of** the emphasis on oral literary creativity/ that these Chicano writers, (whose English-language works are sometimes uninspired,) developed the powerful and arresting language (that characterized their Spanish-language works).

译文： 这样，这些 C 作家们（他们的英语作品有时缺乏灵感）之所以能发展出（称得上是其西班牙语作品的特征的）有力的迷人的语言，/一般是通过强调口头文学的创造性的方式/。

解释： 读者们阅读本句的时候一定感觉极其别扭。首先，我们尽管知道 It has been... that... 这种结构是一种强调语气，但是 It has thus generally been by way of the emphasis on oral literary creativity that... 看上去就极不舒服。当然从语法上讲这么说是可以的；可是我们确实很少见到把 it has been 和 that 之间插入这么多东西的说法。解释一下 by way of 的意思：就是通过什么样的方法、通过某种手段的意思。其英文释义为 by the route of，同义词是 via。

that 以后的内容看上去更费劲，既有长插入语分开主谓语，又有复杂修饰的宾语。

本句之所以结构怪异、意思费解，其原因是作者为了强调这个口头文学的方法。

否则，句子可以写得比较好懂：

Thus, these Chicano writers, whose English-language works are sometimes uninspired, developed the powerful and arresting language (that characterized their Spanish-language works), /generally by way of the emphasis on oral literary creativity/.

意群训练： It has thus generally been by way of the emphasis on oral literary creativity that these Chicano writers, whose English-language works are sometimes uninspired, developed the powerful and arresting language that characterized their Spanish-language works.

序号：127

This declaration, which was echoed in the text of the Fourteenth Amendment, was designed primarily to counter the Supreme Court's ruling in *Dred Scott v. Sandford* that Black people in the United States could be denied citizenship.

难句类型： 复杂修饰 + 插入语　　　**难度：** 3

标志： This declaration, (which was echoed in the text of the Fourteenth Amendment,) was designed primarily /to counter the Supreme Court's ruling (in *Dred Scott v. Sandford*) that Black people in the United States could be denied citizenship/.

译文： 这一（被在十四修正案中呼应了的）宣言主要是被设计/来反对最高法院（在 DSS 一案中的）裁决，即美国黑人能够被剥夺公民权/。

解释： 句中的两个插入语分别起到了两个有效的分割作用：第一个隔开了主句的主语和谓语；第二个分开了做状语的不定式中的宾语及其同位语从句。

意群训练： This declaration, which was echoed in the text of the Fourteenth Amendment, was designed primarily to counter the Supreme Court's ruling in *Dred Scott v. Sandford* that Black people in the United States could be denied citizenship.

序号：**128**

> The broad language of the amendment strongly suggests that its framers were proposing to write into the Constitution not a laundry list of specific civil rights but a principle of equal citizenship that forbids organized society from treating any individual as a member of an inferior class.

难句类型：复杂修饰 + 倒装　　　　**难度**：4

标志：The broad language of the amendment strongly suggests that its framers were proposing to write /into the Constitution/ **not** a laundry list of specific civil rights **but** a principle of equal citizenship (that **forbids** organized society **from** treating any individual as a member of an inferior class).

译文：这个修正案的宽泛的语言强烈地显示出，其制定者不是想把一个详细的公民权的清单写/入宪法/，而是要写入一个平等的公民权的原则，（那就是禁止有组织的社会来把任何个人当作劣等阶级的成员对待）。

解释：本句的倒装还算友好，介词 into 的宾语 the Constitution 比较短，然后马上是 write 的宾语。而且本句的结构也算合理，避免了头重脚轻。如果真按照正常语序来写，那么句子只有更难读懂。即：

The broad language of the amendment strongly suggests that its framers were proposing to **write not** a laundry list of specific civil rights **but** a principle of equal citizenship that forbids organized society from treating any individual as a member of an inferior class **into** the Constitution.

意群训练：The broad language of the amendment strongly suggests that its framers were proposing to write into the Constitution not a laundry list of specific civil rights but a principle of equal citizenship that forbids organized society from treating any individual as a member of an inferior class.

序号：129

This doctrine has broadened the application of the Fourteenth Amendment to other, nonracial forms of discrimination, for while some justices have refused to find any legislative classification other than race to be constitutionally disfavored, most have been receptive to arguments that at least some nonracial discriminations, sexual discrimination in particular, are "suspect" and deserve this heightened scrutiny by the courts.

难句类型：复杂修饰＋插入语＋三重否定＋抽象词　　**难度：**5

标志：This doctrine has **broadened** the application (of the Fourteenth Amendment) **to** other, nonracial forms of discrimination, ／for **while** some justices have refused to find any legislative classification (other than race) to be constitutionally disfavored, **but** most have been receptive to arguments (that at least some nonracial discriminations, sexual discrimination in particular, are "suspect" **and** deserve this heightened scrutiny by the courts) ／.

译文：这一信条把（十四修正案的）使用范围扩展到其他的、非种族形式的歧视上，／因为尽管一些法官拒绝把（任何种族以外的）立法分类视为违反宪法的，可是大多数法官都接受这样的论点，（ 那就是 至少有一些非种族歧视，特别是性别歧视，是值得"怀疑的"并且值得法庭做这种更高规格的审查）／。

解释：句子虽然长，结构却不是太难。相信坚持训练到这里的读者不会再感到句子太长、或者结构太难了。不过这句话还是有两个难点的，一个是其中大量的法律方面的抽象词；另一个是其中的一个三重否定：some justices have refused to find any legislative classification other than race to be constitutionally disfavored，实际上就是：some justices believe that only racial classification may be constitutionally disfavored 或者 some justices regard nonracial discrimination to be constitutionally legitimate。

意群训练：This doctrine has broadened the application of the Fourteenth Amendment to other, nonracial forms of discrimination, for while some justices have refused to find any legislative classification other than race to be constitutionally disfavored, most have been receptive to arguments that at least some nonracial discriminations, sexual discrimination in particular, are "suspect" and deserve this heightened scrutiny by the courts.

4.2 GMAT 阅读难句详解

说明：

1. 以下所列难句的讲解步骤和符号标记的用法与 PART A 完全相同，请参阅 PART A；

2. GMAT 难句的难度确定是基于 GMAT 考试中的阅读的相对难度的，其难度标准低于 GRE 难句的评定标准 0.5 到 1 左右；

3. 考虑到最后读者需要用最新题做模考的实际情况，较新的文章中的句子暂不收录。

序号：001

> Civil rights activists have long argued that one of the principal reasons why Blacks, Hispanics, and other minority groups have difficulty establishing themselves in business is that they lack access to the sizable orders and subcontracts that are generated by large companies.

难句类型：复杂修饰　　**难度：**4

标志：Civil rights activists have long argued that one of the principal reasons (why Blacks, Hispanics, and other minority groups have difficulty establishing themselves in business) is that they lack access [to the sizable orders **and** subcontracts (that are generated by large companies)].

译文：人权活动分子一直认为（黑人、拉美裔和其他少数族裔的美国人之所以难以在商界有所作为的）主要原因就是因为他们缺乏得到 [大规模的订单和（大公司所产生的）分包合同的〕<u>途径</u>。

解释： 主句简单，宾语从句的结构复杂。从句的主语one of the principal reasons被由 why 所引导的较长的定语从句修饰，造成了主语和表语 is 的分离；is 之后又来了个表语从句；其中的宾语被介词结构所修饰，而介词结构中的由 and 连接的第二个介词宾语 subcontracts 又被定语从句（ that are generated by large companies）修饰，是典型的从句套从句的层层修饰。

意群训练： Civil rights activists have long argued that one of the principal reasons why Blacks, Hispanics, and other minority groups have difficulty establishing themselves in business is that they lack access to the sizable orders and subcontracts that are generated by large companies.

序号：002

> Fascination with this ideal has made Americans defy the "Old World" categories of settled possessiveness *versus* unsettling deprivation, the cupidity of retention *versus* the cupidity of seizure, a "status quo" defended or attacked.

难句类型： 复杂修饰 + 抽象词　　　　**难度：** 4[+]

标志： Fascination with this ideal has made Americans defy the "Old World" categories (of settled possessiveness ***versus*** unsettling deprivation, the cupidity of retention ***versus*** the cupidity of seizure, a "status quo" defended **or** attacked).

译文： 对于这种理想的迷恋使得美国人去公然挑战"旧世界"的分类，（即：用稳定的财产来代替不稳定的剥夺；用拥有的欲望取代去掠夺的贪欲；一个"当前的社会状况"被保卫而不是被攻击）。

解释： 相对来讲，本句的词汇的难度要高于其结构的难度。尤其困难的是对两个介词（versus 和 or）的理解。

Versus 有两个词义：**1.** in contest against，＜plaintiff *versus* defendant＞，其同义词是 against；**2.** in contrast with；by way of alternative to，＜peace *versus* war＞，前者与后者比较、或前者代替后者。本句所取的词义肯定是第二个词义中的后一种理解，即前者代替后者，因为 or 作为介词是只有一个意思，即 before 的意思，连接两个名词时指前者优先于后者。

还有两个词需要解释："old world" 不是一般所说的旧世界，而是与美洲相对照的欧洲；英文释义为 often used specifically with reference to European culture，customs，etc. 后面的 "status quo" 是拉丁语，意思是现存的社会状况。

除此之外，在句中的三对用来比较的词汇也都很抽象，但是我们可以发现比较的前项和后项分别是一些有同义词意味的词汇：

前项：possessiveness ／ retention ／ "status quo" defended

后项：deprivation 　／ seizure 　／ "status quo" attacked

原文的这句话说得直白一点，就是美国人反对欧洲传统，要求剥夺财产、贪图劫掠和攻击社会，而反对稳定的社会模式。

意群训练： Fascination with this ideal has made Americans defy the "Old World" categories of settled possessiveness *versus* unsettling deprivation，the cupidity of retention *versus* the cupidity of seizure，a "status quo" defended or attacked.

序号：003

> The nonstarters were considered the ones who wanted stability, a strong referee to give them some position in the race, a regulative hand to calm manic speculation; an authority that can call things to a halt, begin things again from compensatorily staggered "starting lines."

难句类型： 复杂修饰＋省略　　　　**难度：** 3

标志： The nonstarters were considered the ones（ who wanted [1]stability，[2]*who wanted* a strong referee to give them some position in the race，[3]*who wanted* a regulative hand to calm manic speculation；[4]*who wanted* an authority that can call things to a halt，begin things again ／from compensatorily staggered "starting lines" ／）.

译文: <u>落伍者被认为是那些</u>（需要稳定的人，需要一个强有力的仲裁者来在竞赛中给他们一个位置；一只调节性的手来制止住狂热的投机；一个权威来让事情停止，／从一个补偿性错开的"起跑线"上／重新开始）。

解释: 主语nonstarter指那<u>些</u>在竞争中失败的人，英文释义为 someone or something that is not productive or effective；宾语 the ones 后面的、直到全句结束的以 who 引导的定语从句中出现了 4 个列举，来说明被修饰的 the ones 的特点。正如笔者在前面讲过的那样，ETS 的出题者在能用省略的地方都尽量的使用省略，因此后面的三个列举的前面都省略了与第一个列举中相同的 who wanted。

最后的列举中出现了一个词组：compensatorily staggered "starting lines"，指体育竞赛中的短跑的跑道上起跑时的错开的起跑线。这里用来比喻在竞争中处于不利位置的人希望得到一个对其更为有利的规则的帮助。

意群训练: <u>The nonstarters</u> <u>were considered</u> <u>the ones</u> <u>who wanted stability</u>, <u>a strong referee</u> <u>to give them</u> <u>some position</u> <u>in the race</u>, <u>a regulative hand</u> <u>to calm manic speculation</u>; <u>an authority that</u> <u>can call things</u> <u>to a halt</u>, <u>begin things again</u> <u>from compensatorily staggered "starting lines."</u>

序号: 004

> "Reform" in America has been sterile because it can imagine no change except through the extension of this metaphor of a race, wider inclusion of competitors, "a piece of the action," as it were, for the disenfranchised.

请思考: 如果这一句是接着上面所列的那个难句说下来的，那么本句中的"reform"和"change"指的是什么？

难句类型: 复杂修饰＋插入语＋省略＋双重否定　　　**难度**: 5[+]

标志: "<u>Reform</u>"（in America）<u>has been sterile</u> because <u>it</u> <u>can imagine</u> <u>no change</u>/except through the extension of this metaphor of a race/, *except through* wider inclusion of competitors/, *except through providing* "a piece of the action," <u>as it were,</u> for the disenfranchised. ／

译文：（在美国的）所谓的改革是无效的，因为这种改革不能构想出任何变化，/除了通过扩展这个比喻中的竞赛的范围/，/除了通过更广泛地包括竞争者/、/通过给这些没有发言权的人提供一个类似于"参加进来的机会"/。

解释：句子看起来不难，但是在文章中本句的含义极难读懂，是本文的核心难点。这种情况在阅读中极为常见，即如果读者的词汇功底不过关，及时读懂了字面含义，也无法理解句子的真正意图。因此，同学们应该按照笔者后面附录中所讲的"阅读抽象词提速法"对自己的词汇能力做系统的训练，以期为自己的阅读能力打下一个坚实的基础。

首先，本句中所指的 reform 和 change 都是指上一句中后面的四个列举，而后面所说的 disenfranchised 就是指上一个难句中的 nonstarters。本句是接着上一个难句，在说上个句子的结果：刚才说 nonstarters 在竞争中处处被动，因此希望有所变化，稳定下来、重新站位、重新开始；这句说的是这种理想与美国的实际情况的强烈反差：it can imagine no change 等于 it can not imagine any change，如果再加上 except through 就成了一个双重否定，等于在说 The only change the "Reform" can imagine is through……，实际上美国惟一的变化就是把更多的 nonstarter、disenfranchised 这些希望停下来的人卷入他们本来就不占优势的竞争中去，结果对他们而言只能是更为悲惨。这里我们就可以体会为什么作者会在 reform 上面加上一个引号：作者是想表示反语和讽刺，因为不但没有改革，反而是加剧了普遍人民群众的苦难。

本句后面的几个排比中都省略了与前面一样的 except through。句末的 as it were，是仿佛、好像的意思。

意群训练："Reform" in America has been sterile because it can imagine no change except through the extension of this metaphor of a race, wider inclusion of competitors, "a piece of the action," as it were, for the disenfranchised.

序号：005

> We have no pride in our growing interdependence, in the fact that our system can serve others, that we are able to help those in need; empty boasts from the past make us ashamed of our present achievements, make us try to forget or deny them, move away from them.

难句类型：省略 　　　　　**难度：4**

标志： We have no pride /in our growing interdependence/, *we have no pride* /in the fact（that our system can serve others）, */we have no pride* /in the fact（that we are able to help those in need）/; empty boasts（from the past）make us ashamed of our present achievements, make us try to forget or deny them, move away from them.

译文： /对于我们不断增加的相互依赖来讲/, 我们没有任何荣誉; /对于（我们的制度可以服务于他人的）这个事实/也没有任何荣誉; /对于（我们能够帮助那些有所需求的人）这个事实来讲, 也没有任何荣誉; （过去的）空洞吹嘘使得我们耻于目前的成就, 使得我们试图去忘记或否定它们, 摆脱它们。

解释： 本句中的省略逐渐越省越多、变本加厉：第一个逗号后面省略了与前面一样的主谓宾 *We have no pride*; 第二个逗号后面省略的内容进一步增加, 不但省略了第一个句子中的 *We have no pride*, 还省略了第二个短句中的 *in the fact*。

意群训练： We have no pride in our growing interdependence, in the fact that our system can serve others, that we are able to help those in need; empty boasts from the past make us ashamed of our present achievements, make us try to forget or deny them, move away from them.

序号：006

The traditional view supposes that the upper mantle of the earth behaves as a liquid when it is subjected to small forces for long periods and that differences in temperature under oceans and continents are sufficient to produce convection in the mantle of the earth with rising convection currents under the mid-ocean ridges and sinking currents under the continents.

难句类型：复杂修饰 + 专有名词 　　　　**难度：5**

标志： The traditional view supposes that the upper mantle of the earth behaves /as a liquid/ /when it is subjected to small forces for long periods/ **and** that differences（in temperature）（under oceans and continents）are sufficient to produce convection（in the mantle of the earth）/with rising convection currents under the mid-ocean ridges **and** sinking currents under the continents/.

译文： 传统观点认为，地球的上层地幔/当其长期受到小的压力的时候/，其行为/类似于液体/；而且认为（在海洋和大陆下地幔的）（温度的）不同足够产生（地球地幔中的）对流，/在中部海脊之下产生上升对流，在陆地下产生下降流/。

解释： 主句后面带着两个宾语从句，第二个从句离主句的谓语动词 supposes 比较远，这需要读者对读长句子有心理准备。后面这个从句的结构比较复杂，主语 differences 有两个修饰成分，把主语和谓语隔得比较远；with 之后的内容是修饰 produce 的方式状语。

另外本句中的专有名词也比较多，但是本句中的这些单词都是理科文章中的常用单词。

意群训练： The traditional view supposes that the upper mantle of the earth behaves as a liquid when it is subjected to small forces for long periods and that differences in temperature under oceans and continents are sufficient to produce convection in the mantle of the earth with rising convection currents under the mid-ocean ridges and sinking currents under the continents.

序号：007

This view may be correct: it has the advantage that the currents are driven by temperature differences that themselves depend on the position of the continents.

难句类型： 复杂修饰　　**难度：** 4

标志： This view may be correct: it has the advantage that the currents are driven by temperature differences（ that themselves depend on the position of the continents）.

译文： 这种观点可能正确：它有这样的优点，那就是这些流是被温度的不同所推动的，（而温度的不同本身又依赖于大陆板块的位置。）

解释： 本句是一个典型的例子。单词和句子似乎都可以看懂，但是句中所说的几样东西的关系却不一定能够一眼看出。所以请读者注意，读句子的时候不要光看句子的结构，大脑当中一定要去思考句子的含义。这就是笔者在讲课中所极力号召的边读、边想、边记忆的阅读原则。

本句冒号以后所说的 advantage 的具体内容在 advantage 的同位语从句中详细说明，即 currents 依赖 temperature differences，而 temperature differences 又依赖 position；实际的理解中需要把关系倒过来才能清晰地理解原文的因果关系，即：position 推出 temperature differences，后者又推出 currents。

意群训练： This view may be correct: it has the advantage that the currents are driven by temperature differences that themselves depend on the position of the continents.

序号：008

The enclosed seas are an important feature of the earth's surface and seriously require explanation because, in addition to the enclosed seas that are developing at present behind island arcs, there are a number of older ones of possibly similar origin, such as the Gulf of Mexico, the Black Sea, and perhaps the North Sea.

难句类型： 复杂修饰 + 插入语　　**难度：** 3[+]

标志： The enclosed seas are an important feature（of the earth's surface）**and** seriously require explanation / because, in addition to the enclosed seas（that are developing at present behind island arcs）, there are a number of older ones of possibly similar origin, such as the Gulf of Mexico, the Black Sea, and perhaps the North Sea/.

译文：内海是（地球表面的）一个重要特征，而且急需解释，/因为除了当前在弧状岛屿链之后发展的内海之外，还有一些更老的内海可能有相似的成因，比如墨西哥湾、黑海、甚至有可能北海都是如此。/

解释：主句是一个由 and 相连接的并列句。because 之后的所有内容都是主句的状语从句。然而 because 和在意思上与其连贯的 there are... 被比较长的插入语分割，容易使读者的思路不连续。不过本句在意思上不难，读者读起来不至于感到太困难。

意群训练：The enclosed seas are an important feature of the earth's surface and seriously require explanation because, in addition to the enclosed seas that are developing at present behind island arcs, there are a number of older ones of possibly similar origin, such as the Gulf of Mexico, the Black Sea, and perhaps the North Sea.

序号：009

Furthermore, neutrinos carry with them information about the site and circumstances of their production; therefore, the detection of cosmic neutrinos could provide new information about a wide variety of cosmic phenomena and about the history of the universe.

难句类型：复杂修饰 + 倒装　　　**难度**：4

标志：**Furthermore**, neutrinos carry /with them/ information（about the site and circumstances of their production）：**therefore**, the detection of cosmic neutrinos could provide new information（about a wide variety of cosmic phenomena）**and**（about the history of the universe）.

译文：而且，中微子携带了（一些关于其产生的地点和环境的）信息/在其身上/，因此，对中微子的探测能够提供（关于广泛的宇宙现象）和（宇宙历史的）新信息。

解释：本句的惟一难点就是句首出现的倒装：neutrinos carry /with them/ information （about the site and circumstances of their production）的正常语序应该是neutrinos carry information（about the site and circumstances of their production）/with them/。类似本句的结构，其实读者能否快速读懂的关键，就在于笔者前面所讲的大脑是否熟悉这种语序的问题。大家所要做的就是通过多读、熟读、反复读，使大脑能够习惯这种语序，形成下意识的迅速而准确的反应。

意群训练：Furthermore, neutrinos carry with them information about the site and circumstances of their production：therefore, the detection of cosmic neutrinos could provide new information about a wide variety of cosmic phenomena and about the history of the universe.

序号：010

> Consequently, nothing seems good or normal that does not accord with the requirements of the free market.

请思考：Please read between lines. What does the author really mean?

难句类型：倒装 + 双重否定（正话反说）   **难度**：4⁺

标志：**Consequently**, nothing seems good or normal （that does not accord with the requirements of the free market）.

译文：因此，没有任何（不符合自由市场要求的）东西看上去是好的或正常的。

解释：又是一句似易实难的句子。本句的主语 nothing 的定语从句被倒装到了句末，是因为如果按照正常语序 nothing （that does not accord with the requirements of the free market） seems good or normal 显得头重脚轻。

除此之外，本句由于使用了双重否定，句子的意思也不象看起来那么简单。字面上的"没有任何（不符合自由市场要求的）东西看上去是好的或正常的"对读者来讲没有确实的意义，读者一定要理解到实际上作者想说的是"只有符合自由市场的东西才有可能是好的或是正常的"。

意群训练：Consequently, nothing seems good or normal that does not accord with the requirements of the free market.

序号：011

> Accordingly, it requires a major act of will to think of price-fixing (the determination of prices by the seller) as both "normal" and having a valuable economic function.

难句类型：插入语 + 正话反说　　　　**难度**：4 +

标志：**Accordingly**, it requires a major act of will to **think of** price-fixing (the determination of prices by the seller) /**as** both "normal" and having a valuable economic function/.

译文：因此，需要下很大的决心才能把"p-f"（由卖方决定价格）想成是既正常又有着有意义的经济功能的。

解释：it 是形式主语，其真正的内容在 to 后面的不定式中。to **think of** something **as** thing 的固定搭配被插入语(the determination of prices by the seller) 隔开，而且此处的插入语又比较重要，因为它约定了此处的 price-fixing 并不是我们熟知的普通的定价，而特指卖方定价。

这句话的叙述又是一个正话反说：需要下很大的决心才能把由卖方定价看成是既正常的而且有意义的，其实际意义就是：一般来说，卖方定价是不正常的而且是没有意义。

意群训练：Accordingly, it requires a major act of will to think of price-fixing (the determination of prices by the seller) as both "normal" and having a valuable economic function.

序号：012

> In fact, price-fixing is normal in all industrialized societies because the industrial system itself provides, as an effortless consequence of its own development, the price-fixing that it requires.

请思考：句末的 it 指什么？工业社会和卖方定价的关系又是什么？

难句类型：复杂修饰 + 易混指代　　　　难度：4

标志：In fact, price-fixing is normal /in all industrialized societies/ /because the industrial system itself provides, as an effortless consequence of its own development, the price-fixing (that it requires).

译文：实际上，/在所有的工业化社会当中/卖方定价都是正常的，/因为工业制度本身就提供了（作为其自身发展的自然而然的结果的）（它所需要的）卖方定价/。

解释：由于以 because 引导的原因状语从句的结构较为复杂，尤其是最后的修饰宾语 price-fixing 的定语从句中的 it 所代表的事物难以确定，因此 industrial system 和 price-fixing 的关系也就很难一下子看清。

it 之前的名词很多，从语法上来讲既有可能指 price-fixing，有又可能指 industrial system 或 development。但是从句意和逻辑上来讲，it 只能指 industrial system。需要提醒读者的是，在阅读中看到一眼读不懂的东西的时候，与其去分析句子的语法结构，还不如通过理解句子的意思来得准确和迅速。

本句所表达的意思是：卖方定价正常，因为卖方定价既是工业制度的必然结果又是其必要条件；亦即有工业制度必有卖方定价。

意群训练：In fact, price-fixing is normal in all industrialized societies because the industrial system itself provides, as an effortless consequence of its own development, the price-fixing that it requires.

序号：013

That each large firm will act with consideration of its own needs and thus avoid selling its products for more than its competitors charge' is commonly recognized by advocates of free-market economic theories.

难句类型： 复杂修饰　　　　**难度：** 4

标志： [That] each large firm will act /with consideration of its own needs/ **and thus** avoid selling its products for more than its competitors' charge is commonly recognized /by advocates of free-market economic theories/.

译文： 每一个大公司都将/考虑到其自身的需求/，而且这样就会避免比其竞争对手把其商品卖得更贵，这一点通常被/自由市场的经济理论的支持者/所认识到。

解释： 本句一开始就是一个 that 引导的主语从句，而且因为它是由表示并列和递进的 **and thus** 连接的两个句子组成的，因此出奇地长，造成的结果就是不熟悉难句结构的读者读到后面的 is commonly recognized by 的时候，已经搞不清楚是什么被认识到了。

意群训练： That each large firm will act with consideration of its own needs and thus avoid selling its products for more than its competitors' charge is commonly recognized by advocates of free-market economic theories.

序号： 014

> Moreover, those economists who argue that allowing the free market to operate without interference is the most efficient method of establishing prices have not considered the economies of nonsocialist countries other than the United States.

难句类型： 复杂修饰＋插入语　　　　**难度：** 4

标志： **Moreover,** those economists [[who] argue [that] allowing the free market to operate /without interference/ is the most efficient method (of establishing prices)] have not considered the economies [of nonsocialist countries (other than the United States)].

译文： 而且，那些［认为允许自由市场不受干扰地运作是最为有效的（定价）手段的］经济学家们没有考虑到［（除了美国以外的）其他的非社会主义国家的］经济。

解释： 句子的主语those economists被一个很长且很复杂的定语从句修饰，定语从句中又套了一个宾语从句；宾语从句的主语又是一个很长的动名词 allowing the free market to operate without interference，这种层层修饰的结果，就是读者读到句子的真正谓语have not considered 的时候早就把句子的真正主语those economists忘得一干二净了。

造成这种情况的原因有两个，一是这种结构读得少，二是对长句子没有足够的心理预期。解决的办法就是笔者前面反复强调过的训练方法：反复读。后面的讲解不再重复这一点。

意群训练： Moreover, those economists who argue that allowing the free market to operate without interference is the most efficient method of establishing prices have not considered the economies of nonsocialist countries other than the United States.

序号：015

Synder, Daly, and Bruns have recently proposed that caffeine affects behavior by countering the activity in the human brain of a naturally occurring chemical called a-denosine.

难句类型： 复杂修饰＋插入语　　　**难度：** 4⁺

标志： Synder, Daly, and Bruns have recently proposed that caffeine affects behavior / by countering the **activity**（in the human brain）［**of** a naturally occurring chemical（called a-denosine）］/.

译文： Synder、Daly、Bruns 等人近来提出，咖啡因影响人类行为/的方式，是通过抵消（人类大脑中的）［一种自然产生的（叫做 adenosine 的）化合物的］行为/。

解释： 由 that 所引导的宾语从句中的主谓宾都比较简单易懂，而由 by 所引导的作状语的介词结构却很复杂。尤其是 the activity of 被起修饰作用的插入语 in the human brain 切割成the **activity**（in the human brain）［**of...**，初学者读上去会感到很不习惯。

意群训练： Synder，Daly，and Bruns have recently proposed that caffeine affects behavior by countering the activity in the human brain of a naturally occurring chemical called adenosine.

序号：016

> To buttress their case that caffeine acts instead by preventing adenosine binding，Snyder et al compared the stimulatory effects of a series of caffeine derivatives with their ability to dislodge adenosine from its receptors in the brains of mice.

难句类型： 复杂修饰　　　**难度：**5

标志： /To buttress their case（ that caffeine acts /instead by preventing adenosine binding/ ）/，Snyder et al **compared** the stimulatory effects（of a series of caffeine derivatives）**with** their ability（to dislodge adenosine from its receptors in the brains of mice）.

译文： /为了支持他们所说的情况，（ 即 咖啡因/相反是通过防止 adenosine 的附着/而起作用的）/，Snyder 等人比较了（一系列的咖啡因的衍生物的）刺激性效果与它们（在老鼠大脑中把 adenosine 从其接受器上除去）的能力。

解释： 在本句中，逗号以后的主句难以看懂。首先，被 compare... with... 用来比较的双方的语言描述不但复杂，而且充斥着种种专有名词；而且，由于我们以前常见的以 compare... with... 相比较的双方都是不同的事物，而这里比较的是相同事物（caffeine derivatives）的不同类型的效果，因此在读这句话的时候，我们容易钻到"这两者间有可比性吗？"的牛角尖中。其实类似的考虑在现场纯属多余；既然在文章当中出现了这么个比较，就意味着这种语言的表述一定是不存在错误的。读者在阅读现场，特别是 GMAT 考试中遇到这种情况，即对于现场实在无法理解的东西，可以适当往下读上一两句再做理解，往往作者会在下面的叙述中揭开谜底，本句也是如此。

在原文中再往下面读一句话，大家即可发现，本句的 compare... with... 的用法怪异！因为作者比较的并不是 the stimulatory effects of a series of caffeine derivatives 和 their ability to dislodge adenosine from its receptors in the brains of mice 这二者之间的不同，而是在比较有着不同的 stimulatory effects 的不同 caffeine derivatives 之间，其在除去 adenosine 的能力上有何不同，从而找出能够"buttress their case"的规律性来。这里的细微之处不太容易说清楚，请允许笔者对原文做一个类比：

为了证明我的"辣椒是凭借其辣味来使人流泪的"这样一个观点，我 **compared** 各种辣椒使人流泪的效果 **with** 它们的辣味刺激我的味觉的效果。结果我发现，在各种不同的辣椒当中，辣椒的辣味刺激我的效果越强，则我哭得越伤心，这不就验证了我的观点吗？

作为一种高级英语的阅读材料，GRE 和 GMAT 考试中会出现大量的非常规或不常见的生僻的英语用法，请读者注意根据上下文的内容灵活地判断其含义。

意群训练： To buttress their case that caffeine acts instead by preventing adenosine binding, Snyder et al compared the stimulatory effects of a series of caffeine derivatives with their ability to dislodge adenosine from its receptors in the brains of mice.

序号：017

The problem is that the compound has mixed effects in the brain, a not unusual occurrence with psychoactive drugs.

难句类型： 双重否定　　　　**难度：** 3⁻

标志： The problem is that the compound has mixed effects in the brain, (a not unusual occurrence with psychoactive drugs).

译文： 问题是这种化合物在大脑中有着混合的效果，（这对神经刺激药物来讲并不是一个少见的现象）。

解释： 本句非常简单，而且后面的双重否定的语言形式在中文当中也十分常见：我们说"这并不少见"，其实际意思就是"这很常见"。但是笔者仍然在此列出本句，是因为作为一种在 GRE 和 GMAT 考试中经常出现的独特的语言现象，双重否定对于考生的阅读速度和理解上的正确性都形成了较大的威胁，而读者惟一的克服这种威胁的办法就是多练。

意群训练：The problem is that the compound has mixed effects in the brain，a not unusual occurrence with psychoactive drugs.

序号：018

> Who would want an unmarked pot when another was available whose provenance was known，and that was dated stratigraphically by the professional archaeologist who excavated it?

难句类型：复杂修饰 + 倒装　　　**难度**：4⁻

标志： Who would want an unmarked pot ／ when another was available（whose provenance was known，）**and** ［ that was dated ／stratigraphically by the professional archaeologist（who excavated it）／］／?

译文：／当（出处已知、）并［已经/被（挖掘了它的）职业考古学家通过地层分析法/确定了其年代的］别的陶罐能够被得到的时候/， 谁会去想要那些没有标记的瓶瓶罐罐呢？

解释：本句中从 when 开始的状语从句的结构稍有些复杂。其中的主语 another 的修饰成分太长，被倒装到谓语和宾语的后面。其实我们一旦习惯了这种倒装就会觉得它很舒服，否则如果不倒装，如下面的样子，句子会更难懂：

Who would want an unmarked pot ／ when another（whose provenance was known，）**and** ［ that was dated ／stratigraphically by the professional archaeologist（who excavated it）／］／ was available?

这个句子显得头重脚轻，而且状语从句中的主语过长，其中还包含着两重修饰成分，难免读到最后的<u>was available</u>？的时候不知所云。

意群训练：<u>Who would want</u> an unmarked pot when another <u>was available</u> whose prove-nance <u>was known</u>, and that <u>was dated</u> stratigraphically by the professional archaeologist who <u>excavated it</u>?

序号：019

Federal efforts to aid minority businesses began in the 1960's when the Small Business Administration (SBA) be-gan making federally guaranteed loans and government-sponsored management and technical assistance available to minority business enterprises.

难句类型: 复杂修饰　　　**难度:** 5

标志: Federal efforts（to aid minority businesses） began /in the 1960's// when the Small Business Administration (SBA) began **making** federally guaranteed loans **and** gov-ernment-sponsored management **and** technical assistance **available** to minority business enter-prises/.

译文:（帮助少数民族企业的）*联邦政府的努力开始*/于 20 世纪 60 年代/，/那时*小企业管理机构*（简称 SBA）开始使得联邦担保的贷款和政府资助的管理以及技术援助能够为少数民族企业所用。

解释: 在以 when 所引导的状语从句中，begin doing something 是我们熟知的结构，然而 make 的宾语不但很长，而且出现了两个相邻的 and 连接了三个并列的成分，似乎是明显违反语法规则的（按照正常的语法来说，应该是 A，B，and C 这样的结构），可是本句中的情况却不违反语法，因为这两个 and 不是同一个层面的东西：第二个 and 连接的 government-sponsored management **and** technical assistance 是政府的两个资助，而第一个 and 是连接前面的联邦资助和后面的政府资助，也就是说由于在美国联邦和政府不是一回事，所以第一个 and 的层面要高于第二个 and。

本句另外的一个令人难以读懂的地方就在于，由于 make 的宾语过长，所以 make something available 这个固定搭配被分开很远，让人读不出前后的联系。

意群训练：Federal efforts to aid minority businesses began in the 1960's when the Small Business Administration (SBA) began making federally guaranteed loans and government-sponsored management and technical assistance available to minority business enterprises.

序号：020

> Recently federal policymakers have adopted an approach intended to accelerate development of the minority business sector by moving away from directly aiding small minority enterprises and toward supporting larger, growth-oriented minority firms through intermediary companies.

难句类型：复杂修饰 + 固定搭配　　　　**难度：**4

标志：Recently federal policymakers have adopted an approach（intended to accelerate development of the minority business sector /by **moving away from** directly aiding small minority enterprises **and toward** supporting larger, growth-oriented minority firms /through intermediary companies/ /）.

译文：近来的联邦政策的制定者们采用了一个方法，（其目的是要/通过从直接帮助小的少数民族企业的方式/借助于居间的公司/转移到支持更大的、成长性好的少数民族企业的方式来/加速少数民族企业的发展）。

解释：intended to 及其后的一直延续到句末的分词结构是 an approach 的后置定语。问题是这个定语太长，而且包含着长长的状语，没有练过难句的人是很难一眼读懂的。其难懂之处还在于句中的那个被分割开的固定搭配，moving away from... and toward..., 是从……转移到……的意思。

意群训练：Recently federal policymakers have adopted an approach intended to accelerate development of the minority business sector by moving away from directly aiding small minority enterprises and toward supporting larger, growth-oriented minority firms through inter-mediary companies.

序号：**021**

> MESBIC's are the result of the belief that providing established firms with easier access to relevant management techniques and more job-specific experience, as well as substantial amounts of capital, gives those firms a greater opportunity to develop sound business foundations than does simply making general management experience and small amounts of capital available.

难句类型：复杂修饰　　　难度：5

标志： MESBIC's are the result of the belief [that **providing** established firms **with easier access** (to relevant management techniques and more job-specific experience, as well as substantial amounts of capital,) gives those firms a **greater** opportunity (to develop sound business foundations) /**than** does simply making general management experience and small amounts of capital available/].

译文： MESBIC 是这样一种理念的结果，即 提供给健全的公司以更容易得到的（相关的管理技术和更为专业的经验以及大量的资金的）途径这种做法，比仅仅提供大众化的管理经验和少量资金会给那些公司以更大的（发展出健全的商业基础的）可能性。

解释： 主句的宾语 the result of the belief 之后跟着一个长达六行的、延续到句末的由 that 引导的修饰 belief 的同位语从句。从句中的由动名词充当的主语又极长：**providing** established firms **with** easier access (to relevant management techniques and more job-specific experience, as well as substantial amounts of capital)，其中 to relevant 之后的内容是修饰 access 的定语。谓语 gives 之后又是一个双宾语 those firms a **greater** opportunity (to develop sound business foundations)，然后是与 **greater** 相配对的比较的后项 **than**

does simply making...。整个同位语从句的结构其实并不太复杂，就是：**A gives those firms a greater opportunity than does B**，但是因为这里的 A 和 B 都是既长又复杂，opportunity 后面还有不定式作定语，这使得整个句子的阅读难度大大提高。

意群训练： MESBIC's are the result of the belief that providing established firms with easier access to relevant management techniques and more job-specific experience, as well as substantial amounts of capital, gives those firms a greater opportunity to develop sound business foundations than does simply making general management experience and small amounts of capital available.

序号：022

> Most senior executives are familiar with the formal decision analysis models and tools, and those who use such systematic methods for reaching decisions are occasionally leery of solutions suggested by these methods which run counter to their sense of the correct course of action.

难句类型：复杂修饰   **难度：4ˉ**

标志： Most senior executives are familiar with the formal decision analysis models and tools, **and** those（who use such systematic methods for reaching decisions）**are** occasionally **leery of** solutions［suggested by these methods（which run counter to their sense of the correct course of action）］.

译文： 大多数的高级经理人员们是熟悉这些正式的决策分析的模型和方法的，而且那些（使用这种系统方法来做出决定的）*经理们*不时地会警觉于［那些通过这些方法而得出的（与他们自己的对于正确行动方案的感觉相反的）］解决方案。

解释： 先解释一个词：leery 是形容词，指狡猾的，机警的。be leery of 指对某物或某事保持警惕。

整个句子是以 **and** 相连接的两个并列的复合句。后面的句子相对较难读懂，除了刚才的词组有可能不认识之外，本句的主语和 are 后面的表语都比较长，尤其是 are leery of 后面的介词宾语 solutions，又带了一个两重的定语修饰：［suggested by these methods（which run counter to their sense of the correct course of action）］

意群训练： Most senior executives are familiar with the formal decision analysis models and tools，and those who use such systematic methods for reaching decisions are occasionally leery of solutions suggested by these methods which run counter to their sense of the correct course of action.

序号：023

> But the debate could not be resolved because no one was able to ask the crucial questions in a form in which they could be pursued productively.

请思考： 如果本句的下一句是："Recent discoveries in molecular biology，however，have opened up prospects for a resolution of the debate."，则能否用合理化原则推出本句所说的 debate could not be resolved 的原因是什么？

难句类型： 复杂修饰 + 抽象词 + 抽象句意　　　**难度：** 5

标志： **But** the debate could not be resolved／ because no one was able to ask the crucial questions ／in a form（in which they could be pursued productively）／／.

译文： 但是这个争论没法被解决，／ 因为 没有人能够提出一些重要的问题，／以一个（使得这些问题能够被有效地研究的）形式／／。

解释： 请原谅笔者在本书的翻译中所使用的这些颠三倒四的中文语序，笔者做出此痛苦的抉择完全是为了使中文的翻译尽量可以对应上面的英文标志。

本句的语言结构不难，相信大家看了上面的标志就能够自己搞清楚。但是本句的意思却极难理解。首先，pursue 这个单词我们常见，但是在本句中的意思却不容易理解，这就是笔者所说的"抽象词"的特征之一。这种单词一旦出现在阅读中，读者只知道其中文释义"追求"是不行的，而需要迅速地反应出其含义。具体的训练方法，请见后面的附录。在这里其意思是 to proceed along, follow, or continue with（a specified course, action, plan, etc.），联系到本句的实际，对一些问题的 pursue 肯定是去研究它们、跟踪它们来找到线索。

本句的句意之所以难以理解，还在于我们以前所养成的对英文的阅读习惯是只被动地接受文章的语言，而不对它在大脑中主动地加以处理。请记住，不论是中文阅读还是英语阅读，不加思考的阅读永远是无效的阅读！尤其是在 GRE 和 GMAT 的阅读当中，思维的过程是至关重要的。如本句中的 crucial questions 在这里绝对不是那些真正意义上的"问题"，决不是句首的 debate 的同义词；请想一想，我们为什么要提出这些 **crucial** questions？如句中所说，问题提不出来，则 debate 解决不了，那么这些 **crucial** questions 就是……解决这个 debate 的途径。

当然，这里面还有一个很重要的问题，那就是在 GRE 和 GMAT 这些高级英语的阅读中有一个 crucial question 不一定是 question 的现象，笔者称之为"白马非马"。限于本书的篇幅，笔者在此不能详述，只有在另外一本综述 GRE 和 GMAT 阅读方法的书中详细地介绍这个微妙的概念。不过在阅读此篇文章当中，既使读者没有读懂本句，也可以通过下面的一句话用合理化原则推理出本句的意思：Recent discoveries in molecular biology, however, have opened up prospects for a resolution of the debate。现在有了新的研究手段，就能解决 debate 了，意味着刚才的问题就是没有研究手段，缺乏研究途径。这篇文章后面对此句出了一道题，如果读者不能真正看懂本句的意思，那道题是做不对的。

意群训练： But the debate could not be resolved because no one was able to ask the crucial questions in a form in which they could be pursued productively.

序号：024

> During the nineteenth century, she argues, the concept of the "useful" child who contributed to the family economy gave way gradually to the present-day notion of the "useless" child who, though producing no income for, and indeed extremely costly to, its parents, is yet considered emotionally "priceless."

难句类型： 复杂修饰＋插入语　　　**难度：**5

标志：／During the nineteenth century／，she argues，the concept ［of the "useful" child（who contributed to the family economy）］**gave way** gradually **to** the present-day notion ［of the "useless" child（[who]，／**though** producing no income for，and indeed extremely costly to，its parents，／is **yet** considered emotionally "priceless"）］.

译文：／在 19 世纪当中／，她说，［（对于家庭的经济能够起到贡献的）"有用的"小孩］这个观念逐渐地让位于今天的观念，［即：无用的小孩，（[这个孩子]，／尽管不但不会为父母带来任何收入，而且实际上对于父母来说还极其费钱，／仍然被认为在感情上是"无价的"）］。

解释：本句虽然看上去吓人，可是实际上结构很简单：The concept A gave way to concept B。但是由于句子中间夹杂了大量的定语、状语和插入语，把个好好的句子给搞得支离破碎、乱七八糟。然而平心而论，就本句所传达的信息量而言，如果不使用这些修饰成分，确实也无法以如此小的篇幅运载如此大的信息。因此，GRE 和 GMAT 考试的阅读中尽管确实有些人为的、以吓倒考生为目的的难句，但绝大多数的难句既是高级英语文章本身的需要，也是出题者改编、压缩文章的需要。

本句的主干 The concept A gave way to concept B 当中，**gave way to** 这个词组的意思是前者让位于后者。concept A 的语言描述相对简单：the concept ［of the "useful" child（who contributed to the family economy）］，虽然也是复杂修饰，但是一遍还是可以读下来的。concept B 就复杂了，先是有一个 who 引导的定语从句修饰它，然后又在从句中使用了一个表示让步的状语／**though** producing no income for，and indeed extremely costly to，its parents，／，其中还包括了一个插入语，起到了严重干扰读者的作用。

意群训练：During the nineteenth century，she argues，the concept of the "useful" child who contributed to the family economy gave way gradually to the present-day notion of the "useless" child who，though producing no income for，and indeed extremely costly to，its parents，is yet considered emotionally "priceless."

序号：025

Well established among segments of the middle and upper classes by the mid-1800's，this new view of childhood spread throughout society in the late-nineteenth and early-twentieth centuries as reformers introduced child-labor regulations and compulsory education laws predicated in part on the assumption that a child's emotional value made child labor taboo.

难句类型：复杂修饰　　　　难度：5

标志：/Well established among segments of the middle and upper classes by the mid-1800's, / this new view of childhood spread /throughout society/ /in the late-nineteenth and early-twentieth centuries/ /as reformers introduced child-labor regulations and compulsory education laws [predicated /in part on the assumption (that a child's emotional value made child-labor taboo)] /.

译文：/已经牢牢地在 18 世纪的中期在中产阶级和上流社会中确立, /这个新观点/在 19 世纪末和 20 世纪初/传遍了/整个社会/; /当时改革者们引入了童工法和义务教育法, [其出现/是部分地基于这样一个前提, (那就是孩子的感情价值使得童工被禁止)] /。

解释：本句与上一句一样, 也是用最小的篇幅传递了最多的信息。句子的主干就是this new view of childhood spread, 但是作者通过其前和其后的四个状语, 全面地概括了新观点 (this new view) 的产生和发展的整个社会背景。

需要重点解释一下的是最后的这个由 as 引导的状语从句: /as reformers introduced child-labor regulations and compulsory education laws [predicated /in part on the assumption (that a child's emotional value made child labor taboo)] /。在此从句中修饰作为从句宾语的两种法律的从 predicated /in part... 开始直到句末的分词结构, 都用作两种法的定语。predicate A on/upon B 这一搭配的意思是 "以 B 作为 A 的基础" 或 "依据 B 提出 A"。

意群训练：Well established among segments of the middle and upper classes by the mid-1800's, this new view of childhood spread throughout society in the late-nineteenth and early-twentieth centuries <u>as reformers introduced</u> <u>child-labor regulations</u> <u>and compulsory education</u> <u>laws</u> <u>predicated in part</u> <u>on the assumption</u> <u>that a child's</u> <u>emotional value</u> <u>made child labor ta-</u> <u>boo.</u>

序号：026

> "Expulsion of children from the 'cash nexus'... although clearly shaped by profound changes in the economic, occupational, and family structures," Zelizer maintains, "was also part of a cultural process of 'sacralization' of children's lives."

难句类型：插入语 + 倒装　　　　**难度**：5⁻

标志：**Yet** "expulsion of children from the 'cash nexus'... /**although** clearly shaped by profound changes in the economic, occupational, and family structures," / Zelizer maintains, "was also part of a cultural process of 'sacralization' of children's lives."

译文：然而"把儿童从'金钱关系'中排除出去……/尽管是明确地被经济、职业和家庭结构的深刻变化所塑造的，/" Zelizer 认为，"但这也是把儿童的生命神圣化的文化进程的一部分。"

解释：在本句中，文章的作者引用了 Zelizer 的一段原话，造成了大量的插入语和语序颠倒。因为作者的引用是有目的性的，因此对 Z 的语言有删节，而且还要按照 Zelizer 原话说的顺序来讲，所以不是正常语序。如果是不加引用的正常的语序应该是：

Zelizer maintains that although expulsion of children from the "cash nexus" is clearly shaped by profound changes in the economic, occupational, and family structures, it was also part of a cultural process of "sacralization" of children's lives.

如果是加以引用但不必按照原话的顺序，则这句话又应该是：

Zelizer maintains, "although clearly shaped by profound changes in the economic, occupational, and family structures, expulsion of children from the 'cash nexus'... was also part of a cultural process of 'sacralization' of children's lives. "

文章为了照顾 Zelizer 的原话的顺序，把表示让步的状语 although clearly shaped... 倒装到了主语之后。

意群训练："Expulsion of children from the 'cash nexus'... although clearly shaped by profound changes in the economic, occupational, and family structures," Zelizer maintains, was also part of a cultural process of 'sacralization' of children's lives. "

序号：027

Protecting children from the crass business world became enormously important for late-nineteenth-century middle-class Americans, she suggests; this sacralization was a way of resisting what they perceived as the relentless corruption of human values by the marketplace.

难句类型：复杂修饰 + 插入语　　**难度**：4⁻

标志：**Protect**ing children **from** the crass business world became enormously important /for late-nineteenth-century middle-class Americans,/ she suggests; this sacralization was a way (of resisting what they perceived as the relentless corruption of human values by the marketplace).

译文：保护儿童不受充满铜臭气的商业世界的影响 这一点/对于 19 世纪末的美国中产阶级来说/变得极其重要，她说；这种神圣化是一个（抵抗那种被他们视为是市场无情地毁坏了人的价值的现象的）手段。

解释：本句的做主语的动名词结构一上来就很长。分号后面的句子中，a way of 的宾语又是一个动名词结构，其中 resist 的宾语还是一个由 what 引导的名词性从句。对于 corruption 的词义，我们通常只知道"腐败"这个意思，而在此处的意思是 impairment of integrity，virtue，or moral principle，即对人在品行上的伤害或损害。

意群训练：<u>Protecting children from</u> <u>the crass business world</u> <u>became</u> enormously important for <u>late-nineteenth-century</u> <u>middle-class Americans</u>，<u>she suggests</u>；<u>this sacralization</u> was a way of resisting <u>what they perceived</u> as the <u>relentless corruption</u> of <u>human values</u> by the <u>market-place</u>.

序号：028

> The factors favoring unionization drives seem to have been either the presence of large numbers of workers，as in New York City，to make it worth the effort，or the concentration of small numbers in one or two locations，such as a hospital，to make it relatively easy.

难句类型：复杂修饰 + 插入语 + 抽象词　　　　**难度：**4

标志：<u>The factors</u>（favoring unionization drives）<u>seem</u> to have <u>been</u> **either** <u>the presence</u> <u>of large numbers of workers</u>，as in New York City，（to make it worth the effort），**or** <u>the concentration</u> <u>of small numbers</u>（in one or two locations，<u>such as a hospital</u>），（to make it relatively easy）.

译文：（有利于工会组织形成的）因素看起来或者是大量的工人的出现，比如在纽约这样的城市，（使得这种努力值得）；或者是少量的集中（于一两个地方的人，比如医院这种地方），（使其相对较为容易）。

解释：句子的主架构简单，就是 the factors have been either A or B；但是句中对 factors 和 A、B 都加了大量的修饰成分，使得句子变得很长、很复杂。

首先，修饰主语 the factors 的定语中的 drives 在此不是我们通常所知的动词用法，而是作名词，指某种群体性运动或过程，其英文释义为 a strong systematic group effort ＜ a fund-raising drive ＞，同义词是 ENTERPRISE。后面的用 either... or... 连接起来的两种情况中，各有一个插入语作例子，之后又各有一个不定式作插入语前面的情况的后置定语。

需要提醒读者的是，笔者在此所作的语法分析的目的，仍是为了使大家把句子看懂；而一旦看懂之后，就要坚决地抛弃语法分析这一工具；永远不要忘了你阅读的惟一目的，就是在阅读现场迅速地将所读内容看懂。也不要忘了本书的对难句的训练方法，是反复阅读这些难句而不是反复分析这些语法。笔者之所以再次罗嗦此点，实在是担忧本书会给大家带来副作用，以后不再重复。

意群训练： The factors favoring unionization drives seem to have been either the presence of large numbers of workers, as in New York City, to make it worth the effort, or the concentration of small numbers in one or two locations, such as a hospital, to make it relatively easy.

序号：029

Individual entrepreneurs do not necessarily rely on their kin because they cannot obtain financial backing from commercial resources.

难句类型： 倒装 + 双重否定　　　　**难度：** 5

标志： Individual entrepreneurs do not necessarily rely on their kin / because they cannot obtain financial backing from commercial resources/.

译文： 个人企业主不一定是因为他们不能从商业机构那里得到财政支持，才去依赖他们的亲属的。

解释： 相信在没有考过 GRE、GMAT、LSAT 或者练过难句的人当中，绝大多数人会把上面的这句话理解成：

因为个人企业主们不能从商业机构那里得到财政支持，所以他们不一定去依赖他们的亲属。

句意变得荒谬之极，简直不像是正常人类的思维。难怪有人说 GRE 和 GMAT 的阅读不是正常人读的东西。其实本句是一个倒装，because 引导的状语从句被倒装到句末，而正常的语序应该是：Individual entrepreneurs do not necessarily because they cannot obtain financial backing from commercial resources rely on their kin，但是这样的语言同样很蹩脚。作者为了使句子的结构看上去舒服一点，不得不采用现在这样的结构，这也是压缩原文的需要。不信请读者试一下，还用现在的句子长度，如果用清楚的语言来表达，你能够做到吗？

本句还有一个比较简单的双重否定，即"不一定是因为他们不能从商业机构那里得到财政支持，才去依赖他们的亲属"的意思是即使可以得到商业贷款，也可能去找亲属借钱。

意群训练：Individual entrepreneurs do not necessarily rely on their kin because they cannot obtain financial backing from commercial resources.

序号：030

> Since large bees are not affected by the spraying of Matacil，these results add weight to the argument that spraying where the pollinators are sensitive to the pesticide used decreases plant fecundity.

难句类型：复杂修饰　　　难度：5

标志： Since large bees are not affected /by the spraying of Matacil/，these results **add weight /to** the argument ｛ that spraying ［where the pollinators are sensitive to the pesticide （used）］ decreases plant fecundity｝/.

译文： 由于大蜜蜂不受/Matacil 的喷洒的/影响，这些结果加重了/这样一个论点的力度，｛那就是 ［在传粉的昆虫对（被使用的）杀虫剂敏感的地区］ 喷洒杀虫剂，会减少植物的结实性｝/。

解释：前面的由 Since 引导的状语从句简单，复杂的是逗号后面的部分：**add weight to** 这个词组的意思类似于中文所说的"给……增加了力度"。the argument 后面一直到本句结束都是 argument 的同位语从句；从句中的主语 spraying 之后又带了一个 where 引导的状语从句，其中的最后一个单词 used 实际上是前面的 pesticide 的定语，意思是被使用的杀虫剂。但是 used 在句中与 decreases 连用，让人看不出到底那个才是同位语从句的谓语动词。本句是典型的层层修饰。

意群训练： <u>Since large bees</u> <u>are not affected by</u> <u>the spraying of Matacil</u>，<u>these results</u> <u>add</u> <u>weight to</u> <u>the argument that</u> <u>spraying</u> <u>where the pollinators</u> <u>are sensitive to</u> <u>the pesticide used</u> <u>decreases plant fecundity.</u>

序号：031

> The question of whether the decrease in plant fecundity caused by the spraying of pesticides actually causes a decline in the overall population of flowering plant species still remains unanswered.

难句类型： 复杂修饰　　**难度：** 5

标志： The question ｛of ｜whether｜ the decrease（in plant fecundity）（caused by the spraying of pesticides）<u>actually causes</u> a <u>decline</u> ［in the overall population（of flowering plant species）］｝｝ <u>still remains</u> <u>unanswered.</u>

译文： ｛｜是否｜（由于杀虫剂的喷洒造成的）（植物结实性的）下降<u>真的引起了</u> ＼［（开花植物品种的）整体种群数量的］下降｝这个问题<u>仍未解决</u>。

解释： 主语 question 后面是几乎横贯整句的修饰 question 的同位语，将主语和系动词 remains 分成牛郎织女。同位语中的主语又是由一个 whether 所引导的名词性从句来充当，而且 whether 从句中的主语又非常长，由两个定语来修饰；宾语 decline 的修饰成分也不短，使得这个句子看起来很不舒服。本句如果用形式主语的方式大概看上去可以好一点：

It remains still unanswered whether the decrease in plant fecundity caused by the spraying of pesticides actually causes a decline in the overall population of flowering plant species.

不过即使是这么说，句子仍然很复杂。

意群训练： The question of whether the decrease in plant fecundity caused by the spraying of pesticides actually causes a decline in the overall population of flowering plant species still remains unanswered.

序号：032

> Although at first the colonies held little positive attraction for the English——they would rather have stayed home——by the eighteenth century people increasingly migrated to America because they regarded it as the land of opportunity.

难句类型：插入语 + 省略　　　　**难度：3⁺**

标志：Although at first the colonies **held** little positive **attraction for** the English——they would rather have stayed home—— **but** /by the eighteenth century/ people increasingly migrated to America / because they regarded it as the land of opportunity/.

译文： /尽管一开始殖民地对英国人来说没有什么正面的吸引力——他们更愿意呆在家里/——可是/到了 18 世纪的时候/人们越来越多地移民到美国，/因为他们认为那是一片充满机会的土地/。

解释： 对于阅读能力尚未过关的同学来讲，本句有两个容易理解错的地方：一个是前面让步的这句话中的 colonies held little positive attraction for the English，由于前面的这个 colony 既可以指殖民地又可以指殖民者，而后面的 English 又很容易被理解成英国（其实只能理解成英国人），所以有些读者把这句话的意思彻底给搞反了，理解成了英国不能吸引殖民者。其实 A **hold attraction for** B 是 A 能抓住 B 的注意力的意思，即 A 吸引 B，因此原句的意思是：殖民地不能吸引英国人。

第二个容易看错的地方是在插入语之后：因为根据语法一句话中的让步和转折只能出现一次，所以原文在这里实际上是省略了一个 **but**，也就是说插入语后面的内容与前面正相反。有的读者把前面那句理解成了"英国不能吸引殖民者"，在这里就接着理解错，看成了"因此殖民者一有了机会就跑到美国了"，将错就错，居然也能自圆其说，不能不让人怀疑出题者故意在此作了手脚。

意群训练：Although at first the colonies held little positive attraction for the English—they would rather have stayed home—by the eighteenth century people increasingly migrated to America because they regarded it as the land of opportunity.

序号：033

> If the competitor can prove injury from the imports—and that the United States company received a subsidy from a foreign government to build its plant abroad—the United States company's products will be uncompetitive in the United States, since they would be subject to duties.

难句类型：复杂修饰＋插入语＋省略　　　　**难度**：4

标志：**If** the competitor can prove injury from the imports—**and** *can prove* ⎡that⎤ the U-nited States company received a subsidy from a foreign government to build its plant abroad—*then* the United States company's products will be uncompetitive in the United States, since they would **be subject to** duties.

译文：如果竞争者能够证明受到了进口的伤害——*而且能够证明*美国公司在国外设厂时接受了外国政府的资助—— *那么美国公司的产品将*在美国缺乏竞争力，因为这些产品将被征税。

解释：本句有两处省略，一处是插入语中的 and that 之间实际上省略了和前面一样的 *can prove*；另一处是破折号后面，由于句首有了 if，所以此处省去了有重复之嫌的 *then*。**be subject to** 这个词组的意思是受支配、遭受到的意思。

另外，虽然在这里本句的意思易懂，可是在文章中这句话的意思却难以理解，笔者略作解释：此处的 the competitor 实际上指的是在美国设厂的美国以外的竞争者；而这句话的实际意思是，比如日本公司如果在美国有分公司，而美国公司在日本也有合资企业，两家公司都生产同一产品，那么如果日本在美国的分公司能够证明它受到了美国在日本的分公司生产的返销回美国的产品的伤害，或者能够证明日本政府帮助了美国公司在日本设厂的话，则美国要对自己的公司做出惩罚。

意群训练： If the competitor can prove injury from the imports—and that the United States company received a subsidy from a foreign government to build its plant abroad—the United States company's products will be uncompetitive in the United States, since they would be subject to duties.

序号：034

In addition many ethnologists at the turn of the century believed that Native American manners and customs were rapidly disappearing, and that it was important to preserve for posterity as much information as could be adequately recorded before the cultures disappeared forever.

难句类型： 复杂修饰＋倒装　　　　**难度：** 4

标志： /In addition/ many ethnologists （at the turn of the century） believed that Native American manners and customs were rapidly disappearing, **and** *believed* that it was important to preserve /for posterity/ **as much** information （**as** could be adequately recorded） / before the cultures disappeared forever/.

译文： /而且/，（很多本世纪初的）民族人类学家们相信印第安人的习惯和风俗正在迅速地消失，而且以为重要的是/在这些文化永远地消失以前//为后代/保持（能够充分记录下来的）尽量多的信息。

解释： believed 后面带着两个由 that 引导的宾语从句，第二个 that 从句前省略了 believed。这个从句中的主语 it 是形式主语，其具体内容在后面的不定式中。不定式的结构是一个倒装： to preserve /for posterity/ **as much** information （**as** could be adequately recorded） /before the cultures disappeared forever/，其正常语序应该是把 for posterity 放到后面： to preserve **as much** information （**as** could be adequately recorded） /for posterity/ /before the cultures disappeared forever/。其实像本句中的这种倒装并不算什么太难的结构，读者只要读熟了也就掌握了。

意群训练： In addition many ethnologists at the turn of the century believed that Native American manners and customs were rapidly disappearing, and that it was important to preserve for posterity as much information as could be adequately recorded before the cultures disappeared forever.

序号：035

> In such a context, what is recognized as "dependency" in Western psychiatric terms is not, in Korean terms, an admission of weakness or failure.

难句类型： 插入语　　　**难度：** 3

标　志： In such a context, what is recognized as "dependency" in Western psychiatric terms is not, / in Korean terms /, an admission (of weakness or failure).

译文： 在这种情况下，在西方的精神分析的术语中被认为是"依赖"的行为，/在韩国的术语中/，却不被认为是一种失败或弱点。

解释： 本来好好的一个 is not an admission of，被插入语 in Korean terms 硬生生地分开，使初学者头痛不已。其实一旦熟悉了这样的句式，这种东西就没有什么难的；比如笔者现在的状态，一点也不觉得上面的句子有什么别扭的地方，如果不是同学们的提醒，恐怕也不会把这句话收入本书之中。

不过本句确实有一个需要解释的地方。如果只知道 admission 这个单词的中文释义"承认"的话，则句子的意思就会变得很生硬：什么叫做"（被西方认为的）依赖在韩国不是对于弱点的承认"？如果去掉其中的附加成分，就变成了"依赖不是承认"，这如果不是朦胧诗中的修辞手法，则就像是在说江湖黑话一样。其实这里的 admission 的真正含义是 the state of being admitted，就是被认为是……的状态。所以这里的意思是，西方人所说的 dependency，在韩国不是一个被认为是 weakness or failure 的状态。

意群训练： In such a context, what is recognized as "dependency" in Western psychiatric terms is not, in Korean terms, an admission of weakness or failure.

序号：036

> And managers under pressure to maximize cost-cutting will resist innovation because they know that more fundamental changes in processes or systems will wreak havoc with the results on which they are measured.

请思考：*句末的* results *指什么？*

难句类型：复杂修饰　　　**难度**：4 $^+$

标志：**And** managers［under pressure（to maximize cost-cutting）］will resist innovation／because they know that（more fundamental）changes（in processes or systems）will wreak havoc／with the results（on which they are measured）//.

译文：而且［那些在（最大化 cost-cutting 的）压力之下的］经理们将会拒绝创新，／因为他们知道，（更为根本性的）（在工艺或制度上的）变化将会／对被用来考核他们的业绩的结果／产生灾难性的后果。

解释：本句的字面的意思容易读，可是真实含义就不那么好懂了。

先解释一个词：wreak 这个单词，我们的英汉辞典中津津乐道的中文解释是"发泄（愤怒）、报仇"的意思，其实这两个意思 GRE 和 GMAT 的考试中很少用到，而且"报仇"这个词义英语国家中早已是被废弃不用的词义了；常用的意思是"带来（灾难性的后果）"，英文释义是 BRING ABOUT，CAUSE，如本句中的 wreak havoc，就是最经常用到的搭配。havoc 指大灾难。

本句由 because 所引导的原因状语从句中，they know 后面的宾语从句比较难。主要的问题是，changes（in processes or systems）will wreak havoc／with the results（on which they are measured）／中的 results 到底指的是什么。这就不仅仅要求读者只读懂字面上的意思，也要理解所读的内容。其实这个 results 就是指句首的 maximize cost-cutting。请仔细体味一下 the results on which they are measured 和句首的 managers under pressure to maximize cost-cutting 之间的关系。

意群训练: And managers under pressure to maximize cost-cutting will resist innovation because they know that more fundamental changes in processes or systems will wreak havoc with the results on which they are measured.

序号: 037

> Most novelists and historians writing in the early to mid-twentieth century who considered women in the West, when they considered women at all, fell under Turner's spell.

难句类型: 复杂修饰 + 插入语 **难度:** 4

标 志: Most novelists and historians (writing in the early to mid-twentieth century) (who considered women in the West), /when they considered women at all/, fell /under Turner's spell/.

译文: 大多数(在 20 世纪的早期和中期写作的)(考虑到西部妇女的) 小说家们和历史学家们,/如果他们还能考虑到妇女的话/,都受/到了 Turner 的强烈的影响/。

解释: 主语的后置修饰成分既多又长,造成谓语离主语的距离很远;而且主语和谓语之间又被插入语 when they considered women at all 分开,可谓雪上加霜。不过这个插入语也不是乱加上去的,作者其实在暗示这些人很少考虑到西部的妇女。

句末的 fell under T's spell 中的 spell 原来指咒语、魔法,后来被引申为强烈的影响力和吸引力的意思,在此指 a strong compelling influence or attraction。

意群训练: Most novelists and historians writing in the early to mid-twentieth century who considered women in the West, when they considered women at all, fell under Turner's spell.

序号：**038**

> In addition, the ideal of six CEO's (female or male) serving on the board of each of the largest corporations is realizable only if every CEO serves on six board.

难句类型：复杂修饰 + 难解句意　　　　**难度**：5

标志：/In addition, / the ideal[of six CEO's (female or male) (serving on the board of each of the largest corporations)] is realizable /only if every CEO serves on six board. /

译文：/而且/，［六个（男性或女性的）CEO（服务于每一个最大的公司董事会的）］理想/只有当每一个 CEO 都服务于六个董事会的情况下/才可能实现。

解释：除了主语的修饰成分比较长、比较复杂之外，句子的结构没什么可说的；本句的难度主要在于，尽管字字词词都能看懂，可是读者就是搞不懂句子到底是个什么意思，即使有上下文，这个地方也是百分之九十以上的人都无法看懂的难点。实际上这句话在文章中是用于评价"雇用女性 CEO 服务于董事会"这个方案的，其前提是女性 CEO 极少。这句话难以读懂的一个重要原因是其可能实现的 ideal 的荒谬性：本句的意思是，女性 CEO 少，而六个公司都想要女性 CEO，这样一、两个女 CEO 可以加上四、五个男 CEO 组成一个 CEO 团，由六个最大的公司共用，每一个 CEO 就将供职于所有的六个公司。

意群训练：In addition, the ideal of six CEO's (female or male) serving on the board of each of the largest corporations is realizable only if every CEO serves on six board.

序号：**039**

> Increasingly, historians are blaming diseases imported from the Old World for the staggering disparity between the indigenous population of America in 1492—new estimates of which soar as high as 100 million, or approxi-

mately one-sixth of the human race at that time—and the
few million full-blooded Native Americans alive at the end
of the nineteenth century.

难句类型：复杂修饰 + 插入语　　　　**难度：5**

标志： Increasingly, historians are **blaming** diseases（imported from the Old World）**for** the staggering disparity［**between** the indigenous population of America in 1492—new estimates of which soar as high as 100 million, or approximately one-sixth of the human race at that time—**and** the few million full-blooded Native Americans（alive at the end of the nineteenth century）］.

译文： 越来越多地，历史学家们正在把［在 1492 年美洲当地人口数量——最近对此数量的估计升至了一亿或当时人类数字的约六分之一——与（19 世纪幸存的）几百万纯血的印第安人之间数量的］巨大不同归罪于从欧洲传入的疾病。

解释： 这个句子中嵌套了两个固定搭配：一个是 blame A for B，意思是把 B 归罪于 A（注意不要看反）；另外一个是 between... and...。本句难读的原因，是这两个固定搭配所连接的内容都太长，尤其是 **blaming** diseases（imported from the Old World）**for** the staggering disparity［**between**... **and**...］中的"for"之后的内容还包括了 between... and... 这个固定搭配。between 与 and 之间的插入语的长度触目惊心，使得句子的长度愈发臃肿，结构愈发模糊。

意群训练： Increasingly, historians are blaming diseases imported from the Old World for the staggering disparity between the indigenous population of America in 1492—new estimates of which soar as high as 100 million, or approximately one-sixth of the human race at that time—and the few million full-blooded Native Americans alive at the end of the nineteenth century.

序号：**040**

> Virgin-soil epidemics are those in which the populations at risk have had no previous contact with the diseases that strike them and are therefore immunologically almost defenseless.

难句类型：复杂修饰　　　**难度：**4

标志：Virgin-soil epidemics are those {in which the populations (at risk) have had no previous contact [with the diseases (that strike them)] **and** are/therefore/ immunologically almost defenseless}.

译文：处女地流行病是这样一些疾病，{在这些疾病中（危险）人群以前从未接触过 [（那些侵袭了他们的）疾病]，而且/因此/在免疫上几乎是毫无防范的}。

解释：在谈到疾病的时候，populations at risk 的意思是危险人群，at risk 的英文释义为：exposed to a usually specified danger or loss ＜patients at risk of infection＞。本句修饰 those 的定语从句是典型的层层修饰。

意群训练：Virgin-soil epidemics are those in which the populations at risk have had no previous contact with the diseases that strike them and are therefore immunologically almost defenseless.

序号：**041**

> *Spanish tribute records...* The evidence provided by the documents of British and French colonies is not as definitive because the conquerors of those areas did not establish permanent settlements and begin to keep continuous records until the seventeenth century, by which time the worst epidemics had probably already taken place.

难句类型：复杂修饰 + 省略　　　　难度：5

标志： The evidence（provided by the documents of British and French colonies）is not **as definitive**/ because the conquerors（of those areas）did **not** establish permanent settle-ments **and** *did **not*** begin to keep continuous records /**until** the seventeenth century/, /by which time the worst epidemics had probably already taken place/ /.

译文： （由英法殖民者提供的）证据就不那么确定，/ 因为 （这些地区的）征服者/在 17 世纪以前/没有建立起永久的居住点，也没有开始做连续的纪录，/而到那个时候，最严重的流行病可能已经开始了//。

解释： 主句的 The evidence is not as definitive 的最后的两个单词 "as definitive" 的用法比较特殊。这里是与前面的西班牙纪录所做的比较，as 在此作副词，意思是 to the same degree or amount ＜twice as long＞，与常用的 as... as... 的意思相同，但用法不同：只用了一个 as。

另一个比较难的地方是在 because 从句中：在 the conquerors（of those areas）**did not** establish permanent settlements **and** *did **not*** begin 这一部分中，固定搭配 not... until 当中的 not... 的部分被克隆成两个，而第二个 did not 由于前面有一个表示并列的 and，居然被省略掉了，造成了初学者阅读的困难。其实如果熟悉了 GRE 或 GMAT 的句式，读者根本不必去分析语法，只要把注意力集中在句子的意思上，就可以很容易地看出句子的真实含义。

意群训练： The evidence provided by the documents of British and French colonies is not as definitive because the conquerors of those areas did not establish permanent settlements and begin to keep continuous records until the seventeenth century, by which time the worst epidemics had probably already taken place.

序号：042

Unfortunately, the documentation of these and other epidemics is slight and frequently unreliable, and it is necessary to supplement what little we do know with evidence from recent epidemics among Native Americans.

难句类型：复杂修饰　　　　难度：4⁺

标志：/Unfortunately/, the documentation（of these and other epidemics）is slight and frequently unreliable, **and** it is necessary to **supplement** what little we do know **with** evidence [from recent epidemics（among Native Americans）].

译文：/不幸的是/，（这些和其他流行病的）纪录是微不足道的而且经常不可靠，这样就有必要去把 [（印第安人中的）近来流行的疾病] 的证据补充到我们知之甚少的信息中去。

解释：本句的难点主要在表示递进的 and 之后：it 是形式主语，其真正的内容在不定式中。其中容易看错的就是 **supplement A with** B 这个固定搭配的意思是"把 B 补充到 A 中"或"用 B 来补充 A"而不是相反。在句中这个"A"是一个由 what 引导的名词性从句。

意群训练：Unfortunately, the documentation of these and other epidemics is slight and frequently unreliable, and it is necessary to supplement what little we do know with evidence from recent epidemics among Native Americans.

序号：043

Scientists have begun to suspect that this intergalactic gas is probably a mixture of gases left over from the "big bang" when the galaxies were formed and gas was forced out of galaxies by supernova explosions.

难句类型：复杂修饰 + 省略　　　　难度：5

标志：Scientists have begun to suspect that this intergalactic gas is /probably/ a mixture [of gases（left over from the "big bang"）] / when the galaxies were formed **and** gas was forced out of galaxies /by supernova explosions/ /.

译文：科学家们开始怀疑，这种星际间的气体/可能/是一种〔（从"大爆炸"遗留下来的）一些气体的〕混合物，/当时星系被形成，气体/被超新星的爆发/排出到星系之外/。

解释：本句容易读错。有的人把 that 引导的宾语从句中的 left over from the "big bang" when the galaxies were formed 看成了一个整个的部分，都是修饰前面的 gases 的，这样就把从句的主干看成了 this intergalactic gas is a **mixture of A and** B，句子的意思也就理解成"星际间的气体是由 A 与 B 形成的混合物"，其实是错误的，因为 A 在句中是 gases，而 B 则是 gas was forced out of...，是一句话，这两者是不可以并列的。另外，这种理解在意思上也说不通：大爆炸肯定应该是早于星系的形成的。

惟一正确的理解是，mixture 就是 gases 的 mixture；而后面的 when 所引导的时间状语从句是修饰整个宾语从句的，说明混合物形成时的宇宙状态。 when 从句中的 and 是连接两个并列的说明星系情况的句子的。这种在 when 前后的部分都很长的 C when D 的结构，与其把它理解为"当 D 的时候，发生了 C"，在阅读的现场倒不如理解成"C 发生了，当时 D 在发生"来得更清楚、更舒服。

意群训练：Scientists have begun to suspect that this intergalactic gas is probably a mixture of gases left over from the "big bang" when the galaxies were formed and gas was forced out of galaxies by supernova explosions.

序号：**044**

> He noted that the wavelengths of the radiation emitted by a gas would change as the gas cooled, so that as the gas flowed into the galaxy and became cooler, it would emit not x-rays, but visible light, like that which was captured in the photographs.

难句类型：复杂修饰　　**难度**：3$^+$

标志：He noted that the wavelengths 〔of the radiation (emitted by a gas)〕would change /as the gas cooled/, **so that**/as the gas flowed into the galaxy and became cooler/, it would emit **not** x-rays, **but** visible light, like that which was captured in the photographs.

译文： 他指出，[（一种气体发射出来的）辐射的] 波长/当这种气体冷却的时候/将会发生改变，以至于/当气体流入星系并变得更冷的时候/，它所发射出来的不是 X 射线，而是可见光，就好像被照片所捕捉下来的情形那样。

解释： that 引导的宾语从句比较长，但是结构还算简单，需要解释的是最后的"that which"，其实就等于 what。不过阅读现场的这种替换比较耽误时间，读者在现场最快的反应，就是把它看成"具有后面的特征的东西"，英文相当于 one that 或者 ones that。

意群训练： He noted that the wavelengths of the radiation emitted by a gas would change as the gas cooled, so that as the gas flowed into the galaxy and became cooler, it would emit not x-rays, but visible light, like that which was captured in the photographs.

序号：045

> Transported outside the nucleus to the cytoplasm, the mRNA is translated into the protein it encodes by an organelle known as a ribosome, which strings together amino acids in the order specified by the sequence of elements in the mRNA molecule.

难句类型： 复杂修饰＋倒装＋省略＋专有名词　　　**难度：** 5⁺

标志： /**Transported**/outside the nucleus/ /**to** the cytoplasm/ /，the mRNA is **translated**/into the protein (*that* it encodes) / /**by** an organelle (known as a ribosome), { which strings /together/ amino acids /in the order [specified by the sequence (of elements in the mRNA molecule)] /} /.

译文： (*mRNA*) /被传送出细胞核到达细胞质/，mRNA 被/一种（所知叫做 r 的）细胞器官/翻译/成（它所编码的）蛋白质；{ r 把氨基酸/以一种 [被（mRNA 分子中的元素的）序列所规定的〕次序/串联/在一起/ ｝ /。

解释： 本句的难度在 GMAT 文章当中可以说是最高的。很多人把这句话难以看懂的原因归结为专有名词太多，其实看看笔者在上面所作的标志就会知道，这句话难懂的真正原因还在于句子极其复杂的结构。

句首是一个表示被动的过去分词结构作状语。可是这个大状语中又有两个小状语，而且第一个小状语 outside the nucleus 又把 Transported to 拆开；主句当中又有两个状语，同样是第一个状语/into the protein（*that* it encodes）/把 translated by 分开。这个状语中省略了一个定语从句的引导词 *that* 。从 by 之后到句末整个是一个长长的状语，长的原因，是在 ribosome 后面跟了一个结构复杂的非限定性定语从句。这个从句中照例又有两个状语，其中的第一个是倒装：which strings /together/ amino acids 的正常结构是 which strings amino acids /together/。第二个状语中又是层层修饰，令人心烦意乱。整句十分难读，而最令人气愤的是，这个令考生花了很多时间来读的句子，后面居然没有出题。

意群训练： Transported outside the nucleus to the cytoplasm, the mRNA is translated into the protein it encodes by an organelle known as a ribosome, which strings together amino acids in the order specified by the sequence of elements in the mRNA molecule.

序号：046

However, recent investigations have shown that the concentrations of most mRNA's correlate best, not with their synthesis rate, but rather with the equally variable rates at which cells degrade the different mRNA's in their cytoplasm.

难句类型： 复杂修饰 + 插入语 + 省略　　**难度：** 4 +

标 志： **However**, recent investigations have shown that the concentrations（of most mRNA's）**correlate**/best, **not with** their synthesis rate, **but rather** *correlate best* **with** the equally variable rates（at which cells degrade the different mRNA's in their cytoplasm）/.

译文：然而，<u>近来的调查</u><u>显示</u>，（大多数的 mRNA 的）<u>浓度</u>/并不是与其合成速率最/<u>相关</u>，/而是与（细胞在其细胞质中降解不同的 mRNA 的）<u>同样是不同的速率最为相关</u>。

解释：that 引导的宾语从句中，在谓语 correlate 之后直到句子结束的部分是长长的状语，其中嵌套了两层固定搭配：**not...but...**；**correlate with**。这两个固定搭配被组合到一块，变成了 **correlate** best，**not with...**，**but rather with...**。rather 后面省略了与前面一样的 correlate best，使得句子简明扼要。

意群训练：However, <u>recent investigations</u> <u>have shown that</u> <u>the concentrations of</u> <u>most mRNA's correlate best</u>, <u>not with</u> <u>their synthesis rate</u>, <u>but rather with</u> <u>the equally variable rates at which cells degrade</u> <u>the different mRNA's</u> <u>in their cytoplasm</u>.

序号：047

> If a cell degrades both a rapidly and a slowly synthesized mRNA slowly, both mRNA's will accumulate to high levels.

难句类型：复杂修饰   **难度**：3⁺

标志：**If** a cell degrades（**both** a rapidly *synthesized* **and** a slowly synthesized）mRNA / slowly/，**then** both mRNA's will accumulate /to high levels/.

译文：如果<u>一个细胞</u> /*同时 缓慢地*/<u>分解</u>（*一个迅速合成的* 和 *一个慢慢合成的*）mRNA，*则*<u>两种 mRNA</u><u>都会积累</u>/到很高的水平/。

解释：前半个分句的理解极易出错，因为原文实际上省略了很多东西：**If a cell degrades**（**both** a rapidly **and** a slowly synthesized）mRNA /slowly/，实际上是 **If a cell degrades both**（a rapidly *synthesized* ）*mRNA* **and**（a slowly synthesized）mRNA /slowly/的省略形式；而且由于句中同时出现 degrade 和 synthesize、rapidly 和 slowly，所以准确的句义就更难以确定。

意群训练： If a cell degrades both a rapidly and a slowly synthesized mRNA slowly, both mRNA's will accumulate to high levels.

序号：048

> For instance, the mass-production philosophy of United States automakers encouraged the production of huge lots of cars in order to utilize fully expensive, component-specific equipment and to occupy fully workers who have been trained to execute one operation efficiently.

难句类型： 复杂修饰 + 倒装 　　　　**难度：** 4

标志： /For instance/, the mass-production philosophy （of United States automakers） encouraged the production of huge lots of cars /in order to utilize /fully/ expensive, component-specific equipment **and** *in order* to occupy /fully/ workers （who have been trained to execute one operation efficiently） /.

译文： /比如说/，（美国汽车制造商们的）大规模生产的观念鼓励大规模生产汽车，/以/完全/利用昂贵的制造专用零件的设备/，并且*也为了能够*/完全/占据（被训练来高效地执行单一操作的）工人们*的工作时间*。

解释： 作为主语的the mass-production philosophy中的philosophy 如果理解成"哲学"这个意思，其实并不到位。在此是哲学的引伸义：某种人做某些事情时抱有的观念、态度、理念等，其英文释义为：the most general beliefs, concepts, and attitudes of an individual or group。

从 in order to 开始直到句末，是句子的目的状语；其中实际上包含了以 and 相连接的两个 in order to，and 之后的那个 in order to 中省略了与前面相同的 in order。本句初读之下最让人感到别扭的是两个倒装：在 in order to utilize /fully/expensive, component-specific equipment **and** *in order* to occupy /fully/ workers （who have been trained to execute one operation efficiently） 当中，两个 fully 其实都应该被放到后面，正常的说法是：utilize something fully，但是因为第二个 in order to utilize 的宾语workers 加上定语从句的修饰（who have been trained to execute one operation efficiently）后变得很长，如果原文把

fully 放到句末，则句子的结构显得笨拙，因此 fully 被提前；这样，为了句子结构的对称，前一个 fully 也不得不倒装，因此就出现了本句这样的"双倒装"结构。

意群训练： For instance, the mass-production philosophy of United States automakers encouraged the production of huge lots of cars in order to utilize fully expensive, component-specific equipment and to occupy fully workers who have been trained to execute one operation efficiently.

序号：049

Japanese automakers chose to make small-lot production feasible by introducing several departures from United States practices, including the use of flexible equipment that could be altered easily to do several different production tasks and the training of workers in multiple jobs.

难句类型：复杂修饰　　　难度：4

标志： Japanese automakers chose to make small-lot production {feasible /by introducing several departures (from United States practices), [including the use of flexible equipment (that could be altered easily to do several different production tasks) **and** the training of workers (in multiple jobs)] /.

译文： 日本的汽车制造商们选择去进行小规模生产 [其之所以成为可能是/因为通过引入几种（与美国的惯例）不同的方案，[包括使用（能够被很容易地改变来完成几种不同的制造任务的）通用设备和训练（能够做多种工作的）工人/。

解释： chose 的宾语是一个延伸到句尾的不定式。不定式中的宾语 small-lot production 被 feasible by 所修饰，by 的宾语又是一个动名词。注意：动名词中的宾语 departure 不是通常所说的"离开，启程"的意思；当它与 from 连用时，是指与……不一样的方法、策略、操作等等，就等同于 divergence：a deviation from a course or standard。including 之后的内容是修饰 departure 的，其中被复杂修饰了的两个宾语由 **and** 相连接。

意群训练：Japanese automakers chose to make small-lot production feasible by introducing several departures from United States practices, including the use of flexible equipment that could be altered easily to do several different production tasks and the training of workers in multiple jobs.

序号：050

Automakers could schedule the production of different components or models on single machines, thereby eliminating the need to store the buffer stocks of extra components that result when specialized equipment and workers are kept constantly active.

难句类型：复杂修饰　　**难度：**4

标志：Automakers could schedule the production (of different components or models) / on single machines/, /**thereby** eliminating the need {to store the buffer stocks [of extra components (that result /when specialized equipment and workers are kept constantly active/)]} /.

译文：汽车制造商们能够/在一台机器上/安排制造（不同的零件或不同的款式），这样就消除了 {储存 [（/当专业设备和专业工人们不停地运作时/导致的）多余零件的] 缓冲库存的} 需求。

解释：thereby 之后的作状语的分词结构之所以比较难读，仍是因为其复杂的结构：分词的宾语 need 后面带有三层修饰结构。其中需要说明的是 extra components（ that result /when ... 这个结构。这个结构相对复杂，而且读者容易在理解它上面浪费时间。result 这个单词属于少数的几个比较麻烦的、同时具有两种相反的含义的单词之一，既可以指"由于，因为"，也可以指"结果，导致"，到底指什么完全取决于上下文的搭配。在 A that result when B 这个结构中，result 指"发生，产生"的意思，读者可以把这个结构理解成 A 是因为 B 的发生；或者倒过来理解成 B 发生时会导致 A。

意群训练：Automakers could schedule the production of different components or models on single machines, thereby eliminating the need to store the buffer stocks of extra components that result when specialized equipment and workers are kept constantly active.

序号：051

> In recent studies, however, we have discovered that the production and release in brain neurons of the neurotransmitter serotonin (neurotransmitters are compounds that neurons use to transmit signals to other cells) depend directly on the food that the body processes.

难句类型：复杂修饰＋插入语　　　　**难度：**5

标志：/In recent studies/, **however**, we have discovered that the **production** and **release** (in brain neurons) [**of** the neurotransmitter serotonin (neurotransmitters are compounds that neurons use to transmit signals to other cells)] **depend** directly **on** the food (that the body processes).

译文：可是/在近来的研究中/我们发现，（在大脑神经元中的）[对神经传递物质 serotonin（神经传递物质是神经元用来把信号传递给其他细胞的化合物）的] 制造和释放直接取决于（身体所加工的）食物。

解释：that 引导的宾语从句的结构复杂。从句的主语 the production of and the release of 被缩略成 the **production** and **release of**，而且在 the **production** and **release** 和 **of** 之间又插入一个起修饰作用的（in brain neurons），使得句子的结构更难以理解。另外，在 neurotransmitter serotonin 之后出现了一个很长的插入语。这个插入语的与众不同之处在于，一般出现在这个位置的插入语应该是解释紧接在它前面 serotonin 的，而这个插入语解释的是再往前的 neurotransmitter。因此，普通的插入语只是被解释单词的同位语，而这个插入语整个是一个完整的句子。这种情况的出现，是因为 neurotransmitter serotonin 整个是一个名词词组，而作者只想解释其中的 neurotransmitter，如果把句中这么长的插入语放在 meurotansmitter 后面，就会不可避免地把 neurotransmitter 和 serotonin 分得很远，读者根本没法理解。因此，尽管 ETS 胆大妄为，但也不敢冒天下之大不韪，于是出现了本句这样的少见的结构。

意群训练： In recent studies, however, we have discovered that the production and release in brain neurons of the neurotransmitter serotonin (neurotransmitters are compounds that neurons use to transmit signals to other cells) depend directly on the food that the body processes.

序号：052

> Our first studies sought to determine whether the increase in serotonin observed in rats given a large injection of the amino acid tryptophan might also occur after rats ate meals that change tryptophan levels in the blood.

难句类型： 复杂修饰　　**难度：** 5

标志： Our first studies sought to determine whether the increase in serotonin {observed in rats [given a large injection (of the amino acid tryptophan)]} might also occur / after rats ate meals (that change tryptophan levels in the blood) /.

译文： 我们最初的研究试图去确定是否 {在 [被给予了大量（tryptophan 氨基酸的）注射的] 老鼠身上所观察到的} serotonin 的增加也会发生/在那些老鼠吃了（能够改变血液中的 tryptophan 的含量的）食物之后/。

解释： 由 whether 所引导的从句的结构很复杂。主语 the increase in serotonin 的修饰语就是一大堆，远远地隔开了谓语 might also occur；after 引导的从句的结构也不简单，再加上句子中出现了大量的专有名词，使得本句的意思更难读懂。句子的意思其实就是：我们要研究这么一个问题，那就是已知老鼠注射 tryptophan 后 serotonin 增加，求解吃了使 tryptophan 增加的食物后，serotonin 是否增加？

意群训练： Our first studies sought to determine whether the increase in serotonin observed in rats given a large injection of the amino acid tryptophan might also occur after rats ate meals that change tryptophan levels in the blood.

序号：053

> The consumption of protein increases blood concentration of the other amino acids much more, proportionately, than it does that of tryptophan.

难句类型：复杂修饰＋插入语＋　　　**难度：**5

标志： The consumption（of protein）increases blood concentration（of the other amino acids）/much **more**, proportionately, **than** it does that of tryptophan/.

译文：（蛋白质的）消耗增加了（其他氨基酸在）血液中的浓度的程度 在比例上/远远高于蛋白质的消耗增加 tryptophan 在血液中的浓度的程度/。

解释：主语的 consumption 不是普通的消费、消耗，而是特指人体对于食物的摄取。本句从 much more 开始变得不好懂。首先是插入语 proportionately，然后是一连串的以省略为目的的看不清楚的指代：**than** it does that of tryptophan。其实 **than** 之后的内容如果找到与前面的对应，应该是 it 指 the consumption of protein，does 指 increases，that 指 blood concentration。如果把这后半部分补全就是 **than** the consumption of protein increases blood concentration（of tryptophan）。

意群训练： The consumption of protein increases blood concentration of the other amino acids much more, proportionately, than it does that of tryptophan.

序号：054

> This revisionist view of Jim Crow legislation grew in part from the research that Woodward had done for the NAACP legal campaign during its preparation for *Brown v. Board of Education.*

难句类型：复杂修饰　　　　　　难度：4⁺

标志： This revisionist view（of Jim Crow legislation）**grew**/in part **from** the research（that Woodward had done /for the NAACP legal campaign/ /during its preparation for *Brown v. Board of Education* /）/.

译文： 这种（对 Jim Crow 的立法）做出修改的观点/部分地/来源/于 Woodward 为 NAACP 的法律运动所做的研究，当时它（*NAACP*）在为 BBE 一案做准备/。

解释：grew/in Part **from** the research 中，grew from 被 in part 隔开；research 后面的长长的定语从句，是本句看不清的主要原因，因为后一个状语 during its preparation for *Brown v. Board of Education* /中的 its 不是指 Wookward，而是指 NAACP，这与读者顺序往下阅读的思路相冲突，感觉上很别扭。

意群训练： This revisionist view of Jim Crow legislation grew in part from the research that Woodward had done for the NAACP legal campaign during its preparation for *Brown v. Board of Education* .

序号：055

Woodward confessed with ironic modesty that the first edition "had begun to suffer under some of the handicaps that might be expected in a history of the American Revolution published in 1776."

难句类型：复杂修饰 + 倒装　　　难度：5⁻

标志： Woodward confessed /with ironic modesty/ that the first edition "had begun to suffer /under some of the handicaps { that might be expected /in a history [of the American Revolution（published in 1776）/]} /."

译文： Woodward/以一种令人感到奇怪的谦虚/招认说，第一版"已经开始遭受到

{可以被预计到的/在〔（1776年出版的）关于美国大革命的〕历史书中/出现的} 那样的缺陷"。

解释：confessed 与 that 之间被插入了一个状语/with ironic modesty/，而且这个状语实际上又是一个倒装结构，其正常的位置应该在句末。在 ironic modesty 中，ironic 的意思不是通常所讲的"讽刺的"的意思，而是指反常的、令人感到奇怪的。其名词 irony 所对应的英文释义为：（1）：incongruity between the actual result of a sequence of events and the normal or expected result（2）：an event or result marked by such incongruity。

宾语从句中的谓语 had begun 的宾语是一个不定式 to suffer；suffer 的状语 under some of the handicaps 后面又跟着一个修饰 handicaps 的一个复杂修饰的定语，定语中又有状语，使得句子拖拉不堪。

意群训练：Woodward confessed with ironic modesty that the first edition "had begun to suffer under some of the handicaps that might be expected in a history of the American Revolution published in 1776."

序号：056

> Yet, like Paine, Woodward had an unerring sense of the revolutionary moment, and of how historical evidence could undermine the mythological tradition that was crushing the dreams of new social possibilities.

难句类型：复杂修饰＋省略　　　**难度**：4

标志：**Yet**, like Paine, Woodward had an unerring sense (of the revolutionary moment), **and** *Woodward had an unerring sense* {of how historical evidence could undermine the mythological tradition [that was crushing the dreams (of new social possibilities)]}.

译文：然而，就像 Paine 一样，Woodward 有着一种（对于革命性的时刻的）正确的感觉，而且 {对于历史证据如何能够削弱那种〔粉碎了（新的社会可能性的）梦想的〕神话式的传统也有一种正确的感觉。

解释：unerring 这个单词本身就是一个双重否定：没错的 = 正确的。本句的 **and** 其实是连接两个并列的句子的，不过 and 之后的句子的主、谓、宾 (*Woodward had an unerring sense*) 因为与前面的相同，所以全部被省略。本句的意思在文章中不是很好理解，因为在 how 以后有很多暗指：historical evidence 暗指 W 的对历史的重新解释；mythological tradition 暗指以 Jim Crow 立法为代表的传统观点；the dreams of new social possibilities 暗指黑人追求社会上的平等地位的梦想。

意群训练：Yet, like Paine, Woodward had an unerring sense of the revolutionary moment, and of how historical evidence could undermine the mythological tradition that was crushing the dreams of new social possibilities.

序号：057

Joseph Glarthaar's *Forged in Battle* is not the first excellent study of Black soldiers and their White officers in the Civil War, but it uses more soldiers' letters and diaries—including rare material from Black soldiers—and concentrates more intensely on Black-White relations in Black regiments than do any of its predecessors.

难句类型：复杂修饰 + 插入语 + 省略 + 倒装　　　　**难度**：5⁻

标志：*Although* Joseph Glarthaar's *Forged in Battle* is not the first excellent study [of Black soldiers and their White officers (in the Civil War)], **but** it uses **more** soldiers' letters and diaries—including rare material from Black soldiers—and **concentrates** /**more** intensely/ **on** Black-White relations (in Black regiments) **than** do any of its predecessors.

译文：Joseph Glarthaar 的《战火的洗礼》虽然不是第一项 [关于（在内战期间的）黑人士兵和他们的白人军官的] 优秀研究，但是它比以前的任何研究都使用了更多的书信和日记（包括从黑人士兵那里得到的珍稀资料）并且更为强烈地集中于（在黑人部队中的）黑白关系上。

解释：前面的分句省略了 *Although*。**but** 之后的分句的结构较为复杂：**and** 连接个两个并列的比较，一个是 **more** letters and diaries，一个是 concentrates **more** intensely on，这两个比较的后项都是句尾的 **than** do any of its predecessors，这就相当于前面的比较省略了比较的后项。后一个比较中有一个倒装：<u>**concentrates** /**more** intensely/ **on** Black-White relations（in Black regiments）thando any of its predecessors</u> 的正常语序应该是：<u>**con-centrates on** Black-White relations（in Black regiments）/**more** intensely/ **than** do any of its predecessors</u>。**more** intensely 被提前到**concentrates** 和 **on** 之间，实际上是同时打乱了句子中的这两个固定搭配。作者之所以这样写，是因为 and 后面的比较与前面共用了一个 than，如果按照刚才的语序，容易被人理解成 than 是第二个比较所独用的。

意群训练： <u>Joseph Glarthaar's *Forged in Battle* is not the first excellent study of Black soldiers and their White officers in the Civil War, but it uses more soldiers' letters and diaries—including rare material from Black soldiers—and concentrates more intensely on Black-White relations in Black regiments than do any of its predecessors.</u>

序号：058

> While perhaps true of those officers who joined Black units for promotion or other self-serving motives, this statement misrepresents the attitudes of the many abolitionists who became officers in Black regiments.

难句类型： 复杂修饰＋省略　　　　　　　**难度：** 4

标志： /**While** perhaps *this statement is* true of those officers（ who joined Black units for promotion **or** other self-serving motives）/，***but*** this statement misrepresents the attitudes [of the many abolitionists（ who became officers in Black regiments）].

译文： /尽管这对于那些（为了升职或其他个人动机而参加黑人部队的）军官来讲可能是真的/，可是这种陈述却误传了［很多（后来成为了黑人部队的军官们的）废奴主义者的］态度。

解释： abolitionist 这个单词在很多的有关种族问题的 GRE 或 GMAT 的文章中都会

出现，特指那些主张废除种族奴隶制的人。

while 引导的分句中的 while perhaps true of 实际上省略了主语和谓语 *this statement is*。后面的分句中又省略了转折连词 ***but***。

意群训练： While perhaps true of those officers who joined Black units for promotion or other self-serving motives, this statement misrepresents the attitudes of the many abolitionists who became officers in Black regiments.

序号：059

Moreover, arguments pointing out the extent of both structural and functional differences between eukaryotes and true bacteria convinced many biologists that the precursors of the eukaryotes must have diverged from the common ancestor before the bacteria arose.

难句类型：复杂修饰　　难度：4

标志： **Moreover**, arguments {pointing out the extent [of **both** structural **and** functional differences (**between** eukaryotes **and** true bacteria)]} convinced many biologists that the precursors (of the eukaryotes) must have diverged /from the common ancestor/ /before the bacteria arose/.

译文： 而且，一些个{指出了[（eu 和真细菌之间的）结构和功能上的不同的]程度的}论据使得很多生物学家们相信，（eu 的）祖先们一定是/在细菌的出现之前//从其共同祖先那里/分化出来的。

解释： 主句的主语arguments 在被层层修饰了之后变得极长，令读者看到convinced 的时候已经不知道它是谓语，也不知道主语在哪里了。convinced 带着一对双宾语，第一个是many biologists，第二个是that引导的宾语从句。

意群训练： Moreover, arguments pointing out the extent of both structural and functional differences between eukaryotes and true bacteria convinced many biologists that the precursors of the eukaryotes must have diverged from the common ancestor before the bacteria arose.

序号：060

New techniques for determining the molecular sequence of the RNA of organisms have produced evolutionary information about the degree to which organisms are related, the time since they diverged from a common ancestor, and the reconstruction of ancestral versions of genes.

难句类型：复杂修饰＋省略　　　**难度**：5

标志：New techniques ｛for determining the molecular sequence ［of the RNA（of organisms）］｝ have produced evolutionary information［about the degree（to which organisms are related），*about* the time（since they diverged from a common ancestor），**and** *about* the reconstruction（of ancestral versions of genes）］.

译文：｛确定［（生物体的）RNA 的］分子序列的｝新技术产生了有关进化的信息，［这些信息是关于（生物体的相关的）程度、关于（它们从一个共同祖先那里分化出来的）时间、并且关于（对于祖先的基因版本的）重建的］。

解释：要是单看主、谓、宾，句子倒是简单：New techniques have produced evolutionary information。然而问题在于主语和宾语都被长长的定语所修饰。主语的修饰成分是标准的层层修饰，而宾语的修饰成分则是三个并列的介词结构，而且后两个当中省略了介词 about。

意群训练：New techniques for determining the molecular sequence of the RNA of organisms have produced evolutionary information about the degree to which organisms are related, the time since they diverged from a common ancestor, and the reconstruction of ancestral versions of genes.

序号：**061**

These techniques have strongly suggested that although the true bacteria indeed form a large coherent group, certain other bacteria, the archaebacteria, which are also prokaryotes and which resemble true bacteria, represent a distinct evolutionary branch that far antedates the common ancestor of all true bacteria.

难句类型：复杂修饰＋插入语　　　难度：5⁻

标志： These techniques have strongly suggested that /**although** the true bacteria indeed form a large coherent group, **but** certain other bacteria, [the archaebacteria, (which are also prokaryotes **and** which resemble true bacteria)], represent a distinct evolutionary branch that far antedates the common ancestor (of all true bacteria).

译文： 这些技术强烈地显示出，/尽管真细菌确实形成了一个大的、一致的种群，但是有一些其他的细菌，[即（也是 pro 的而且很像真细菌的）原始细菌]，代表着一个独特的进化分支，这个分支远远地早于（所有真细菌的）共同祖先。

解释： 主句的谓语 suggested 后面跟着直到句尾才结束的一个长长的宾语从句。此宾语从句的与众不同之处在于，其中居然还有两个表示让步和转折的分句，这在除了 GRE、GMAT 和 LSAT 考试之外的英语考试中是极少见到的。在表示转折的分句（此句的句首省略了 **but**）中，主语 certain other bacteria 后面跟着修饰它的同位语 the archaebacteria，之后又是修饰这个同位语的两个并列的定语从句（which are also prokaryotes **and** which resemble true bacteria）。同位语及其定语在句中都是作为插入语出现的，而且有效地起到了分割开主语与谓语的作用。

意群训练： These techniques have strongly suggested that although the true bacteria indeed form a large coherent group, certain other bacteria, the archaebacteria, which are also prokaryotes and which resemble true bacteria, represent a distinct evolutionary branch that far antedates the common ancestor of all true bacteria.

序号：062

> The new tax law allowed corporations to deduct the cost of
> the product donated plus half the difference between cost
> and fair market selling price，with the proviso that deduc-
> tions cannot exceed twice cost.

难句类型：复杂修饰＋否定　　　　**难度：**4⁺

标志：The new tax law **allowed** corporations **to** deduct the cost of the product donated **plus** half the difference（**between** cost **and** fair market selling price），/with the proviso（that deductions cannot exceed twice cost）/.

译文：新税法允许各家公司减去被捐献产品的成本，再减去（在成本与公平市场价格之间的）差值的一半，/其限制性条款（是减免不可超过成本的两倍）/。

解释：句子的结构虽然不算难，但是其意思却很难理解对。尤其是deduct the cost of the product donated **plus** half the difference（**between** cost **and** fair market selling price）一句中居然出现了肯定与否定（正与负的）的四则运算：deduct A plus B 不是指减去 A 然后加上 B，而是指减去 A 再减去 B，即 S－（A＋B）＝S－A－B。作为本句的 B 的 half the difference（**between** cost **and** fair market selling price）实际上指的是利润的一半。

后面的 proviso（that deductions cannot exceed twice cost），指的是这样的一种限制：减免不得超过两倍成本，即作为其减免基数的、用来计算减免的（成本＋利润）不得超出成本的三倍，这主要是为了防止纳税公司作假。注意句尾的cannot exceed twice cost 不能随便地把它替换成cannot exceed cost twice，后者的意思变成了不能超过成本的三倍。

意群训练：The new tax law allowed corporations to deduct the cost of the product donated plus half the difference between cost and fair market selling price，with the proviso that deductions cannot exceed twice cost.

序号：**063**

> Unfortunately, emancipation has been less profound than expected, for not even industrial wage labor has escaped continued sex segregation in the workplace.

难句类型：倒装　　　　**难度：**4⁻

标志：/Unfortunately/, emancipation has been **less** profound /**than** expected/, /**for not even** industrial wage labor has escaped continued sex segregation（in the workplace）/.

译文：/不幸的是/，解放没有/设想的/那么深入，因为即使是工业中的工资劳动力也没有逃脱工作场所中的持续的性别歧视。

解释：本句中的由 for 引导的原因状语从句看上去很不舒服：**not even** industrial wage labor has escaped... 的正常语序应该是 **even** industrial wage labor has **not** escaped...；如果作者为了强调而把 not 放到句首，那么 has 则应该提前，则句子应该被倒装成 **not even** has industrial wage labor escaped...。本句的 not 提前但是 has 没有被倒装的原因是 not 并不是第一个单词，第一个是 for。但是本句仍然令初学者感觉很别扭。

意群训练：Unfortunately, emancipation has been less profound than expected, for not even industrial wage labor has escaped continued sex segregation in the workplace.

序号：**064**

> To explain this unfinished revolution in the status of women, historians have recently begun to emphasize the way a prevailing definition of femininity often determines the kinds of work allocated to women, even when such allocation is inappropriate to new conditions.

难句类型：复杂修饰＋省略　　　　**难度：**5

标志： ╱To explain this unfinished revolution（in the status of women）╱, historians have recently begun to emphasize the way [that a prevailing definition（of femininity）often determines the kinds of work（allocated to women）, ╱even when such allocation is inappropriate to new conditions╱].

译文： ╱为了解释这个（女性地位的）未完成的革命╱, 历史学家们近来开始 强调 [（对女性特点的）一个流行的定义经常决定着（分配给女性的）工作的种类] 的这种方式, ╱即使这种分配不适用于新情况╱。

解释： 我们知道, 修饰 way 的定语从句的引导词通常可以被省略, 如 He felt indignant about the way they had treated him。但是本句中由于修饰 the way 的定语从句实在太长, 看完从句后很难把它与被修饰的 the way 联系到一起, 就好像原文是并列地讲了两句话一样, 显得本句似乎不符合语法。希望读者们在现场阅读的过程当中, 只要可以正确地理解文章的意思, 就不要去琢磨它是否符合语法；只有迅速地读懂文章的意思, 才是我们的惟一目的。

意群训练： To explain this unfinished revolution in the status of women, historians have recently begun to emphasize the way a prevailing definition of femininity often determines the kinds of work allocated to women, even when such allocation is inappropriate to new conditions.

序号：065

> For instance, early textile-mill entrepreneurs, in justifying women's employment in wage labor, made much of the assumption that women were by nature skillful at detailed tasks and patient in carrying out repetitive chores; the mill owners thus imported into the new industrial order hoary stereotypes associated with the homemaking activities they presumed to have been the purview of women.

难句类型： 复杂修饰＋插入语＋倒装　　　　**难度：** 5[+]

标志：/For instance/, early textile-mill entrepreneurs, in justifying women's employment in wage labor, made much of the assumption[that women were/by nature/ skillful (at detailed tasks) **and** patient (in carrying out repetitive chores)]; the mill owners thus **imported into** the new industrial order hoary stereotypes [associated with the homemaking activities (*that* they presumed to have been the purview of women)].

译文：/例如/，早期的纺织厂主们在说明在工资劳动中雇用妇女的理由时，做了很大程度上的假设，即妇女/天生/就擅长（做细活）并且（在从事重复性的杂务这方面）很耐心；厂主们这样就把［关于（被他们视为妇女的天职的）家务劳动的＼］陈腐的老套引入了新的工业秩序之中。

解释：先解释两个词：justify 在此的意思不是我们通常所说的"使合法"，而是指"为……提供理由，解释说明"的意思，其英文释义为：to supply good or lawful grounds for，warrant；其同义词有 show sufficient grounds for，countenance，confirm，show cause excuse，explain。purview 在此的意思也不能简单地理解为中文所说的"范围"，而是特指某人或某事物所能够负责或控制的、有局限性的圈子，其英文释义为 the extent or limit of control，activity，or concern。

本句前面的分句的结构就比较复杂：主语和谓语被长长的插入语分开；宾语 assumption 后面还跟了一个长长的同位语从句。后面的分句的结构更为难读，这主要是因为出现了一个"由 import A into B 转变成 import into B A"这类的倒装结构。按照正常的语序，import 之后应该紧接着其宾语hoary stereotypes，但是因为在本句中这个宾语被长度惊人的定语［associated with the homemaking activities (*that* they presumed to have been the purview of women)］所层层修饰，为了避免句子的头重脚轻，作者把介词及其宾语 **into** the new industrial order 提前，而 import 的宾语则被放到了句末。

意群训练：For instance, early textile-mill entrepreneurs, in justifying women's employment in wage labor, made much of the assumption that women were by nature skillful at detailed tasks and patient in carrying out repetitive chores; the mill owners thus imported into the new industrial order hoary stereotypes associated with the homemaking activities they presumed to have been the purview of women.

序号：066

> More remarkable than the origin has been the persistence of such sex segregation in twentieth-century industry.

难句类型：大型倒装　　　　难度：3

标志：More remarkable /than the origin/ has been the persistence[of such sex segregation (in twentieth-century industry)].

译文：/比最初的情况/更为引人注目的，是［这种性别歧视（在 20 世纪的）］持续。

解释：整个句子是一个彻头彻尾的大型倒装，句子的"主＋系＋表"的结构被翻了过来，成了"表＋系＋主"。本句的正常语序应该是：

The persistence [of such sex segregation (in twentieth-century industry)] has been more remarkable /than the origin/.

句子被倒装的原因有两个：一是主语被复杂地修饰之后变得太长，倒装有利于句子的结构均衡，避免头重脚轻；二是作者为了强调句首的 more remarkable。

意群训练：More remarkable than the origin has been the persistence of such sex segregation in twentieth-century industry.

序号：067

> According to a recent theory, Archean-age gold-quartz vein systems were formed over two billion years ago from magmatic fluids that originated from molten granitelike bodies deep beneath the surface of the Earth.

难句类型：复杂修饰＋语＋专有名词　　　难度：4

标志：/According to a recent theory/，Archean-age gold-quartz vein systems were **formed** /over two billion years ago/ /**from** magmatic fluids ［that originated /from molten granitelike bodies（deep beneath the surface of the Earth）/］/.

译文：/根据一个近来的理论/，太古代的金－石英矿脉系统是/在二十亿年以前/ /从［来/自（地球表面以下很深的）融化了的像花岗岩似的部分/的＼］岩浆流当中被形成的。

解释：本句中的固定搭配 be formed from 之间被插入了一个状语/over two billion years ago/，实际上是起到了一个插入语的作用。另外，本句中充斥着种种专有词汇，恐怕很多人之所以读不懂，是因为被这些东西所吓倒的。其实仔细看一看，除了 magmatic 之外，并没有真正意义上看不懂的词汇：Archean-age 和 granitelike 这两个词可以通过词头和词根猜出其意思，而 magamtic 其实不认识也无所谓，作一个首字母提炼"m"即可。

意群训练：According to a recent theory, Archean-age gold-quartz vein systems were formed over two billion years ago from magmatic fluids that originated from molten granitelike bodies deep beneath the surface of the Earth.

序号：068

> However, none of these high-technology methods are of any value if the sites to which they are applied have never mineralized, and to maximize the chances of discovery the explorer must therefore pay particular attention to selecting the ground formations most likely to be mineralized.

难句类型：复杂修饰＋否定　　　　**难度**：3⁺

标志：**However**，none of these high-technology methods are of any value /**if** the sites（to which they are applied）have never mineralized/，**and**/to maximize the chances of discovery/ the explorer must therefore **pay** particular **attention to** selecting the ground formations（most likely to be mineralized）.

译文：然而，/如果（被应用到其之上的）地点从未被矿化的话/，则没有一个这样的高技术手段会有任何用处，而且/为了最大化发现的机会/，探矿者因此就必须对选择（最有可能被矿化的）地质构成给予特别的注意。

解释：句首的none of these high-technology methods are of any value /if...的说法是不符合中文习惯的。首先，我们习惯于把 if 放到前面；另外，我们不会说"没有一个这样的高技术手段会有任何用处"，而是会说"所有这样的高技术手段都不会有任何用处"。所以我们的读者只有通过多读、多练来熟悉这种表达方式，才能够彻底排除掉难句子这个阅读中的语言障碍，向着与文章的思想打交道这个阅读的高级境界前进。

意群训练：However, none of these high-technology methods are of any value if the sites to which they are applied have never mineralized, and to maximize the chances of discovery the explorer must therefore pay particular attention to selecting the ground formations most likely to be mineralized.

序号：069

> In order for the far-ranging benefits of individual ownership to be achieved by owners, companies, and countries, employees and other individuals must make their own decisions to buy, and they must commit some of their own resources to the choice.

难句类型：复杂修饰 + 特殊结构　　　**难度**：4⁺

标志：/**In order**/**for** the far-ranging benefits（of individual ownership）/ **to** be achieved /by owners, companies, and countries/ /, employees and other individuals must make their own decisions（to buy）, **and** they must **commit** some of their own resources **to** the choice.

译文：/为了/使（个人所有权的）深远益处/ /被所有者、公司和国家/都得到/，雇员和其他人必须做出自己的（购买的）决定，而且他们必须为其抉择付出他们自己财富的一部分。

　　解释：句首的目的状语的结构特殊。正常情况下，目的状语中的动作执行者与主句中的主语应该相同，则只需说"In order to do something，主语……"。可是在本句中，目的状语中的动作执行者是 owners, companies, and countries；而主句的主语则是 employees and other individuals，二者不同，所以出现了句首的被动语态的结构：读者理解它的时候可以将其拆开，看成是/for the far-ranging benefits（of individual ownership）/ 与 /**In order to** be achieved by/这两个状语的叠加。

　　不过笔者仍然不推荐这种理解方式。最好的办法，就是将这句话读熟以形成这种语感，这样，就能够在阅读现场迅速地理解句子的含义。

　　后面的**commit** some of their own resources **to** the choice 中的 commit A to B 是固定搭配，是为了某目的 B 而付出某代价 A 的意思，其英文释义为：to hand over or set apart to be disposed of or put to some purpose，< to *commit* something to the trash heap >。

　　意群训练：In order for the far-ranging benefits of individual ownership to be achieved by owners, companies, and countries, employees and other individuals must make their own decisions to buy, and they must commit some of their own resources to the choice.

附录一　练习工具

下图是一个双功能练习卡。笔者在自己学习 GRE 和 GMAT 期间，曾经制作和使用了这么一个卡片，有两种功能：

1. 左上脚的缺口可以用来背单词。通常词汇书的生词在左，解释在右。在背完第一遍单词之后，复习时一定要自己盖住右边的解释，来回想左边单词的意思。可是实际操作当中，经常会不经意间看到右边的词义，令人不胜烦恼。利用笔者所制作的这个卡片来背左边的英文单词的时候，是看不到右边的单词释义的；只有向下移动卡片才能看到其中文的解释，这样既克服了想要得过且过地急于看答案的惰性，又避免了不小心先看到了解释的麻烦，可谓一举两得。

2. 卡片中央的长条形的小窗口是为了防止读者养成"回视"的不良习惯的。每一个人都有惰性，而回视是造成阅读速度上不去的恶性循环的主要原因：回视→阅读速度慢→心情波动→注意力不集中→回视。打破这个怪圈的入手之处就是克服回视这一恶习。

卡中间的窗口，用来显示正在被阅读的内容。一旦此行读完，读者将卡片向下平移，阅读下一行。读者初用此卡时需要调节卡的移动速度，最后找到一个合适的平衡点。需要注意的是，一旦读者下决心改掉回视的毛病，就一定要坚持住不可迁就自己，卡片一旦移下来，就不要再移回去；哪怕没有读懂，也在所不惜。坚持住一段时间，读者就会逐渐形成一个好的习惯。希望本书的读者在练习读过五遍以上的难句时，能够利用此卡做不回视的训练。

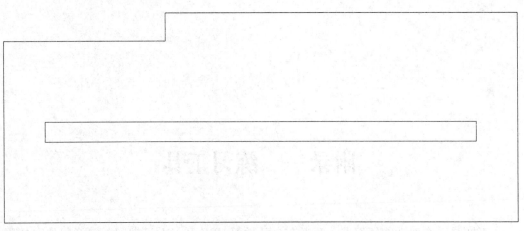

（本卡尺寸，读者可以根据实际需要自行设计）

附录二　难句自测

　　以下是十个难度适中的句子，其难度远远高于 GRE 和 GMAT 文章中普通的句子的难度水平，略低于本书中所录的难句。如果读者在 6 分钟内可以基本上完全读懂其中的 8 个句子，并且可以一遍读懂其中的 4 个，则恭喜你，你阅读句子的能力已经完全过关。

　　测试方法：以下句子的行宽、行距以及字体的大小与本书中所列出的难句的格式完全一致。每个句子的下面都有一个成绩纪录卡，如下：

　　阅读遍数：1 □　　2 □　　3 □　　　是否读懂：基本读懂 □　　基本没读懂□

　　读完一个句子，都按照自己阅读时的情况在相应的选项上做一个标记。时间（6 分钟）一到，立即停止阅读。

注意事项：

　　1. 如果读者感到不能适应这种没有上下文的阅读，感觉读不进去，也是正常现象。因为任何句子失去了文章的环境，必然难以理解。这也是笔者在前面推荐读者最好把难句训练与阅读文章结合起来的原因。这种情况下，读者请不必拘泥于时间的要求，只需力求将句子的意思看懂即可。

　　2. 句中如有生词或专有名词，请迅速用合理化原则推理出其大致含义，如做不到，请做首字母提炼；自我评价阅读成绩时，不应考虑这些生词是否理解。

　　3. 请读者千万不要陷入对句子的语法进行分析的误区之中，记住，你在阅读时的惟一目的就是要把句子的意思看懂。

　　4. 注意阅读速度与理解力上的平衡点，不要在时间压力下读得过快。要抱着宁可时间不够用，也要把句子读懂的想法来读。实际上，如果读者确实对本书的难句按照笔者的要求做过认真的训练，时间其实是足够用的。

5. 在阅读过程中，请集中注意力，尽量不要回视。

6. 不必拘泥于测试结果。由于笔者在前面的第一条注意事项中所说过的原因，这个测试的结果不好，并不能代表你在文章中的阅读结果也不好。

No. 1

> For example, a fluorescent dye whose excitation spectrum changes when it gains or loses a hydrogen ion can serve as an indicator of pH, since the fluorescence will change intensity as the environment becomes more acidic or more alkaline.

阅读遍数：1 □　2 □　3 □　　是否读懂：基本读懂 □　基本没读懂 □

No. 2

> The predator is searchingly aggressive, inner-directed, tuned by the nervous system and the adrenal hormones, but aware in a sense closer to human consciousness than, say, a hungry lizard's instinctive snap at a passing beetle.

阅读遍数：1 □　2 □　3 □　　是否读懂：基本读懂 □　基本没读懂 □

No. 3

> Social structure was in fact so fluid—though recent statistics suggest a narrowing of economic opportunity as the latter half of the century progressed—that to talk about social classes at all requires the use of loose economic categories such as rich, poor, and middle class, or eighteenth-century designations like "the better sort."

阅读遍数：1 □　2 □　3 □　　是否读懂：基本读懂 □　基本没读懂 □

No. 4

They have demonstrated, however, that a variety of the complex molecules currently making up living organisms could have been present in the early ocean and atmosphere, with only one limitation: such molecules are synthesized far less readily when oxygen-containing compounds dominate the atmosphere.

阅读遍数：1 □　2 □　3 □　　是否读懂：基本读懂 □　基本没读懂 □

No. 5

Although, at present, scientists cannot explain how these relatively small molecules combined to produce larger, more complex molecules, some scientists have precipitously ventured hypotheses that attempt to explain the development, from larger molecules, of the earliest self-duplicating organisms.

阅读遍数：1 □　2 □　3 □　　是否读懂：基本读懂 □　基本没读懂 □

No. 6

These structures are thematic, and they spring, not surprisingly, from the central fact that the Black characters in these novels exist in a predominantly White culture, whether they try to conform to that culture or rebel against it.

阅读遍数：1 □　2 □　3 □　　是否读懂：基本读懂 □　基本没读懂 □

No. 7

When, in the seventeenth century, Descartes and Hobbes rejected medieval philosophy, they did not think of themselves, as modern philosophers do, as proposing a new and better philosophy, but rather as furthering "the warfare between science and theology."

阅读遍数: 1 □ 2 □ 3 □ 是否读懂: 基本读懂 □ 基本没读懂 □

No. 8

With respect to their reasons for immigrating, Cressy does not deny the frequently noted fact that some of the immigrants of the 1630's, most notably the organizers and clergy, advanced religious explanations for departure, but he finds that such explanations usually assumed primacy only in retrospect.

阅读遍数: 1 □ 2 □ 3 □ 是否读懂: 基本读懂 □ 基本没读懂 □

No. 9

But those who reject the idea of rhetoric because they believe it deals in lies and who at the same time hope to move people to action, must either be liars themselves or be very naive; pure logic has never been a motivating force unless it has been subordinated to human purposes, feelings, and desires, and thereby ceased to be pure logic.

阅读遍数: 1 □ 2 □ 3 □ 是否读懂: 基本读懂 □ 基本没读懂 □

No. 10

In the *Civil Rights Cases* of 1883, for example, the Court invented the "state action" limitation, which asserts that "private" decisions by owners of public accommodations and other commercial businesses to segregate their facilities are insulated from the reach of the Fourteenth Amendment's guarantee of equal protection under the law.

阅读遍数：1 □　2 □　3 □　　是否读懂：基本读懂 □　基本没读懂 □

附录三 阅读抽象词提速法

从某种意义上来说，我们在考试现场大脑的运作方式与我们那时要面对的电脑的运作方式有类似之处，都要根据一些数据和信息进行运算，然后得出运算的结果，也就是答案。因此，提高阅读速度就涉及到提高大脑运算速度的问题。当然，不同的人之间，这种绝对运算速度是有差异的，但是所有的人都可以通过一个方法来提高其阅读速度，也就是通过消除一些延误我们大脑运转速度的因素来提高我们的阅读速度。

GRE 和 GMAT 文章的特殊性就在于其涉及到的因素之多，是其他任何部分都无法与之相比的，因此才在两种考试中都成为最难的一个部分。如果说文章是高楼大厦，段落就是房间，句子就是一面面的墙，单词就是一块块的砖。以上几个环节中的任何一个环节出了问题，都会影响我们对整篇文章的理解。为了解决上述问题，本书着重研究了如何克服 GRE 和 GMAT 难句的问题，这里来谈一谈单词的问题。

刚才我们把人脑和电脑做了一个类比。然而在阅读中，阅读者的大脑的运算过程有其特殊性：读者在答题前必须先通过阅读文章来把大量的信息输入大脑，然后才能对它加工处理。这就好比电脑在运行大型软件之前先要把大量数据输入计算机的内存一样。我们知道，除了考虑计算机的 CPU 速度以外，计算机的内存大小是决定其运行速度快慢的最为重要的参数：因为计算机需要把计算中最频繁使用的数据放到内存里，因此内存大的计算机也较快。前面我们讲 GRE 难句的时候，曾经提到过一个大脑容量的问题，其实这个大脑容量所起的作用就与计算机的内存的作用相似。我们读文章时，从文章中吸取的信息，都是放到这个内存中，以供大脑对这些信息做加工处理之用。问题是，任何一个人，其脑容量再大，也是有限的。尤其是当大家读难句的水平和词汇水平还不高时，如果这些你不理解的东西都把你的脑容量占用了，你根本谈不上真正跟上文章思路去进行阅读理解，而且你大脑即便是在试图理解文章，你的运算速度也一定非常慢，原因就在于，越是你不懂的东西，它占用你大脑的容量就越大。比如计算机在打开 office、photoshop 等软件时，因为这些软件占用内存比较大，所以速度就慢。

关于 GRE 难句，我们前面有专门的解决方案，那么在阅读中什么样的词汇占用我们大脑的容量比较大、大脑处理起来比较慢呢？就是我们今天要讨论的东西，我们把其称之为阅读抽象词。

什么叫做抽象词：

判断一个词是不是阅读抽象词，有以下三个标准：

第一，并非 GRE 或 GMAT 词汇书里的生词，而是一个你认识的词；

第二，一句话解释不清楚；

第三，你在阅读的时候，突然想不明白这个词放在句子当中（或文章当中）是什么意思了。

首先，请大家不要误解笔者的意思，笔者说它不是 GRE 或 GMAT 词汇，并非是说 GRE 和 GMAT 词汇里没有阅读抽象词，正相反，大多数的 GRE 和 GMAT 词汇都属于抽象词范畴；不过这里面涉及一个如何背单词的问题，过一会儿再讲。我主要是要说这样一些词汇：所有的人都认识，但是意思抽象、信息量大，如果出现在文章或句子中，其意思难以迅速理解。如下面的句子：

例句： ... be a descriptive distinction rather than an empirical observation and consequently lacks explanatory value.

这句话所用的单词大家都认识，可是为什么不易读懂呢？就在于构成这句话的单词全是一些这样的抽象词。下面列了一些抽象词，大家看一看，有没有大家不认识的？

psychological law reality emotion appraise
intensity correspond observation identical mistakenly perceive

都认识。比如这个 law，小学就学了，可是谁能用一句话给这个 law 下一个定义？一句话解释不明白，就意味着其信息量也是很大的，占用我们大脑的内存也就越大。而这样的词，在文章或句子中出现，想象其含义比较困难，这就造成我们同学在阅读中出现这样一个奇怪现象：明明是认识的词，突然在阅读中就不知道是什么意思了。如果需要在考试现场来思考单词在文章中的含义，必然会导致思维的停顿和思路的被打断，大大地影响我们的阅读速度。就刚才所举的例句而言，如果阅读这句话的时候还要停下三、四次来想那几个抽象词在句中是什么意思，这一句话是不是要读上半天？

问题我们已经找出来了，那么如何去解决掉呢？

阅读抽象词训练法

第一步，在阅读完每一篇 GRE 或 GMAT 文章之后，按照上面所说的三个标准找出这些抽象词来。

第二步，把这些单词记在小本上或存在电脑里，也可以补充到本书所列出的三百多个抽象词中；读文章或者背单词感到疲劳了，就可以拿来翻一翻，想一想。

注意这里所说的想的方法。比如在刚才作为例子所举出的抽象词中的 appraise，大家应该都其中文释义叫做"评估"。可是如果你只知道在现场的阅读中把它翻译成中文的"评估"，再去想"评估"的意思是什么，这种速度是无法满足 GRE 和 GMAT 考试对阅读的要求的。那么什么叫 appraise？比如说这瓶矿泉水，我们对其评估的过程是这样的：先把它拿出来观察，找出其性质特点与同类（或一个标准）做比较，根据优缺点对其价值做出估测，然后再找到它在当前市场情况下的合理价位，这么一个完整的过程才叫做 appraise。如果我们到考场上去把 appraise 翻译成"评估"，再去想这些过程，纯属浪费时间；最快的办法，就是一看到 appraise 这个单词，你就下意识地、直觉性地反映出这样一个过程来。

我们同学从小学英语的办法，就是记住一个单词的英文拼写和其中文释义，然后再到阅读文章中去搞翻译：先把英语单词翻译成中文单词，再把中文单词串联成一句中文的话，最后按照翻译出来的中文来理解文章的意思。这样做不但不能满足 GRE 和 GMAT 考试的时间要求，而且碰到抽象词的时候往往也不灵：英语的抽象词翻译成中文的释义，这个中文释义也是抽象的！比如 philosophical 翻译成中文"哲学的"，该不理解还是不理解。

因此，笔者所说的训练抽象词的方法，就是把一些我们阅读时在瞬间突然反应不出其意思的、抽象的英文词汇找出来，然后在平时花一些时间把这些英文单词出现在文章中的真正意义想清楚。我们训练 GRE 抽象词，就是把考试时需要花的时间，兑换成你平时训练时花的时间。读者们提高自己的阅读速度的一个有效的途径，就是找出这些抽象词来，利用自己的零碎时间，想象一下这些单词出现在文章当中的真正含义，每天积累、每天研习；在大脑中把这些英文单词的真正意义想象得越熟练，则你在阅读中对词义的反应也就越快。

这样的训练过程也是一个积累的过程。其实在 GRE 和 GMAT 的各种题材的文章中，涉及到的抽象词是有限的，最多也不会超过一千个词汇，而具体到每个人身上，也就只有那么几百个：因为笔者在教学中经过观察发现，不同的人对于不同的抽象词的理解程度也是不同的；在你那里算是抽象的单词，到了他那里就理解得很好，这是与学习者的知识背景和生活经验相关的。

对于抽象词的积累与对难句的积累过程类似：一开始越积累越多，坚持训练到了一定程度，就会越来越少，直至完全消失，也就那么一个来月的工夫。每天练习的时间不必多，有半小时足矣；关键在于每天都要练。还是那句老话：贵在坚持。

笔者在后面的附录四当中列出了这样的一些抽象词和抽象词组。然而由于编写本书的时间太仓促，笔者未能对这些单词在文章中的用法和其真正的意义给出详细的解释，这是本书的一大遗憾。希望在再版时能够把注释补充进来。

需要说明的一点是，抽象词因人而异，无法统一，所以本书所给出的抽象词不应成为所有读者的标准。如果大家发现有些单词可以理解得很透彻，则可以从书中划去；而且笔者也承认，由于没有充足的时间，本书所搜罗的四百余个抽象词和抽象词组也不一定完整。如果读者在阅读当中遇到本书中没有给出的抽象词，请自行补充。

附录四　阅读抽象词与抽象词组

PART A　阅读抽象词

abolitionism

academic

acceptance

accidental

accommodate

acknowledge

acknowledgement

acquisition

address

adjustment

aesthetic

anecdotal

antithesis

apparently

apportion

appraise

approach

approximation

apt

architectural

argue

art

artifact

aspect

assess

assume

assumption

attain

attitude

attune

authenticate

authorization

availability

beset

boom

border (v.)

broad

capable

channel

characteristic

characterization

charting

claim

classical

clerical

clinical

coexistent

coherently

coincidently

commend

commentary

commit

competent

complex

comprise

conception

conceptual

conclusion

conditional

configuration

confine

confrontation

confuse

congenial

consequently

considerably

consign

constitute

constitution

construct

construction

consume

consumption

contemplate

contemporary

contend

contentious

continuously

contravention

conventionalize

conventionally

correspond

corrupt

council

counteraction

counterexample

critical

crucial

debate

defend

definition

demanding

democracy

denote

departure

depiction

derivative

descriptive

devise

devoted

diagnose

dimension

discernible

discerning

discharge

discursive

dismal

dismay

dispute

dissemination

dissension

dissolution

distinction

distinguish

distinguished

doctrine

domain

draft

dramatize

drawing

dubious

ecclesiastical

edition

effect

elementary

emancipation

emotional

empirical

emulate

encompass

encounter

encouraging

energetic

enfranchisement

engage

engagement

epistemology

established

establishment

ethics

ethnic

event

exceed

exclusively

expense

explanatory

extension

facility

feeling

fitness

fortuitous

foster

framework

function

functional

fundamental

gain

general

generalization

genuine

genus

given

global

grateful

ground

hard-nosed	insult	mechanism
horizontal	intellectual	mental
identical	intensely	merit
identification	intensity	midst
identify	intentional	mistakenly
illusory	interact	momentous
implication	interpretation	morality
impression	intricacy	multiple
impression	intriguing	necessarily
impulse	intuitive	negation
inadvertent	inversion	negative
incentive	invert	nonviable
incidence	investigation	notable
incomparable	inveterate	nuclear
incompatibility	irrational	numerously
incorporate	judgment	object
indicate	justification	objective
individualism	justify	observation
inert	law	observational
inevitably	lawsuit	occurrence
infinite	league	official
informal	legacy	omission
inherently	literalize	ongoing
inhibit	literally	organization
innocent	literary	orientation
innuendo	literature	originality
inordinately	logic	panic
inquiry	maintain	particularly
insofar	mandate	pedagogical
inspiration	margin	perceive
instance	mastery	percept
institution	means	perception
insufficient	mechanically	perceptive

perceptual	prompt	representation
perfunctory	property	repute
perplexed	proportionately	rescue
perplexity	proposal	reservation
pervasive	provision	resolution
phenomena	psychological	resourceful
physical	psychologist	respectively
pictorial	purposive	respond
picture	pursuit	responsible
pinpoint	qualified	responsive
plague	qualitatively	revise
plausible	quantitatively	rightness
pleading	radical	rigorously
pledge	rather	salvation
polarity	ration	saturated
positional	reaction	scheme
positive	readily	secure
possibility	reality	seductive
practical	realm	seem
precisely	rear	senate
presence	reception	sequential
pretend	receptive	servitude
previously	recognizable	signal
prey	recount	specter
principal	refute	speculation
principle	regional	speculative
privacy	regulate	sphere
privately	regulation	statement
problematic	remarkable	stationary
proceed	remedy	stature
process	remembrance	statute
procure	render	stimuli
prominence	repetitive	strait

striking	training	unerring
strip	trait	unremitting
structural	trample	untangle
studied	transcription	vain
substantial	unavailing	value
substitute	unconscionable	virtual
suffrage	underlying	virtue
synthesize	underplay	visionary
technical	understanding	whereas

PART B　阅读抽象词组

a wide range	explain away
accede to	farewell performance
account for	if only
act on	in any event
aesthetic experience	in favor of
as it were	in passing
as long as	in spite of
attest to	in the first place
be aimed at	intent on
be bereft of	internal to
be bound to	in the guise of
be compensated for	in view of
be directed at	must be careful about
biological remains	naturalistic modes of expression
composers of Beethoven's stature	nonaesthetic emotion
confer on	not least by a sense of form
conferred by	one of the questions of interest
ecological stabilization	only if
economic interest	order of magnitude
emotional life	other than

perceive as

point to

properties of reality

psychotic fantasy

raise issues

regardless of

scholarly journals

selectively neutral

serve to do

shore up

sit in judgment on

so called

substitute for

take into account

take responsibility for

technically unconventional

the notions of Black identity

unattributable to

verges on

vivid imagination

work on

附录五　读者来信

下面是一封读者来信，其人基础较弱，第一次考前跳过难句，考场失利后痛定思痛，强攻难句，一番苦功之后高奏凯歌。这类事例在学习难句的同学中十分有代表性，在此将此信附上，希望给大家以示范和激励。功不唐捐，若非一番寒彻骨，哪得梅花扑鼻香？

一次背诵的真实经历

大家好！我叫肖云，2011 年 5 月份我从单位获得了一次公费到长江商学院就读全日制英文 MBA 课程的机会，当时我的心情是很复杂的，既有欢喜，又有忧愁。欢喜的是因为我获得了一次绝好的自我提升机会，忧愁的是单位只负责推荐以及学费，进入长江商学院的面试和 GMAT 成绩，需要我自己搞定。面试比较好办，只要有足够的准备时间，加上本身的工作经验也较为丰富，相信达到长江商学院的要求不难。但是 GMAT 成绩让我发了愁，我的英语基础并不好，6 年前大学四级考了 462 分（425 分相当于及格），而且相信其中还含有运气的成分。我曾经还有过侥幸的心理，询问长江商学院是否可以先上课，以后再补 GMAT 成绩，可长江商学院答复：因为是全英文的MBA 项目，GMAT 成绩是硬性标准，考不到预定的成绩，就会看不懂案例、听不懂课、理解不了教授的思路、毕不了业。

在得到让我死心的答复之后，我下定决心，开始了艰难的 GMAT 备考过程，但是，当我第一次翻开 GMAT 真题时，我是非常崩溃的，尤其是阅读的文章，我根本看不懂意思。就像一个想要在射箭比赛中获得冠军的选手，突然发现自己连拿起弓箭的力气都还不具备。

这个时候，我询问了几个考过 GMAT 考试的朋友，自己应该怎么办。当时，我得到的答复主要有以下二种：

1. 强化阅读技巧（如：核心词阅读法），硬着头皮往下做题；

2. 从基本功抓起，背单词和看长难句，直到能流畅读懂文章意思之后，再开始做题；

在得到这二个答复之后，我有过犹豫，后来经过简单的分析之后，我选择了第一种方法，并且开始通过网络和书籍疯狂的查找阅读技巧。而当时没有选择第二个方案的原因是：首先，我已经背过 TOEFL 单词，新东方老师说词汇量已经足够了，其次，我自认为 GMAT 长难句无外乎就是在阅读当中挑选了一些句子，即使是我做阅读题，同样也可以接触长难句。这样我就可以一练技巧，二在实战阅读题中练习长难句，一举两得了。但后来的事实证明，我的这个错误决定耽误了我近一个月的宝贵时间，也让我差一点失去了就读长江商学院的机会。

关于具体如何在不注重"内功"，只关注"技巧"的道路上摔跟头的过程，我就不详细叙述了。但给我警醒的关键事件是：我参加一战，惨败，非常惨烈。当时看到成绩之后，整个人都崩溃了，不知道是如何回的家，回到家之后，也是倒头就睡。上午考的试，下午一直睡到晚上快 9 点，午饭、晚饭都没有吃，后来实在饿得不行了，起来煮了一包方便面吃，然后继续睡，感觉很痛苦。

到了第二天之后，慢慢的开始清醒了，觉得这样下去不是办法，一战的惨败已经事成定局了，最关键的是要分析原因。我仔细回想了我之前复习的整个过程，突然发现了关键问题是：我过于注重技巧的训练，而忽略了"内功"的修炼，到了考场，加上紧张的考试氛围，题目都不太能看懂，就算是我掌握了再好的技巧也使用不出来，就像是一个拳击手修炼了无敌的拳谱，可是连对手在哪里都看不清楚。

这时，可能有同学要问了，难道考前用技巧解的题都不对吗？答案是：用技巧解题了，正确率不差。但这就是出现问题的关键，考前我在用技巧训练的时候，详细的归纳了什么样的题目应该使用什么样的技巧，什么样的文章类型，应该采用什么样的阅读顺序，看到什么样的关键词，应该警醒这个可能就是正确答案的意识等等。但关键问题就是，考前解题，我是知道这个题是什么类型，应该用什么技巧，但到了真实考场，基本是没有接触过的新题，而且难度还要略微难一些，我在题目意思都不能完全看明白的情况下，根本就谈不上使用技巧的问题。

这时，我想起了之前朋友给的建议，只关注技巧可能不行，我意识到还要从"内功"抓起，我从书柜中找出了新东方杨鹏老师的《GRE&GMAT 阅读难句教程》，但是当时，我并没有想到要去背长难句，只是觉得这个东西对我会有帮助。由于离长江商学院要求提供 GMAT 成绩的日子越来越近的原因，我也开始变得有些焦虑，拿起书之后，也没有管前言和长难句训练原理等讲解内容，直接就奔着 GMAT 句子开始了复习。但是不到一个星期的时间，我有点崩溃了，如果只是阅读一遍句子和杨鹏老师的讲解就往下翻也没有问题，但是效果欠佳，一天下来看的句子不少，但是看完之后不多久，印象就不深了。到了第二天，杨鹏老师的讲解大概还记得一些，但句子本身却印象比较模糊了。

在这样的痛苦中，我实在是没有办法了，当时有一种黔驴技穷的感觉，单词也背过了，技巧也总结了不少，看不懂题，就读长难句，也依然不得法。这时，我在想，我是不是应该上 GMAT 学习网站上，再看看别人的学习心得，总结一下自己的问题，还怎么样能够改进。就这样，我看到了一篇帖子，内容很短，大概意思就是：3 个月成功杀 G，花了 1 个多月看了 28 遍杨鹏长难句，尤其是每天早上和晚上基本都要看一遍，到后来，前面的 50 个句子，基本都熟悉的已经可以背出来了。

看完之后，我可能和别人想的不太一样，我当时的想法是：既然看了 28 遍，而最后的效果是变的非常熟悉句子，甚至前 50 个句子已经可以背下来了。那为什么不刚开始就把句子背下来呢？同样都是刺激大脑皮层，与其温和的刺激 28 遍，还不如凶猛的刺激 2－3 遍，也许效果会更好，能背下来的就不只是前 50 个句子，而是所有的句子了。

在有了这个想法之后，我就开始有念头要背句子了，但当时并没有完全下决心，因为在别人的学习心得上，还提到一点，说杨鹏长难句实际上并不只是长难句的集合，如果有时间应该把杨鹏老师在书中讲解的长难句原理、训练方法也都好好的看一看。我这才意识到，我有点过于焦虑了，并没有好好静下心来阅读这本书。这时，我打开书，从前言的内容开始看起，看完之后，这下更加肯定了我要背句子的念头。而且我在杨鹏老师的讲解中，还读到了这样的话："最快的方法，往往就是最'笨'的方法"、"古人说，惟上智与下愚者不移，意思是只有最聪明和最傻的人才能坚持到底、矢志不移"。这些话，到现在都还让我记忆犹新。这个时间，还有一个小插曲，我在看杨鹏老师训练方法的时候，我有一个同样备考 GMAT 的朋友打电话给我，说强烈建议我要看一下杨鹏长难句这本书，效果很好，而且我还有着和杨鹏老师些许相似的经历：工作多年之后，要重新参加出国考试。现在这个朋友已经实现梦想在美国读书了，真是非常感谢他。

在下了决心之后，我正式开始了背诵句子的过程，我首先做了一个计划，GMAT 总共 69 个句子，GRE 总共 129 个句子，因为在书中杨鹏老师也提到了因为 GMAT 前身也是 ETS 出的题，所以 GRE 和 GMAT 的长难句套路基本是一样的，在训练阅读能力的时候，两者可以通用。所以，我决定把这 198 个句子都背了。具体的背诵方法如下：

1. 以 5 个句子为一组；
2. 每天至少背诵一组句子；
3. 背诵完的句子，第二天和第三天各复习一遍；

按照这个计划，我开始了艰难的背诵过程，头几天，背诵的特别痛苦，专业词汇

不认识、语法结构不熟悉、句子太长记不住。再加上并没有完全静下心来，有时候，背着背着就跑偏了，想到别的事情上面去了。导致有些长句子，甚至要花将近2个小时才能完成熟悉、理解到记住，其中还包括句子结构分析和意群训练。

在刚开始的一段时间，我向单位请了年假学习，可以每天6点就起来背诵句子，中间累了就做语法题，换一换脑袋。但到了后期，单位已经不能给我全天假期学习了，我必须要上午回单位上班，我就改变了背诵时间，上午8点起床去单位上班，12点下班，随便吃点东西，打车回家，大约1点半，然后睡觉到下午6点，在吃点晚饭之后，7点开始背诵，直到凌晨4点。因为除了之前早上背诵效果特别好以外，我发现晚上我的背诵效果也比较好，心很静，而下午可能因为天气比较热的原因，背诵效果不太好，我就用来睡觉了。

就这样，我坚持了一个多月，有时候在梦里都想着背诵的长难句，整个过程下来，人也瘦了十多斤。

有些同学可能会问了，说这个过程是不是极其痛苦啊？开始几天是这样的，但之后慢慢的就不会了，实际上，到了最后的一段时间，我还有一些享受的感觉。而这种享受的感觉是来自于我真正的投入了进去，到了后期，看文章、看句子，不需要大脑过多的反应，犹如行云流水一般顺畅。记句子的效率也是越来越高，而且有一次，我记得是在下午6点左右，刚刚睡觉起来没多久，当时拿起一个不算太复杂的新句子，大概看了15分钟，把杨鹏老师的解释都看了一遍，然后就去洗澡了，没想到，在洗澡的时候，不自觉的脑子当中就回想起了刚刚看的那个新句子，突然发现自己无意之中，居然把这个句子已经背下来了。那种感觉真是非常的舒畅。

最后，背完这198个句子，结果确实出乎我的意料之外，我发现我在不知不觉中，阅读能力已经得到了大幅度的提升，以前看的似懂非懂的文章，现在一下子就清晰了很多。我现在还记的很清楚的一个例子是，之前我看OG上有一篇讲关于文物的文章，我在没有背诵句子之前，总是看的似懂非懂，包括博物馆如何对文物进行编号，博物馆遇到存放文物的问题，作者为什么支持考古学家在市场上出售文物等等观点，都是似懂非懂。但在背诵完句子之后，我发现OG上的阅读题目，我已经可以保证至少80%的正确率。虽然，OG上的题目确实比真实考场上的题目要偏简单一些，但对于我自己来说，这已经是一个非常大的突破了。

当然，结果也就像我期望的一样，虽然没有上700分，但如愿以偿的考到了长江商学院要求的成绩，而且是在我数学没有发挥好的情况下。

不过，同学们千万不要认为背诵长难句带给我的好处就完了。在我进入长江商学院念书之后，我发现虽然有同学可能GMAT成绩不比我差，甚至更高一些。但是我因为背诵长难句而打下了扎实的基础，在阅读教材和案例上，有些同学不能很快理解的句子，我可以比较快的把握意思。而且，在我没有任何商业课程（比如：会计、投资等）基础的情况下，我的成绩也不算差，还运气比较好的获得了去加拿大 Queen's university 交换一个学期的机会。我想背诵长难句带给我的帮助是功不可没的。虽然，我当时并没有考上 700 分，但有一部分也是时间原因，我需要赶在固定的时间点给长江商学院提供成绩。而我现在差不多完成了长江商学院核心课程的紧张学习之后，也准备在接下来的时间，再继续报考一次 GMAT，肯定能考上 700 分，并了却自己的一件心事。

　　不管怎样，我要感谢杨鹏老师。谢谢您！